NO GOOD WITHOUT REWARD

The Other Voice in Early Modern Europe:
The Toronto Series, 13

The Other Voice in Early Modern Europe: The Toronto Series

SERIES EDITORS Margaret L. King *and* Albert Rabil, Jr.

Recent Publications in the Series

Madre María Rosa
Journey of Five Capuchin Nuns
Edited and translated by Sarah E. Owens
2009

Giovan Battista Andreini
Love in the Mirror: A Bilingual Edition
Edited and translated by Jon R. Snyder
2009

Raymond de Sabanac and Simone Zanacchi
Two Women of the Great Schism: The Revelations *of Constance de Rabastens by Raymond de Sabanac and* Life of the Blessed Ursulina of Parma *by Simone Zanacchi*
Edited and translated by Renate Blumenfeld-Kosinski and Bruce L. Venarde
2010

Oliva Sabuco de Nantes Barrera
The True Medicine
Edited and translated by Gianna Pomata
2010

Louise-Geneviève Gillot de Sainctonge
Dramatizing Dido, Circe, and Griselda
Edited and translated by Janet Levarie Smarr
2010

Pernette Du Guillet
Complete Poems: A Bilingual Edition
Edited by Karen Simroth James
Translated by Marta Rijn Finch
2010

Antonia Pulci
Saints' Lives and Bible Stories for the Stage: A Bilingual Edition
Edited by Elissa B. Weaver
Translated by James Wyatt Cook
2010

Valeria Miani
Celinda, A Tragedy: A Bilingual Edition
Edited by Valeria Finucci
Translated by Julia Kisacky
Annotated by Valeria Finucci and Julia Kisacky
2010

Enchanted Eloquence: Fairy Tales by Seventeenth-Century French Women Writers
Edited and translated by Lewis C. Seifert and Domna C. Stanton
2010

Leibniz and the Two Sophies: The Philosophical Correspondence
Edited and translated by Lloyd Strickland
2011

In Dialogue with the Other Voice in Sixteenth-Century Italy: Literary and Social Contexts for Women's Writing
Edited by Julie D. Campbell and Maria Galli Stampino
2011

Sister Giustina Niccolini
The Chronicle of Le Murate
Edited and translated by Saundra Weddle
2011

No Good without Reward:
Selected Writings

A BILINGUAL EDITION

LIUBOV KRICHEVSKAYA

⁓

Edited and translated by

BRIAN JAMES BAER

Iter Inc.
Centre for Reformation and Renaissance Studies
Toronto
2011

Iter: Gateway to the Middle Ages and Renaissance
Tel: 416/978–7074   Fax: 416/978–1668
Email: iter@utoronto.ca   Web: www.itergateway.org

CRRS Publications, Centre for Reformation and Renaissance Studies
Victoria University in the University of Toronto
Toronto, Ontario M5S 1K7 Canada
Tel: 416/585–4465   Fax: 416/585–4430
Email: crrs.publications@utoronto.ca   Web: www.crrs.ca

Iter and the Centre for Reformation and Renaissance Studies gratefully acknowledge the generous support of James E. Rabil, in memory of Scottie W. Rabil, toward the publication of this book.

Library and Archives Canada Cataloguing in Publication

Krichevskaia, Liubov´
No good without reward : selected writings / Liubov Krichevskaya ; edited and translated by Brian James Baer.
(The other voice in early modern Europe : the Toronto series ; 13)
Text in English and Russian.
Issued also in electronic format.
Co-published by: Centre for Reformation and Renaissance Studies.
Includes bibliographical references and index.
ISBN 978–0–7727–2110–5

1. Krichevskaia, Liubov´—Translations into English. 2. Krichevskaia, Liubov´.3. Russian literature—Women authors—Translations into English. 4. Russian literature—Women authors. 5. Russian literature—19th century—Translations into English. 6. Russian literature—19th century. I. Baer, Brian James II. Victoria University (Toronto, Ont.). Centre for Reformation and Renaissance Studies III. Title. IV. Series: Other voice in early modern Europe. Toronto series ; 13

PG3337.K67A1995 2011
891.78'309   C2011–905285–7

Credit: Portrait of a young woman, c.1833–34 (oil on canvas) by Louis August Schwiter (1805–89) Musee des Beaux-Arts, Orleans, France/ Giraudon/ Bridgeman Art Library. XOR387358.

Cover design: Maureen Morin, Information Technology Services, University of Toronto Libraries
Typesetting and production: Iter Inc.

Contents

Acknowledgments   ix

Introduction   1
    The Other Voice   1
    The Historical Context   3
    Biography and Works   8
    Analysis of Krichevskaya's Works   12
    Conclusion   35

Preface   38

To My Readers [Foreword to *My Moments of Leisure*] (1817)   41
Several Excerpts from a Journal Dedicated to My Friends (1817)   42
    My Comments   44
    A Plan for a Temple of Love in the Heart   46
    Thoughts   47
Blind Mother, or The Reward of Virtue Tested; A Drama in Three Acts (1818)   49
No Good without Reward; A Comedy in Three Acts (1826)   84
Two Novellas (1827)   117
    Corinna   117
    Emma   141
Count Gorsky, a Novel (1837)   165
Selected Poetry (bilingually, on facing pages)   268
    To Rtishchev (1817)   269
    To a Frame without a Picture (1817)   269
    A White Sheet of Paper (1817)   271
    On the Militia of 1812 (1817)   273
    The Dniepr. May 25, Evening (1817)   275
    To Gr——ry F——ch Kv——ka in Answer to His Verses of
       September 17 (1817)   275
    Another Song (1817)   277
    Truth (1817)   277
    In Answer to the Question: Why Do I Sleep So Much? (1817)   279
    From the Banks of the Ternovka (1824)   279

Bibliography   280

Index   283

Acknowledgments

This volume would not have been possible without the generous support of friends, colleagues, and students. A travel grant from the Office of Research and Sponsored Programs at Kent State University allowed me to travel to the University of California, Berkeley, Library, the only place in the United States where Krichevskaia's works are available. Thanks also go to Colleen Mulvey and Tatyana Ptichkin, who helped me obtain texts by Krichevskaya, to Svetlana Barber of Kent State University for her insightful editing suggestions, and to my great friend Natalya Olshanskaya of Kenyon College for her help in the selection and translation of Krichevskaya's works and for her unflagging moral support throughout this project. Students in my graduate course on literary and cultural translation—Nadezhda Korchagina, Deborah Hoffman, Olga Drozdova, Justin Bearden, Anisya Danilova, Marina Zatsepina, Ilya Elnatanov, and Andrey Kononov—also provided excellent input regarding the translation of specific passages. I also wish to recognize my colleagues at the Institute of Applied Linguistics at Kent State, who were always ready and willing to discuss the various translation-related issues I encountered in this project. The editorial advice of series editor Al Rabil was also greatly appreciated. Finally, I owe a special debt of gratitude to Helena Goscilo, whose extensive and insightful comments on the manuscript greatly improved the quality of the translations and of my analysis. Moreover, this is not the first time my work has benefited from her generosity and willingness to share her vast storehouse of knowledge, and I hope it won't be the last. That being said, any remaining errors or infelicities in the translations are mine alone.

Introduction

Friend of the gentle Muses! You dispense their
gifts
As much with brilliance as with modesty.
Your voice rang out among us first,
And all Ukraine applauds thee
LXX ... CC ... , 1816[1]

The Other Voice

Many readers will be surprised to find Liubov Yakovlevna Krichevskaya, a writer born in the first year of the nineteenth century, in a series entitled the Other Voice in Early Modern Europe. However, the "early modern" age, that is, "the period in which Russia was transformed from an essentially medieval, feudal culture into a modern, secularized, European empire,"[2] is generally acknowledged among Russian historians to have begun later and lasted much longer than the comparable period in the West. In terms of literature, Marcus Levitt explains, the early modern period extends into the early nineteenth century: "During what might be called the 'early modern' period ... , the 'classical' hierarchical system of genres underwent three basic transmutations in Russia before it was finally dethroned in the nineteenth century: the seventeen-century baroque; mid-eighteenth-century Russian classicism; and the sentimentalism of the later eighteenth and early nineteenth century."[3] In fact, of the forty-nine writers included in the volume *Early Modern Russian Writers*, over a third lived well into the nineteenth century. And while Krichevskaya's cosmopolitan contemporary Alexander Pushkin would be honored as

---

1.This poem, signed with the cryptograph "LXX ... CC ...," was dedicated to L. Krichevskaya. It appeared in the journal *Ukrainskii vestnik*, volume two, issue 4, of 1816, alongside the first two published verses of Krichevskaya, "Vera, Nadezhda, Liubov" and "R——vu."

2. Marcus Levitt, introduction to *Early Modern Writers, Late Seventeenth and Eighteenth Centuries*, ed. Marcus Levitt, vol. 150 of *Dictionary of Literary Biography* (Detroit, New York, and London: Bruccoli Clark Layman, and Gale Research, Inc., 1995), ix.

3. Ibid., xi.

"the father of modern Russian literature," Levitt argues that those authors who, like Krichevskaya, wrote outside of Pushkin's influence and continued to develop sentimental forms belong still to the early modern age.[4] Accepting the relatively recent dating of this period, readers may be all the more surprised at the dearth of women writers, at least in the scholarly literature. In fact, only two women are included in the above-mentioned volume: Catherine the Great and her friend Princess Ekaterina Dashkova. Moreover, their wealth and status make them hardly representative voices of the time. And so, the work of Krichevskaya, long unavailable in either English or Russian, promises to lend greater insight into the other voice in the literature of that turbulent and still understudied period known as early modern Russia.

Appearing on the Russian literary scene during the reign of Alexander I (1801–1825), Krichevskaya stands out in the history of Russian literature for a number of reasons. Not only did she manage to publish her work in the early nineteenth century, a time when there were very few successful women writers in Russia, but she did so in the provincial city of Kharkov, located in Little Russia, or present-day Ukraine, not in Russia's "two capitals"—St. Petersburg and Moscow, the undisputed centers of Russian literary culture of the time. Moreover, she was one of only a small group of writers—male or female—who attempted to live off their literary earnings, in her case to support her widowed mother and unmarried younger sisters. Driven by financial need as well as writerly ambition, Krichevskaya was nonetheless constrained by the modesty and self-abnegation expected of women at the time, leading her to reflect in her literary work on the idea of woman's agency, that is, how and to what extent women might control their lives and direct their destiny. Krichevskaya's prose fiction alternately displays great confidence, desperate hope, and profound ambivalence that a woman's exercise of selfless virtue will indeed be rewarded in this life with the financial security and domestic happiness she sought, while her poetry is also punctuated by moments of utter despair, as in the poem "Another Song," where her lyric subject makes the abject declaration, "The poor of this world ought not to love!"

---

4. Ibid., xiv.

In a literary tradition that has marginalized and obscured the contribution of its women writers, Krichevskaya has for too long now been "hidden from history." Alessandra Tosi claims that the neglect of women writers like Krichevskaya was institutionalized by the Soviet scholarly establishment, whose teleological view of literary history privileged realism, relegating early nineteenth-century sentimentalism, for all practical purposes, to the dustbin of history.[5] Such a dismissive evaluation of this mode of writing had very real consequences for the subsequent study of this literature. As Tosi explains, "[I]t not only swept away the complexity and richness characterising this age of Russian fiction, but also resulted in there being only a sparse number of both scholarly studies on the period and, crucially, new editions of early nineteenth-century works."[6] Due to the unavailability of Krichevskaya's works, even scholars of Russian women's literature make only the most cursory mention of her literary output, if they acknowledge it at all.[7] However, as an unmarried provincial woman of modest means pursuing a professional career as a writer in the early nineteenth century, Krichevskaya occupies a unique place in Russian letters, and a comprehensive analysis of her work promises to shed new light on the development of early nineteenth-century Russian literature and on the role played in it by women writers.

The Historical Context

Liubov Krichevskaya lived through a rather turbulent time—politically, socially, and culturally—in Russian history, famously chronicled by Leo Tolstoy in the novel *War and Peace*. This era was marked by

5. Alessandra Tosi, *Waiting for Pushkin: Russian Fiction in the Reign of Alexander I (1801–1825)*, Studies in Slavic Literature and Poetics, 44 (Amsterdam and New York: Rodopi, 2006), 12. I follow Tosi in not capitalizing "sentimentalism," "pre-romanticism," and "romanticism" in recognition of the fact that the highly syncretic nature of Russian literature at the time makes it difficult to set chronological boundaries or to describe these modes of writing as discrete "schools" (ibid., 207).

6. Ibid.

7. For example, the biographical sketch of Krichevskaya in Adele Marie Barker and Jehanne M. Gheith, eds., *A History of Women's Writing in Russia* (Cambridge: Cambridge University Press, 2002), 332, is incomplete, leaving out any mention of her major works, such as the epistolary novel *Count Gorsky* (*Graf Gorskii*, 1837).

the accession to the Russian throne of the more liberal-minded Alexander I, the Napoleonic Wars with the burning of Moscow and the Russian occupation of Paris, the liberal Decembrist revolt of 1825, and the repressive reign of Nicholas I that followed. This was a time of intense social and cultural tumult in Russia. As Tosi notes, "The early nineteenth century is a momentous time for Russian cultural life. The new freedom enjoyed by Russians at the beginning of Alexander's 'liberal' reign injected new life into artistic activities in general, and into the literary arena in particular. The number of Russians taking up the pen soared, and began to include non-aristocratic writers and female authors, whilst literary institutions such as societies and journals proliferated."[8]

Despite the increasing number of women writers, the early nineteenth century was an age dominated by men, quite unlike the preceding century, during which four women occupied the Russian throne and Princess Dashkova served as the first president of the Russian Academy of Science. Krichevskaya was born less than a decade after the death of Catherine the Great and only three years after the latter's son and heir, Paul I, issued the law of succession that instituted male primogeniture, which excluded women from inheriting the crown. The presence of women in politics was greatly reduced, and women's influence was largely restricted to social venues, such as salons and artistic patronage. As Catriona Kelly notes, "the emergence of women's writing in Russia was linked with a *decline* in women's real political and economic powers."[9] Not surprisingly, the idea of woman's power, or agency, is at the heart of Krichevskaya's work.

Krichevskaya began her literary career in the second decade of the nineteenth century, during that flowering of Russian literature referred to as the Golden Age, when a pleiad of extremely talented—and almost exclusively male—lyric poets appeared. Among them was arguably Russia's greatest poet, Alexander Pushkin, who made his literary debut in 1814, just two years before Krichevskaya did. However, the fact that Pushkin (1799–1837) and Krichevskaya were almost perfect contemporaries does more to highlight the differences

8. Tosi, *Waiting for Pushkin*, 12–13.

9. Catriona Kelly, *A History of Russian Women's Writing, 1820–1992* (Oxford: Clarendon Press, 1994), 8.

in male and female literature than to point out any similarities, and helps to explain the increasing marginalization of women's writing in Russia. The literary output of the cosmopolitan Pushkin was marked by a highly sophisticated use of romantic irony, something few women writers of the time were free to imitate, confined as they were to more naïve, sentimental modes.[10] Only a generation before, one of Russia's most popular and respected authors, Nikolai Karamzin, had championed the sentimental tale, but by the 1820s male authors were largely abandoning sentimentalism or lampooning it. However, very few women authors were able to escape "the prescriptions of sentimentalism as *the* feminine trend."[11] And while sentimentalism exerted a similar influence on women writers in the West, the Russian case, Tosi argues, "is more extreme in terms of both the hold and the long-term effects sentimental views had on women writing."[12]

In order to give a better sense of the intensely hybrid cultural context in which Krichevskaya pursued her art, it is interesting to note that not all the female authors who took up the pen at that time in Russia wrote in Russian. French was then the first language of Russia's aristocratic elite, and while men were typically forced to learn Russian in their formal schooling in order to pursue careers in the civil service or the military, Russian women were under little compulsion to learn the national language, at least not until the Napoleonic Wars set off a wave of patriotism. And so, three of Krichevskaya's female near-contemporaries—Natalia Golovkina (1769–1849), Yulia Krüdener (1764–1825), and Zinaida Volkonskaya (1792–1862)—wrote almost entirely in French.[13]

The first decades of the nineteenth century also witnessed the establishment of Bible societies, which spread pietism through the educated classes of Russian society and, as Catriona Kelly notes, "encouraged women to express their spirituality in a way that the Or-

---

10. For a discussion of romantic irony in the works of Pushkin, see Monika Greenleaf, *Pushkin and Romantic Fashion: Fragment, Elegy, Orient, Irony* (Stanford: Stanford University Press, 1994).

11. Tosi, *Waiting for Pushkin*, 134.

12. Ibid., 213.

13. For more on these writers, see Iuri Lotman, "Russkaia literatura na frantsuzkom iazyke," in Iu. M. Lotman. *Izbrannye stat'i: V trekh tomakh* (Tallinn: Aleksandra, 1994), 3: 350–368.

thodox Church of Russia historically had not."[14] Such "enthusiastic religiosity" was perhaps a reaction to the restricted roles available to women in the public sphere; in any case, it is strongly evident throughout Krichevskaya's oeuvre, but especially in her lyric poetry. In the late twenties and early thirties, however, the Russian reading public's taste for poetry waned, and many authors, such as Krichevskaya and her more famous contemporary Pushkin, turned increasingly to prose.

The city of Kharkov, where Krichevskaya spent her entire life, may have been far from the cultural centers of St. Petersburg and Moscow, where the poets of Pushkin's pleiad spent their time among Russia's cosmopolitan elite, but it was no backwater. Although it was indeed provincial according to a number of indices—its population in 1802 was just over 10,000, while that of St. Petersburg in 1800 was close to 220,000, and "until the 1830s even the city's main roads were not always passable by carriage"[15]—it underwent rapid expansion and development throughout Krichevskaya's life. Located at the confluence of the Uda, Lopan, and Kharkov Rivers, it served as a major trading point between the north and south of the Russian Empire from the end of the eighteenth century. At that time it became known as a vibrant educational and cultural center, serving an enormous geographic region that included much of Ukraine, portions of the Caucasus, and some southern Russian provinces, as well as the Don region. In 1796 it was made a provincial capital, and in 1799 it became a Russian Orthodox archdiocese, whose Cathedral of the Dormition was adorned with an iconostasis designed by Francesco Bartolomeo Rastrelli, the architect who transformed the face of St. Petersburg under the Empresses Anna and Elizabeth II.

The most significant event in the evolution of Kharkov's cultural life was undoubtedly the founding in 1804 of Kharkov University, one of four universities chartered by the reform-minded tsar Al-

---

14. Catriona Kelly, "Sappho, Corinna, and Niobe: Genres and Personae in Russian Women's Writing, 1760–1820," in *A History of Women's Writings in Russia*, ed. Adele Marie Barker and Jehanne M. Gheith (Cambridge: Cambridge University Press, 2002), 37–61, at 47.

15. L. Makedonov, s.v. "Khar'kov," *Entsyklopediia*, ed. I. E. Andrevskii (St. Petersburg: F. A. Brokgauz-I. A. Efron, 1903), 74: 109–17, at 115.

exander I, and the second-oldest university in Ukraine.[16] In 1824, the university press began publishing the *Ukrainian Journal* (Ukrainskii zhurnal), which, together with the Kharkov-based journal *Ukrainian Herald* (Ukrainskii vestnik), became an important publication venue for the young Krichevsksaya. The city's cultural expansion was especially rapid during Krichevskaya's adolescence, following the Napoleonic Wars. For example, in 1812 the Kharkov nobility founded a beneficent society to educate the children of those with insufficient resources. In 1813 the Society of Sciences was established, in 1816 a section of the Bible Society, in 1817 the Student Society of Lovers of the Russian Word, in 1820 the Student Bible Community, and in 1823 the Bible Community of Gymnasium Students. Kharkov would become a center of Ukrainian romantic nationalism in the 1830s, something which seems to have had little effect on Krichevskaya, although it catapulted her cousin Grigory (Hrihorii) Kvitka-Osnovianenko to lasting fame as a Ukrainian writer.

Despite the founding of universities, each with its own press, and the emergence of new journals during the reign of Alexander I, it was still quite an achievement to be published in Russia, especially for a provincial woman writer. Consider the fact that in the first five years of the nineteenth century, "the average number of books published in Russia was 400 volumes per year and steadily increased to 585 in 1825."[17] Moreover, in a society with an illiteracy rate of 96 percent, the reading public was fairly sophisticated, restricted as it was "to a small elite, mainly represented by the high society of Moscow and St. Petersburg."[18] On top of all that, there was the issue of censorship. The fact that Krichevskaya managed to publish three volumes of her fiction and another volume of historical anecdotes, which she edited, is certainly testimony to her talent and drive.

16. The University of Lviv was founded in the seventeenth century when western Ukraine was under Polish rule.

17. Tosi, *Waiting for Pushkin*, 34.

18. Ibid., 35.

Biography and Works

Krichevskaya was born on the family estate near Kharkov in 1800, and her career as a writer was, in many respects, as much a necessity as it was a vocation. Her father died when the author was only twelve, leaving her and her four younger sisters without a dowry and, therefore, for all intents and purposes, unmarriageable. Moreover, as the eldest child, Krichevskaya became responsible for the welfare of her entire family, and so it would seem to be no coincidence that all of her heroines are fatherless, and in her novel *Count Gorsky* the heroine, whose name is also Liubov, experiences the death of her father at a very early age. And while mother-daughter relationships are portrayed with great warmth and sympathy in her work, providing for a widowed mother is nonetheless an agonizing burden for many of her heroines of modest means (in, e.g., *Blind Mother* and *No Good without Reward*), who must choose between the care of their mothers and their own happiness.

If her father's death necessitated that Krichevskaya pursue a literary career to support herself (and her family), her first cousin Kvitka-Osnovianenko made such a career a real possibility for the young girl. In an age when women writers "depended on the goodwill of the male writers who edited journals" to get published,[19] Kvitka-Osnovianenko, as an editor of *Ukrainskii vestnik*, as well as an active supporter of Kharkhov theatricals, appears to have played an important role in Krichevskaya's professional life.[20] Kvitka-Osnovianenko no doubt helped his cousin to get published in the journal he edited and may have been responsible for the staging of Krichevskaya's play *No Good without Reward*. And while it seems from Krichevskaya's poetry and other writings that she and her cousin were very close, Kvitka-Osnovianenko's support for the young writer may have also been inspired by more abstract principles. A social progressive, Kvitka-Osnovianenko was, among other things, a founder of the Kharkhov Institute for Noble Girls (Institut blagorodnykh devits), reflecting a

---

19. Kelly, "Sappho, Corinna, and Niobe," 56.

20. It is interesting to note that while Kvitka-Osnov'ianenko wrote in Ukrainian, his cousin Liubov did not. Although fluent in at least French and Russian, Krichevskaya probably did not read and write in Ukrainian.

commitment to expanding educational opportunities for women.[21] The proceeds from Krichevskaya's first book-length publication, the two-volume collection of selected works, *My Moments of Leisure* (Moi svobodnye minuty, 1817–18), went to support this school. In any case, it is clear that Kvitka-Osnovianenko encouraged his cousin to write, going so far as to praise her literary talent in verse, to which Krichevskaya responded in the poem "To Gr——ry F——ch Kv——ka. In Answer to His Verses of September 17," thanking her cousin "for all you wished for me," and chiding him for his compliments: "Dear friend! Why did you praise me so/And place me among the very good?"

Such a reaction may have been inspired at least in part by Krichevskaya's self-consciousness over her limited education, which she describes briefly in a footnote to the poem "To Rtishchev" and in the preface to *My Moments of Leisure*. The education she received was directed by her "gentle, good-hearted mother" (1: iv) and involved for the most part the study of religion, or catechism, as she describes it.[22] Nevertheless, Krichevskaya insists that she was content with her modest education—"Thank God! I feel that this is enough for a truly Christian life" (1: iv)—although she does note that it was perhaps insufficient for one hoping to assume "the lofty title of writer" (1: iv), underscoring the challenges women faced in trying to accommodate Christian humility with writerly ambition.

Krichevskaya's description of her limited education was certainly exaggerated; her translations from French and the breadth of her reading suggest that her education extended a good deal beyond the study of the catechism—thanks to her intellectual curiosity and discipline. Her heroines also tend to take the improvement of their minds very seriously. The eponymous heroine of her novella *Emma*, for example, "would be practicing a difficult piece of music

21. S. Shakhovskii, introduction to *G. F. Kvitka-Osnov'ianenko. Povesti* (Kiev: Radians'kii Pis'mennik, 1954), 5.

22. However, one should not, perhaps, make too much of the gender implications of such an education. Kvitka-Osnovianenko, who belonged to the nobility and who, like Krichevskaya, spent his entire life in and around Kharkov, had a similar religion-based education. As he himself put it, "I lived in a time when education did not go very far" (Shakhovskii, introduction, 4).

or traveling through Greece with Anacharsis" in her free time while her sister was "hopping about at a ball." Moreover, we know from her short autobiographical essays that Krichevskaya read widely. In fact, she liked to copy down in a notebook all the edifying passages she came across, although she notes with some humor that many writers express completely opposite opinions with equal conviction—occasionally, on the very same page![23] This interest in entertaining and instructive quotations from works of literature and history led to one of Krichevskaya's greatest publishing successes: *Historical Anecdotes and Selected Quotations of Famous People* (Istoricheskie anekdoty i izbrannye izrecheniia izvestnykh liudei, 1826), largely taken from French sources. The breadth of her reading is also suggested by the authors she cites in her novel *Count Gorsky*, a virtual who's who of Russian romanticism: Pushkin, Ivan Kozlov, Alexander Bestuzhev-Marlinsky, and Vasily Zhukovsky. In any case, while Krichevskaya's description of her education may be overly modest, it nonetheless reflects the reality that women of her day, no matter what their social station, generally did not have access to an education in such prestigious disciplines as classical languages, law, and the hard sciences.

Attempting to live off her earnings as a writer, Krichevskaya may have been the first "professional" woman writer in Ukraine.[24] Such a literary career was only just imaginable in Russia at a time when, as Joe Andrew notes, "the reading public was modestly expanding [and] there was increased professionalization and commercialization of literature."[25] Moreover, a system of female patronage was emerging, evidenced by the dedication of *Count Gorsky* to Princess Emelia Petrovna Trubetskaya by an "appreciative Liubov Krichevskaya," "filled with true gratitude for a kind deed rendered in days of sorrow"—most probably following the death of her mother in the early 1830s and the subsequent loss of property. Nevertheless, social mores of the time constrained women writers—including those, like Krichevskaya, who

---

23. "Moi zamechaniia" (My Comments), in *Moi svobodnye minuty* 1817, 1:138).

24. I. V. Zborovets' and O. P. Nasonova, "G. F. Kvitka-Osnov'ianenka i L. Ia. Krichevs'ka," *Radians'ke Literaturoznavstvo* 11 (November 1978): 44.

25. Joe Andrew, trans., *Russian Women's Shorter Fiction: An Anthology, 1835–1860* (Oxford: Clarendon Press, 1996), viii.

entertained professional ambitions—to present their work as ama-
teurish, unprofessional, the fruits of their spare time.

Outside such dedications and isolated passages in her verses
and semiautobiographical prose, relatively little is known of the life of
Liubov Krichevskaya, including how and when she died. Court papers
from the late 1830s indicating a legal dispute with her brother over
their mother's small estate and a letter from Krichevskaya to the literary critic Pyotr Pletnev asking him to intercede with Grand Duchess
Maria Nikolaevna for patronage underscore the increasing material
difficulties Krichevskaya faced toward the end of her life. It was certainly no easy task to live as a professional writer at that time—for anyone, let alone a woman. Consider, for instance, the difficulties faced
by Krichevskaya's contemporary, the much better-connected Pushkin,
dubbed by André Maynieux "a professional writer in the full sense of
the term."[26] The absence of copyright laws alone was a major impediment to those who sought to live off their literary earnings. Moreover,
for women, writing was not generally considered "a respectable long-
term profession, comparable with, say, a position at court."[27] This is
reflected in the fact that "most women writers of that period apologize
for writing,"[28] a phenomenon reflecting what Sandra Gilbert and Susan Gubar describe as an "anxiety of authorship."[29]

As was typical of authors of her time, Krichevskaya wrote in
virtually all literary genres, publishing a collection of lyric poetry (*My
Moments of Leisure*, 1817), dramas (*Blind Mother*, 1818, and *No Good
without Reward*, 1826), short prose fiction (*Two Novellas: Corinna and
Emma*, 1827), and a novel (*Count Gorsky*, 1837). Her gradual move
from lyric poetry to prose fiction appears to reflect the shifting tastes

26. André Maynieux, *Pouchkine: Homme de lettres et de la littérature professionelle en Russie* (Paris: Librarie des Cinq Continents, 1966), 15.

27. Kelly, "Sappho, Corinna, and Niobe," 42.

28. Yael Harussi, "Women's Social Roles as Depicted by Women Writers in Early Nineteenth-Century Russian Fiction," in *Issues in Russian Literature before 1917: Selected Papers
of the Third World Congress for Soviet and East European Studies* (Columbus, OH: Slavica,
1989), 40.

29. Sandra M. Gilbert and Susan Gubar, *The Madwoman in the Attic: The Woman Writer
and the Nineteenth-Century Literary Imagination*, 2nd ed. (New Haven, CT: Yale University
Press, 2000), 45.

of the time. In 1826, Krichevskaya published her only nonfictional work, *Historical Anecdotes and Selected Quotations of Famous People*. Zborovets and Nasonova note a distinct antimonarchic tone in some of the stories, which ridicule the capriciousness of kings. Such a tone was, of course, in keeping with the general aspiration among Russia's elite in the years following the defeat of Napoleon for greater constraints on the will of the monarch, as embodied in a constitutional monarchy or even a republic. However, there is no direct confirmation elsewhere in Krichevskaya's writing of liberal political leanings. Krichevskaya's last published work was her longest, the epistolary two-volume novel *Count Gorsky*. It seems to have been the least successful—both financially and critically—of all her works. The last recorded mention of the author occurred in 1841 in a letter by Kvitka-Osnovianenko to his friend, the literary critic Pletnev. With that, one of the first professional women of letters in the Russian Empire virtually disappeared from literary history.

Analysis of Krichevskaya's Works

In December 1833, on the cusp of a minor boom in Russian women's writing that would take place in the 1830s and 1840s, historian and bibliographer M. N. Makarov published a piece in the St. Petersburg journal *Damskii zhurnal* (Ladies' Journal), entitled "Materials for a History of Russian Woman Authors" (Materialy dlia istorii ruskikh [sic] zhenshchin-avtorov), which consisted of seven short biographies of contemporary woman writers (two of whom earned their literary reputation as translators of French and German literature). All of the women published their work in Russia's "two capitals"—St. Petersburg and Moscow—except for Krichevskaya, described in the opening lines of her biographical sketch as "a native of Little Russia, the daughter of a Kharkov civil servant of modest means, who was brought up in Kharkov" (49). The biography ends with the promising remark: "If this Little Russian writer is given the necessary support, her prose could rank among the finest in comparison with that of other Russian woman writers" (150). This compliment, however, also implies that a comparison of her prose with that of Russian male authors was unthinkable.

Recognition in such a journal was an enormous accomplishment for a provincial woman writer such as Krichevskaya, who would spend her entire life in and around the city of Kharkov, "far from the capitals,"[30] something that inspired repeated protestations of humility from the author. For example, in a footnote to her first published work, the poem "To Rtishchev," which appeared in the journal *Ukrainskii vestnik* in 1816, Krichevskaya offers elaborate justifications for the "impudence" of putting her work before the public. She explains that her cousin, who was then an editor of the journal, convinced her to do so. It was he, she insists, who "wanted her voice to be heard throughout Ukraine."[31] She does admit to moments when she dreams of assuming the title of writer (*pisatel'nitsa*), "but, thank God, such moments of blindness are rare" (92).

In the preface to her selected works, Krichevskaya develops even more elaborately what Kelly refers to as the "modesty topos." After expressing the hope that her trusting reader might enjoy at least one hour of pleasure from her work, she writes, "No! I do not delude myself with that sweet dream. Neither the voice of vanity nor the requests and approval of my friends could compel me to assume such boldness as to hope that I might provide my readers with some moments of pleasure."[32] She then apologizes for the "countless mistakes" her work must contain, asking her readers to correct them. And finally, she notes that the greatest pleasure for her in publishing her work is the thought that it might encourage her most honorable public to render new acts of beneficence toward the orphans served by the Kharkov Beneficent Society: "Who among you would refuse to be a benefactor to humanity in need?"[33] It must have been unthinkable for a young woman from the provinces—she was merely sixteen or seventeen when the first volume of her selected works was published!—to flout the pose of modesty that was de rigueur for women writers of the time. Moreover, the title of her selected works, *My Moments of Leisure*, and the verses it contains, marking family occasions or recording pi-

30. Mikhail Sh. Fainshtein, *Pisatel'nitsy Pushkinskoi pory: Istoriko-literaturnye ocherki* (Leningrad: Nauka, 1989), 138.

31. Krichevskaya, "R—vu," *Ukrainskii vestnik* 4 (1816): 91, footnote.

32. Krichevkskaya, preface, *Moi svobodnye minuty*, 1: iii.

33. Ibid., 1: v.

ous meditations ("A Prayer on My Brother's Birthday," "A Prayer While Gazing at the Crucifixion," "On the Death of the Most Delightful N. N. Ia——a," "To Two Name Day Celebrants," and "On the Birthday of O. Ia. E——a"), so typical of the poetry one might find in any young girl's album of that period, present Krichevskaya first and foremost as a devoted and deeply religious daughter—in other words, a humble amateur. Nevertheless, as Kelly remarks, "Krichevskaya's work, like that of the Moskvina sisters' verses, is often clumsy in phrasing and stumbling in metre, but … has a spontaneity missing from the more polished efforts published in *Aonidy, Priiatnoe i poleznoe provozhdenie vremeni*, or later *Damskii zhurnal* and the *European Herald*."[34]

The importance of modesty for a woman writer is underscored in an advertisement from the publisher—probably written by Kvitka-Osnovianenko himself—on the last page of *Count Gorsky*, which assures readers that they will find no "vanity or conceit" in Krichevskaya's works. The publisher then notes that the profits from Krichevskaya's first published work went to the Kharkov Institute for Noble Girls. (Krichevskaya had earlier claimed that they would go to orphans.). However, her next work, *Two Novellas: Corinna and Emma* (1827), was published by Krichevskaya with the "extraordinary aim" of supporting her mother, which was praised by Kvitka-Osnovianenko in *Damskii zhurnal*: "It seems to me that her mother's fate is extremely enviable: to receive bread from the hands of her daughter. And what self-sacrifice! Evident here is a child's love in all its brilliance: in order to sweeten her mother's days, the daughter undertakes to present before the public her thoughts, opinions, and modes of explication, declaring, 'Judge me, accuse me, but give my mother the means to rescue herself from poverty.'"[35] It is interesting that Kvitka's description of his cousin's motives makes her into the very image of her own self-sacrificing heroines, blurring life and fiction in a way typical of sentimentalism. At the end of the advertisement, readers interested in purchasing either *No Good without Reward* or *Two Novellas: Corinna and Emma* are advised to write to "His Excellency Grigory Kvitka." We can assume that profits from these works went to the author. (In-

34. Kelly, "Sappho, Corinna, and Niobe," 49.

35. Grigorii Kvitka[-Osnov'ianenko], "O novom sochinenii Liubovi Krichevskoi [On a Recent Work by Liubov Krichevskaya]," *Damskii zhurnal* 18 (1827): 314–315, on 314.

cidentally, the cost of shipping was more than twice the cost of the volume itself.)

The modesty assumed by woman authors, scholars note, may have served to discourage the almost exclusively male critics from focusing on the stylistic and other "defects" of their work. I place "defects" here in quotation marks to remind us that sentimental literature of the kind produced by Krichevskaya has been marginalized or entirely forgotten by the male-dominated scholarly tradition, which long held almost exclusive power to define "good" literature from "bad." What Jane Tompkins says of American sentimental fiction holds no less true of the Russian variant: "The very grounds on which sentimental fiction has been dismissed by its detractors, grounds which have come to seem universal standards of aesthetic judgment, were established in a struggle to supplant the tradition of evangelical piety and moral commitment these novelists represent. In reaction against their world view, ... twentieth-century critics have taught generations of students to equate popularity with debasement, emotionality with ineffectiveness, religiosity with fakery, domesticity with triviality, and all of these, implicitly, with womanly inferiority."[36] To read the works of a writer like Krichevskaya, then, is to enter an alternative literary universe, organized by different values, by a different logic. Sentimental literature, Tompkins asserts, represents nothing less than "a monumental effort to reorganize culture from a woman's point of view ... [and] this body of work is remarkable for its intellectual complexity, ambition, and resourcefulness."[37] Evident throughout Krichevskaya's work is the way in which sentimentalism, as the philosophy or way of thinking behind this mode of writing largely "by, for, and about women,"[38] elevated the importance of emotional sensitivity, downplaying that of reason or intellect.[39] In this way, sentimentalism, or the

---

36. Jane Tompkins, *Sensational Designs: The Cultural Work of American Fiction, 1790–1860* (New York: Oxford University Press, 1985), 123.

37. Ibid., 124.

38. Ibid., 126.

39. The sentimental movement arose later in Russia than in Western Europe (Kelly, "Sappho, Corinna, and Niobe," 51). The term "sentimentalism" was coined at the end of the nineteenth century by literary critics to describe a literary movement that came into being in Russia at the end of the eighteenth century; the term used by those writers themselves

cult of sensibility, offered women a new source of cultural authority, based in morality, a direct result of what Barbara Heldt refers to as the "feminization of virtue."[40] Analysis of Krichevskaya's fiction, then, must focus on how, "out of the ideological materials at [her] disposal, … [she] elaborated a myth that gave women the central position of power and authority in the culture."[41]

Sentimental narratives, which reflect the power of feminine virtue and maternal love to save the world, allowed the orphaned Krichevskaya to make sense of her predicament and must have given her hope. Women's unique claim to moral virtue is reflected in Krichevskaya's work in, among other things, the tag names she often gives to her heroines: Sofia, meaning "Holy Wisdom," Aurora, or "dawn," and Mrs. Dobroliubova, or "lover of goodness.'" And while her antagonists are distributed more or less equally between the sexes (Count Priamov in *Blind Mother* and Count Vetrov in *No Good without Reward*, but Laura in *Corinna* and Princess Zelskaya in *Count Gorsky*), superior virtue is the exclusive attribute of her heroines. Sophia, the heroine of her first drama, *Blind Mother; The Reward of Virtue Tested* (1818), is described as "an angel in human form" who, "in addition to the unparalleled care she provides her mother, […] gives solace to everyone who comes to her in need. What am I saying? Everyone who comes to her—no! She seeks out the poor and helpless and shares with them all she has. When you see her and speak with her, it seems she doesn't belong to this world. She hasn't a single desire, a single intention for herself alone."[42] One might easily ascribe to such a heroine the "terrible perfection" described by Heldt, and Krichevskaya makes clear that perfect virtue is often earned through

---

was "sensibility" (*chuvstvitel'nost'*). Joe Andrew refers to Russian women's writing in the latter half of the nineteenth century as "Neo-Sentimentalism," but the tradition appears to have been unbroken, making the term somewhat misleading. Although, as Kelly points out, *sentimentalizm* was largely used as "a term of abuse" (*A History of Russian Women's Writing*, 51), I choose to use the popular term in order to argue that the negative connotations given it by literary critics are in many ways unfair and inaccurate, especially the associations made by Soviet scholars between sentimentalism and political reaction (Orlova, introduction, 5).

40. Barbara Heldt, *Terrible Perfection: Woman and Russian Literature* (Bloomington: Indiana University Press, 1987), 12.

41. Tompkins, *Sensational Designs*, 125.

42. Krichevskaya, *Moi svobodnye minuty*, 1: 30, 2: 30, 2: 35.

terrible suffering. For example, Sofia's selfless act of giving up her beloved Modest in order to marry Doctor Merl, who has promised to restore her mother's sight, causes her profound anguish. Almost twenty years later, in her second drama, *No Good without Reward* (1826), Krichevskaya's heroine is again caught between two female roles: wife and daughter. "If I provide peace of mind for my mother," the heroine wonders in the opening scene, "will I ever have it for myself?"[43] Devotion to an ailing, widowed mother by a loving heroine stands in the way of a romantic love match, a topos of sentimentalism traceable to Karamzin's short story "Poor Liza" (1792). In any case, as Tosi points out, "these conflicts between roles that are equally precious according to the sentimental canon ... do not lead to insights into the heroine's psychological motives."[44]

Also typical of sentimentalism is the way Krichevskaya's selfless heroines inspire the male characters to greater virtue. In the novella *Emma*, for example, the Major rescues an infant from a burning house only *after* Emma herself has rushed toward the flames without thought for her own safety. Later, Emma presents as a birthday gift to her friend and protector Baron G. "a list of all the unfortunate people living in the vicinity of his estate. She included only those whom she herself couldn't help."[45] In the drama *No Good without Reward*, the heroine's beloved, Erast—who shares the name of the weak-willed hero of Karamzin's "Poor Liza"[46]—attempts to prevent her from wedding the villainous Count Vetrov by ineptly challenging the latter to a duel, which he simply refuses. It is the heroine's selfless gesture of giving away all her money to a blind beggar that brings about the drama's happy resolution, after she has already interceded with Vyska-

---

43. Krichevskaya, *Net dobra bez nagrady* [No Good without Reward] (Kharkov: V Universitetskoi tipografii, 1826), 3.

44. Tosi, *Waiting for Pushkin*, 221.

45. Krichevskaya, *Dve povesti: Korinna i Emma* [Two Novellas: Corinna and Emma] (Moscow: V Universitetskoi tipografii, 1827), 80.

46. Russian sentimental writers tended to rely on a rather limited repertoire of names for their characters, such as Liza, Sophia, Maria (Masha), Modest, and Erast. If these names served as intertextual references to previous sentimental works, then the concept of intertextuality at the time was broad, for the works often had little in common in terms of plot, although they contained similar sentimental devices and clichés.

zov, moving him to excuse a promissory note. And in the novel *Count Gorsky*, the heroine waits patiently and without reproach for her wayward husband to come back to her, going so far as to suffer the death of their firstborn child alone and in secret so as not to shame him into returning. He does eventually return to her, but only after his lover in St. Petersburg has abandoned him for another, more brilliant match.

For Krichevskaya, superior virtue places women in a position to instruct men, who are often portrayed as morally weak and easily led astray (Stradaev in *No Good without Reward* and Prince Belsky and Count Gorsky in *Count Gorsky*). For example, she offers this description of the kind-hearted Baron G. in *Emma*: "[W]hen his heart experienced love, it was always for women who were virtuous, intelligent, and kind. Such women school a man in the most advantageous aspects of his character, making him attractive at every stage of life. Such a man needn't fear the loss of his youth; he will always be a favorite among women." The moral lassitude of men is a major theme in the novel *Count Gorsky*, in which Prince Belsky cynically seeks to take advantage of the Gorskys' marital discord to make advances on the Countess, but is unequivocally rebuffed, while Count Gorsky is handily seduced by the society temptress, Princess Zelskaya. Note Krichevskaya's fondness for symmetry; she gives rhyming surnames to the two characters who threaten the Gorskys' marriage. The name "Belsky," however, comes from the Russian word for *white*, while "Zelskaya" comes from the Russian word for *poison*, suggesting that while Krichevskaya's fiction generally portrays women as more virtuous than men, female antagonists are presented in much darker terms than their male counterparts. These women, such as Laura in *Corinna* and Princess Zelskaya in *Count Gorsky*, appear as preternaturally evil and unredeemable, while male antagonists are portrayed as simply weak and in need of the moral guidance of a virtuous woman. In other words, women are at the moral poles in Krichevskaya's work, while the male characters occupy a vast moral gray area. This may explain why Krichevskaya made Count Gorsky the eponymous hero of her novel instead of the angelic Countess. Because Gorsky is merely weak-willed and spoiled, he is capable of change, which according to Aristotle defines the protagonist, while the Countess is as perfectly virtuous at the outset of the novel as she is at its conclusion—and the evil Princess Zelskaya is beyond redemption.

Also notable in the novel is the fact that three handsome, young male characters (Prince Belsky and the two Count Gorskys, father and son) are attracted to older, more experienced women. In an age when husbands were typically much older than their wives, this curious motif appears to challenge the "canons of masculine and feminine behavior (which presuppose naiveté on the part of the woman and experience on the part of the man)."[47] The motif is also in direct opposition to the traditional sentimental narrative involving the innocent girl and the experienced rake. At the same time, Krichevskaya's treatment of older women is nuanced insofar as the evil Princess Zelskaya is included in this group alongside the highly virtuous Liubov Alekseevna Svetlova, the heroine's grandmother, and Liubov Ivanovna Gorskaya, the heroine herself. Krichevskaya refuses to draw a necessary connection between female experience and danger or vice, although she does distinguish the behavior of the two virtuous women from that of the conniving, cosmopolitan Zelskaya—who, significantly, lives in the imperial capital, St. Petersburg. The first two guide the younger men who court them to more appropriate matches (with younger women), while the last shamelessly encourages and entertains the attentions of her younger admirers.

While it is certainly true that "the sensitive and obedient heroines filling polite fiction in the early nineteenth century reflected and, at the same time, endorsed the patriarchal system of values in place in Russian society,"[48] we should nevertheless recognize the socially progressive aspects of sentimentalism, as well as Krichevskaya's own unique contribution to that cluster of gender concerns referred to in Russia from the early nineteenth century on as the "woman question." Most obviously, perhaps, sentimentalism challenged the social conventions that determined who was an acceptable partner in marriage.

---

47. Nancy K. Miller, *The Heroine's Text: Readings in the French and English Novel, 1722–1782* (New York: Columbia University Press, 1980), 100. Interestingly, Joe Andrew notes that two of Krichevskaya's contemporaries, Elena Gan and Maria Zhukova, also "valorize the older woman." In *Narrative and Desire in Russian Literature, 1822–49: The Feminine and the Masculine* (New York: St. Martin's Press, 1993), 147.

48. Tosi, *Waiting for Pushkin*, 212.

In Krichevskaya's play *Blind Mother*, for example, Sophia is a poor commoner in love with Modest, the son of the wealthy and aristocratic Count Priamov. Initially, the Count refuses his son permission to marry the virtuous Sofia, arguing for the inviolability of class: "[Y]our stations are different. Good sense would never approve such a union" (*Moi svobodnye minuty*, 2: 20). Suspicious of the "system of sentimentality that has settled in every mind" (2: 27), the Count mocks those who think that "to love is for them a necessity and the only reason we are born into the world" (2: 19). He also suspects that Sophia loves his son for his wealth. However, he is eventually so moved by Sophia's selflessness that he declares her to be a "noble soul" (*blagorodnaya dusha*; 2: 34). This marks a crucial moment in the sentimental text, when certain key words that initially referred to economic or class distinctions, such as *poor* and *noble*, are transformed into metaphors for moral or emotional states, representing the ultimate victory of sentimental over material values.[49] Similarly, the adjective "blind," which is first used to describe Mrs. Liubomirova's physical condition, becomes a metaphor when, toward the end of the play, the Count declares, "Finally, a happy incident has opened my eyes" (2: 90). Now seeing the injustice of his traditional beliefs and prejudices, he gives his blessing to the union of Modest and Sophia.

Krichevskaya goes even further in promoting the primacy of sentiment by challenging the traditional relationship of physical reality and one's inner emotional state. In a short untitled essay contained in volume 1 of *My Moments of Leisure*, she suggests that the emotions through which we view the surrounding world effectively create that world, a view with strikingly contemporary resonance. "When we look at everything with trust," she writes, "we come upon good people everywhere; everyone appears disposed to us with their whole heart.

49. This device was made popular in one of Russia's first and most popular works of sentimental literature, Karamzin's "Poor Liza" (Bednaia Liza, 1792), the heroine of which is poor in the sense of economically disadvantaged but in the course of the story becomes "poor" in the figurative sense, as an object of sympathy. Translated into "the language of the heart," "poor" becomes a metaphor and, as such, it makes the economically oppressed members of the lower classes available to humanizing sympathy. Karamzin's story was followed by A. E. Izmailov's "Poor Masha" (Bednaia Masha, 1801) and N. P. Milonov's "Istoriia bednoi Mar'i" (Story of Poor Maria, 1805). Fyodor Dostoyevsky resurrected the device in his first published work, *Bednye liudi* (Poor Folk, 1846).

When we don the glasses of sorrow, everywhere we see disappoint-ments that resemble malice. Ah! Our hearts contain both heaven and hell!" (1: 148–149). She concludes with the remark that there is more hell in our hearts than heaven because "we do not attempt to govern our emotions" (1: 149).

The privileging of sentiment was also deployed by writers of both genders to challenge social convention and oppressive author-ity in all forms. The plot of arranged marriages, legal unions forced upon the younger generation by parents or older relatives, as well as self-sacrificing marriages by "innocent young women" who wish to rescue beloved parents or obey domineering ones, all provided fodder for the society tale—a genre subsequently expanded into the novel. The genre, which flourished in the late 1820s and the 1830s, offered a forum for addressing women's estate while savaging the beau monde. (Vladimir Odoevsky's "Princess Mimi" (1834) exemplifies the gen-re's emphasis on and criticism of the conjugal imperative for young women and the amoral callousness of high society.) A young woman's entry into society, public exposure of private relations via accident or gossip, triumphs and humiliations in luxurious upper-crust settings, and social mobility, among other things, constituted the very stuff of the society tale, which often relied on the device of the frame (the em-bedded narrator) to trace the (usually destructive) persistence of the past in the present. Especially writers concerned with spiritual values and residing in the provinces (as Krichevskaya did) would view such typical settings of the privileged metropolitan classes—the resplend-ent ballroom, the salon, the opera house, the theater, and so forth—as corruptive and superficial. It is no accident that Count Gorsky over-hears inaccurate gossip about his wife in such a milieu, that Countess Gorskaya is "insulted" by her jaded rival while attending a theatrical performance in the capital, and that those invested in the social whirl, such as Bibi, end up badly. (Incidentally, such alliterative foreign names as Bibi, which underscore the character's frivolity and/or that of the entire high society milieu, would become a standard feature of the society tale, as in Odoevsky's "Princess Mimi" and "Princess Zizi.") This negative image of society anticipates sundry literary variations on the corrosive potential of "society." Through the persona of Count Gorsky, Krichevskaya explicitly rejects the grand whirl of "superficial" social life in the capital for the "authenticity" of intimate life in the country (a topos linking sentimental glorification of unspoiled nature with Russian realism's focus on the gentry estate as the locus of "normal" everyday life, especially in the works of Ivan Turgenev and Leo Tolstoy).

All the plots of Krichevskaya's prose fiction are built on the concept of a soul mate, which was central both to sentimentalism and to romanticism. This concept implies that the heart must be free and unfettered to find its one true partner. However, both Sofia in *Blind Mother* and Aurora in *No Good without Reward* are threatened with the prospect of marrying someone they do not truly love in order to save their mothers. It is significant that the anguish is no less for Sofia, who faces marriage to the kindly Dr. Merl, than it is for Aurora, who faces marriage to the superficial and conniving Count Vetrov—because neither man is the heroine's one true love. In the novel *Count Gorsky*, a deathbed promise made by the eponymous hero of the novel to his mother poisons the married life of the young Gorskys by casting a pall of suspicion over his motivation: did he marry out of love or duty? Similarly, in *Corinna* a deathbed promise made by Mr. N. to his father commits him to marrying Laura instead of his true love, Corinna. This results in Corinna's death and Mr. N.'s madness. Although Krichevskaya is careful to present the parent's motivations in the best light, the effect of such constraints placed irrevocably on the hearts of her characters is tragic. These parents exercise a tyranny over the hearts of their beloved children, a tyranny that is no less destructive for being unwitting.[50]

Of course, by elevating the moral and cultural authority of women, sentimentalism lent unprecedented literary power to women writers, transforming what had previously been considered inherent weaknesses—an unsystematic education, emotionality—into strengths: women were believed to have greater, less mediated access to their emotions, which were at the heart of the literature of sentiment. The thematic shift "from the outside world of the heroes' ac-

---

50. It is possible that such pleas for freedom of the heart may serve to encode political aspirations. For a discussion of the relationship between romance and politics in Russian literature, see Brian James Baer, "Between Public and Private: Re-Figuring Politics in Pushkin's *Boris Godunov*," *Pushkin Review* 1, no. 1 (Winter 1999): 25–44.

tions to the intimate world of the individual's emotions" was a crucial part of the "feminization" of Russian society and culture in the early nineteenth century.[51] Krichevskaya demonstrated the authority sentimentalism offered woman writers in an early poem that reads as a kind of poetic credo, "To Rtischev. On the Advice That, Having Read a Description of Nature by Voltaire, I Describe His Garden" (1817).[52] Following a reference to Voltaire, a central figure of the Enlightenment, Krichevskaya advances the major tenets of sentimentalism. First, she explains to her addressee, there is no need to refer to "the skill of other minds" (*iskusstvo chuzhykh umov*) in fashioning a poem. Instead, one should put one's own feelings into verse. In this way, Krichevskaya downplays the kind of formal training that exalts poetic predecessors and demands intertextual references and formal imitation. The only legitimate poem is one that comes directly from the heart, meaning that anyone who, as we might say today, is "in touch" with his or her emotions, can write a poem. Imitation, then, is not only unnecessary, it may actually distort the poet's own feelings. Supporting her argument with references to nature rather than (high) culture, Krichevskaya notes, "A robin won't take the sweeter song/ That to the nightingale belongs." By rejecting imitation, Krichevskaya downplays the role of classical education and makes the unfettered heart the ultimate source of poetic authority. It is a point she reiterates in the shorter poem "To a Frame without a Picture" (1817), where she writes, "Not by intellect and subtle skill,/A painting's made of our most pleasing sentiment."

The degree to which such sentimental notions empowered women to write is underscored here by the fact that the addressee of the poem "To Rtischev" is a man, which is obvious in Russian from the surname's masculine ending. Krichevskaya, then, is instructing a man on the art of poetry after rejecting his advice that she look to another man, Voltaire, as a model for her work. To the extent that Voltaire here serves as a metonymy for the Enlightenment, Krichevskaya's rejection of the great French writer can be seen as a rejection of the

---

51. Tosi, *Waiting for Pushkin*, 198.

52. The poem was first published in 1816 in *Ukrainskii vestnik* under the title "To R——u." Although the full name of the addressee is not given, the ending nonetheless indicates that it is a man.

reason championed by the Enlightenment in favor of the tenderness advocated by sentimental writers. Not incidentally, Krichevskaya contrasts the Russian word *um*, which is grammatically masculine, meaning "reason," to the word *nezhnost*, meaning "tenderness," which is grammatically feminine.

Krichevskaya's identity as a woman writer is also addressed in the poem "On the Militia of 1812," in which she positions herself somewhere between the traditionally gendered public and private spheres. Unable to take up the sword in the face of the enemy invasion, she nonetheless takes action. Putting down the needle and picking up the pen, she argues against the deleterious influence of Rumor (*Molva*), which she personifies throughout. To the extent that rumor, or gossip, is presented in much of the literature of the time as the provenance of women—as in Odoevsky's "Princess Mimi" (1834) and Elena Gan's "Society's Judgment" (1840)—it is significant that Krichevskaya fights against rumor, which she names that "terrible friend of truth."

If the values promulgated by sentimentalism lent new authority to women writers, they may have lent particular authority to *provincial* women writers like Krichevskaya, at least in theory, as the countryside became a privileged topos for the sentimental ideals of innocence and sincerity. In the anonymous sentimental tale "Modest and Sofia" (Modest i Sofiia, 1810), for example, the narrator offers the following rapturous description of the heroine, who has spent her entire life in the countryside: "Sofia cannot be in any way compared with you, glittering society beauties! She's a provincial [*provintsialka*]! … Her blue eyes were a mirror of her tender heart; her face, so sweet and good, revealed a meek, sensitive soul. And her outward appearance did not deceive. Sofia didn't wish to distinguish herself in society: the humble violet was the symbol of her behavior; but every well-educated person who spoke with her for several minutes regretted having to leave her."[53] Krichevskaya's heroines—Emma, Corinna, and Countess Gorskaia—express a marked preference for the countryside and by extension have little interest in society life (*svetskaia zhizn'*). And while Krichevskaya introduces motifs from the society tale into her prose fiction, she never restricts any of her works exclusively to

53. Anonymous, "Modest i Sofiia," *Russkaya sentimental'naya povest'*, ed. P. A. Orlova (Moscow: Izdatel'stvo Moskovskogo Universiteta, 1979), 292.

the city; the duplicity of society is always presented in contrast to a sentimentalized and idealized depiction of country life. It is no coincidence, then, that the virtuous Countess Gorskaya lives on their country estate while her husband carries on an affair with Princess Zelskaya in St. Petersburg, which by that time already functioned as "a symbol of Europe in Russia, of alienation, madness and despair and, above all, artificiality."[54] Incidentally, the heroine's surname, Gorskaya, means "mountainous" and so serves to associate her with nature, while Zelskaya, meaning "poisonous," underscores her rival's wicked nature. When Countess Gorskaya finally confronts Princess Zelskaya face to face, it is in a theater, a topos made famous in such works as Jean-Jacques Rousseau's "Lettre à M. d'Alembert sur les spectacles" (1758) and Pierre Choderlos Laclos' *Les Liaisons dangéreuses* (1782) as a metonymy for the superficiality and insincerity of society life. After defeating her rival on her own turf, so to speak, Liubov brings her husband back to the countryside, where they live an idyllic life of domestic bliss. As Tosi points out, "intimate relationships in the secluded space of the countryside provide a key chronotope in the literature of feeling,"[55] and secluded locales, filled with sentimental associations, play a crucial role in Krichevskaya's prose fiction. Consider the Edenic island in *Emma*, the garden pavilion in *Corinna*, and the grave of the Gorskys' son in *Count Gorsky.*

While sentimentalism may have indeed empowered woman writers, and specifically, provincial woman writers, it should nonetheless be noted that the agency imagined for women is highly circumscribed and mediated. As Tosi points out, "it may be argued that sentimentalism had the merit of creating a congenial atmosphere for women to take up the pen, in so far as praise of feminine aesthetic faculties offered women the opportunity to write. The price for such a safe cocoon, however, was an aesthetically narrow horizon and a psychologically binding set of tenets."[56] As suggested by the titles of Krichevskaya's two dramas, *Blind Mother, or the Reward of Virtue Tested* and *No Good without Reward*, her heroines are able to effect change only indirectly when their selfless virtue is rewarded by

54. Andrew, *Narrative and Desire in Russian Literature,* 1822–49, 94.

55. Tosi, *Waiting for Pushkin,* 202.

56. Tosi, *Waiting for Pushkin,* 215.

Providence, often in the guise of an authoritative male figure, such as Count Priamov in the former and Pravdin in the latter. Moreover, the innate authority of these male characters is underscored by their names: Priamov, from the Russian work *priamoi*, meaning "straight," "upright," "direct," and Pravdin, from the Russian word *pravda*, meaning "truth."

The circumscribed nature of women's agency is also a central theme of the novel *Count Gorsky*, in which the heroine successfully wins back her wayward husband through a combination of seemingly endless patience and selflessness. She not only refrains from reproaching the Count for his infidelity but defends his reputation to others; and she even provides him with money although she knows he will spend it on her rival! The novel ends with a letter from Count Gorsky's close friend and confidant, Alexander Lvov, who notes that while women suffer most from marital discord, they only increase their woes with "complaints and cries, often insincere, and reproaches, often exaggerated and unproven." Therefore, he advises women to practice "humility, modesty, and more faith, which is an endless source of comfort for all misfortunes." This is precisely how Countess Gorskaya achieves her goal of preserving her marriage. "What a triumph for her virtue," declares Alexander, "when her husband with total repentance and burning love threw himself at her feet! And she—she alone authored his happiness."[57] Her power as a wife, rather like the power of Krichevskaya herself as a writer, is won according to the logic of Christian virtue—through almost total self-abnegation. The kind of agency practiced by the Countess clearly speaks to the fact that there were very few options then open to women faced with marital infidelity.

The circumscribed nature of women's agency is also underscored in a passage from her "Excerpts from a Journal Dedicated to My Friends" (1817), which begins with the pronouncement, "A woman and a rose can nowhere be hidden." Krichevskaya then relates an incident in which she picked a rose in memory of a friend and placed it in her reticule. Later, while the hostess is offering her opinions on women's behavior—"Ah, how nice it is when a young girl

57. Krichevskaya, *Graf Gorsky* [Count Gorsky] (Kharkov: V Universitetskoi tipografii, 1837), quotations on 193–194, 193, 197.

behaves well!"—she suddenly smells the rose hidden in Krichevskaya's bag. Krichevskaya then connects the rose to the discussion of women's behavior, declaring, "No matter how hard a good girl tries to hide herself, her principles and talents will always reveal her."[58] Unable to draw attention to herself, the well-mannered girl must "be," not "do," abdicating her agency in the hope that someone will eventually discover her talents and virtues.

While in her prose Krichevskaya appears to have absolute faith that a woman's virtue and talents will indeed be recognized and rewarded, she offers a much less confident picture in selected poems. Alongside lyric verses on the themes of "Christian humility, love of family, and friendship,"[59] Krichevskaya gives full vent to her despondency over the fact that virtue does not always find its reward in this world.[60] In two of her most anguished poems, "From the Banks of the Ternovka" and "Another Song," Krichevskaya expresses the blackest despair over her inability to author her own happiness. The first poem, which she signed with the cryptonym L. K., describes the poet's grief over a failed romance and ends with a cri de coeur: "One thing, 'Farewell!', has darkened all my days/And now, as before, I am nothing!" In "Another Song," the poet complains that she can find no solace as people "cannot feel another's pain/Or grief that isn't tearing them in two," and concludes with the hopeless declaration: "The poor of this world ought not to love!" Such works suggest that Krichevskaya was not a blind adherent of sentimentalism. She was clearly in dialogue with its values, entertaining real doubts about the moral agency it proposed for women.

---

58. Krichevskaya, "Excerpts from a Journal Dedicated to My Friends," in *Moi svobodnye minuty*, 1:130, 132.

59. T. F. Neshumova, "Krichevskaya, Liubov Iakovlevna," *Russkie pisateli, 1800–1917: Biograficheskii slovar'*, ed. P. A. Nikolaev (Moscow: Bol'shaia Rossiiskaia Entsyklopediia, 1994), 3: 158.

60. The desperate voice of some of Krichevskaya's verses may also be a product of sentimentalism. Kelly argues that "the Sentimentalist tradition also offered some women poets, particularly those from outside the aristocracy, the chance to voice real pain" ("Sappho, Corinna, and Niobe," 49). In that respect, it is interesting to note that Krichevskaya entitled her 1824 poem "From the Banks of the Ternovka," rather than "On the Banks of the Ternovka." The poet is not suffering in silence, but sending her despair out into the world in search of a sympathetic reader.

There are other passages in her writing when Krichevskaya seems to be describing not simply sadness, but something more akin to chronic depression. For example, in her journal she notes that, "[t]here is sorrow that for no particular reason oppresses our soul." And in the four-line poem entitled "In Answer to the Question: Why Do I Sleep So Much?" Krichevskaya alludes to a general despair she feels over her unlucky fate and her inability to change it. The critic M. N. Makarov picked up on this depressive streak, noting a "melancholy contemplation of [her] deficiencies" that recurs in her writing.[61] As a writer, however, Krichevskaya found herself to be in something of a bind, for while the experience of strong, often sorrowful emotions was, as she put it, "my school," she also recognized that one must regulate those emotions lest we make our world a hell by donning "the glasses of sorrow."

It would be interesting to know how Krichevskaya, a professional woman of letters, viewed the act of writing, whether as an exercise of woman's agency or as compensation for the few social and professional roles available to her. Unfortunately, while she clearly patterned aspects of her fictional heroines after herself, she made none of them a writer. Nonetheless, she does appear consciously to inscribe herself within a European tradition of women writers. As if invoking "models of an authoritative female voice,"[62] she gave the eponymous heroines of her two novellas, *Corinna* and *Emma* (1827), names that are not only strikingly non-Russian but that are also the titles of novels by two of the most popular and important woman writers of the early nineteenth century: Madame de Staël and Jane Austen, respectively.[63] The enormous popularity in Russia of de Staël's novel *Corinne*,

61. M. N. Makarov, "Materialy dlia istorii ruskikh zhenshehin-avtorov," *Damskii zhurnal* 51–52 (December 1833): 150.

62. Katherine Hodgson, *Written with the Bayonet: Soviet Russian Poetry of World War Two* (Liverpool: Liverpool University Press, 1996), 208.

63. Krichevskaya may have been making reference to another well-known French novel of the time, Sophie Ristaud Cottin's *Claire d'Albe* (1799), giving the heroine the name Aurora, from the Latin for "dawn," highly unusual in Russian literature. Albe, the surname of Cottin's heroine is French for 'dawn.' But more striking is the fact that both works are structured around the separation of two lovers and the misunderstanding that ensues; both lovers think the other has fallen out of love. Cottin's novel, however, is a tragedy and, although didactic, contains some rather graphic sensuality for the time, while Krichevskaya's is a comedy and, as with most nineteenth-century Russian prose, is highly chaste.

which was published in France in 1807 and in a Russian translation in 1809, makes it very likely that Krichevskaya was acquainted with the novel, and similarities in plot suggest that she indeed patterned her work, however loosely, after that of her French counterpart. It is much less certain that she read Austen's work in English, although it is indeed possible that she read a French translation of the novel. The first French translations, by Isabelle de Montolieu, were popular, in part because Montolieu, who had "an immense following of her own," sentimentalized the English author, putting her more in line with Continental tastes.[64] In doing so, Montolieu also brought Austen more in line with Krichevskaya's literary voice, which exhibits little of the subtle irony and restraint of Austen's prose.[65] As Noel King remarks, "[Montolieu's] work is characterized by a rigid morality and an ecstatic love of virtue that scarcely accords with Jane Austen's frank avowal to Fanny Knight: 'Pictures of perfection, as you know, make me sick and wicked.'"[66]

Krichevskaya's *Emma*, however, has very little in common with Austen's *Emma* of 1816, which was translated by Montolieu into French under the title *La Nouvelle Emma*. The two contrasting sisters in Krichevskaya's novella, who both marry at the novel's end, more closely resemble the sisters in *Sense and Sensibility* and *Pride and Prejudice*, and it is indeed tempting to imagine Krichevskaya, one of five dowryless sisters, encountering the Bennet family in Austen's *Pride and Prejudice*, with its five unmarried daughters, or the three Dashwood sisters in *Sense and Sensibility*, who were left in straightened circumstances by the premature death of their father.[67] It may be in fact

64. Noel J. King, "Jane Austen in France," *Nineteenth-Century Fiction* 8, no. 1 (June 1953): 5.

65. Isabelle Bour argues that Montolieu's sentimentalizing translations found an audience on the Continent, in particular in France, because "the novel of sensibility was not as worn out a genre in France as it was in Britain in the 1800s, by which time it was largely discredited and abundantly parodied, after being transformed, and undermined, by Gothic fiction." "The Reception of Jane Austen's Novels in France and Switzerland: The Early Years, 1813–1828," in *The Reception of Jane Austen in Europe*, ed. Anthony Mandel and Brian Southam (London: Continuum, 2007), 13.

66. King, "Jane Austen in France," 7.

67. Excerpts from *Pride and Prejudice* appeared in French translation in the Swiss journal *Biblioteque Britannique* in 1813. It later appeared in 1822 in a complete translation by Eloïse Perks as *Orgueil et préjugé*. Perks notes in her preface that the novel was "extremely success-

that Krichevskaya took her Emma from Austen but not from the novel of that name. For some reason, Montolieu decided to translate Margaret, the name of the youngest sister, in *Sense and Sensiblity*, as Emma. In addition, this sister is thirteen at the time of their father's death, the same age as Krichevsksaya when her father passed away, significantly altering her family's circumstances and her marriage prospects. Moreover, Krichevskaya's *Emma* suffers from the same character flaw as Austen's Elinor: she loves too deeply. In any case, Krichevskaya's Emma, like Austen's, is a comedy, ending in the happy marriage of the heroine, while her *Corinna*, like de Staël's, is a tragedy, ending in the eponymous heroine's untimely death, suggesting that the Russian writer was indeed making an intertextual nod to her more famous female forebears. Regarding names, it should also be noted that, despite the rather black-and-white morality of the novellas, Krichevskaya abandons the moralistic practice of using tag names, which featured so prominently in her dramas and which would reappear, albeit with more subtlety, in her novel, *Count Gorsky*. The dropping of tag names is, in turn, accompanied by greater psychological insight.

Both of Krichevskaya's novellas are internally structured according to the contrastive poetics so popular among sentimental writers of the time.[68] *Emma* features two sisters, one melancholic and bookish, the other high-spirited and scatterbrained, while *Corinna* features two female rivals, one innocent and good, the other worldly and cruel. The fact that Krichevskaya pairs these two novellas—a comedy and a tragedy—suggests that she deployed this poetics of contrast on a metaliterary level as well. The contrast of comedy and tragedy is further elaborated in the narrative forms of the two tales. *Emma*, the comedy, is recounted by an omniscient narrator of undetermined gender, while *Corinna*, the tragedy, is a frame narrative; the heroine's story is told by a man, her cousin, to another man, and contains a lengthy narration by a third, her ex-lover, Mr. N.

---

ful in France" (Bour, "The Reception of Jane Austen's Novels in France and Switzerland," 16). *Sense and Sensibility* was the first of Austen's novel to be translated in its entirety into French, by Mme Montolieu, in 1815, as *Raison et sensibilité*. *Emma* appeared one year later in Montolieu's translation as *La Nouvelle Emma*, clearly intended to benefit from the enormous popularity enjoyed by Rousseau's *La Nouvelle Heloïse*.

68. Tosi, *Waiting for Pushkin*, 141.

The theme of framing is in fact central to the novella, as Corinna is an artist, in contrast to her French namesake, who is a poet.[69] At the country estate where the fatherless Corinna lives with her mother, she has created a beautiful garden with a pavilion filled with her own touchingly rendered paintings of herself and her mother. However, when the innocent Corinna meets Mr. N.—in her garden pavilion— and falls in love, she finds herself increasingly powerless to frame her own story. Mr. N., it turns out, is affianced to her cousin, Laura, and is bound by a vow made to his dying father to marry her. Corinna's final undoing occurs at a grand ball hosted by Laura when Mr. N. throws himself at Corinna's feet on the balcony and Laura throws open the doors, exposing them to the reproachful eyes of the guests.[70] Corinna is thus framed both literally—Mr. N. and Corinna appear on the balcony as a tableau vivant—and figuratively: she has been made to appear guilty of an indiscretion. Her good name ruined, she gradually wastes away and dies.

While Laura appears at first glance to be Corinna's only nemesis in the story, the admiring gaze of the male characters increasingly objectifies her, framing the woman artist as a work of art and robbing her of the agency her talent might have provided her. In fact, Mr. N. and the narrator first set eyes on her in a portrait housed within a golden frame, the first allusion in the novella to the metaphor of the gilded cage. Later, in Corinna's pavilion, they come across another portrait of the heroine: "An unfinished painting on an easel was also a true, ideal reflection of the one who'd painted it." They then come upon a tambour, or embroidery frame, containing yet another representation of Corinna. And so it is not surprising that when Mr. N. visits her pavilion at a later date, he stands at the entrance before announcing himself so that he can admire her in silence—as if she were a painting. Corinna is later described at a social gathering once again as an object of visual pleasure: "Everyone's gaze was focused on her [the Countess] and Corinna—Corinna, whose beauty was indescribable!"

69. Another major difference is that Krichevskaya's *Corinna* has none of the political subtext of de Staël's novel, the full title of which is *Corinne, ou l'Italie*.

70. Krichevskaya suggests in this climactic scene just how complex the social gaze that entraps Corinna is. Corinna realizes the full horror of the incident when she catches sight of her mother, who is looking at the guests, who in turn are gazing at Corinna.

Similarly, at Laura's ball, the narrator declares, "Truly, Corinna was the ball's finest decoration."

The apotheosis of Corinna as work of art comes in death, when she is quite literally objectified, having become an inanimate object. Beholding her in the coffin, the narrator offers the following description: "Corinna ... even in death was an indescribable creature. In the dark of night, surrounded by burning candles, she resembled a marble statue. Galatea herself, emerging from beneath Pygmalion's chisel, couldn't have been more lovely." The (woman) artist has now been permanently reduced to a work of art, with the reference to Pygmalion and Galatea underscoring the issue of gender. In fact, from the opening paragraph of the novella, Krichevskaya does not merely thematize vision but genders it, even sexualizes it, when the first narrator describes his approach to the city of K. Ordering the top of his carriage to be lowered so that he could enjoy an unobstructed view of the surrounding countryside, he remarks: "As I looked around, I felt proud of nature and of the fact that I had been chosen to enjoy it [her]." (Nature, *priroda*, is grammatically feminine in Russian.)[71]

Corinna, it must be pointed out, appears to participate in her own objectification, as she makes herself the idealized and sentimentalized subject of almost all her own paintings. This self-reflexivity, however, may serve as a metaphor for women writers who "were trapped," as Kelly puts it, "in a net of topoi that precluded original expression."[72] John Berger describes the dilemma this way: "Men look at women. Women watch themselves being looked at ... The surveyor of woman in herself is male: the surveyed female. Thus she turns herself into an object—and most particularly an object of vision: a sight."[73] Moreover, the fact that Corinna is the subject—or rather, the object—of her own paintings suggests not only an inability or unwillingness to work at a greater level of abstraction but also an inability to imagine any future for herself outside her childhood home, as the exclusive theme of her artistic work is her relationship with her

71. In order to bring out the gendered nature of vision that is so central to this story, I chose to translate *priroda*, "nature," as "Mother Nature," which then allowed me to use the feminine object pronoun *her* after the verb "enjoy."

72. Kelly, "Sappho, Corinna, and Niobe," 48.

73. John Berger, *Ways of Seeing* (New York: Penguin, 1977), 47.

mother. To the extent that the theme of framing is associated in the novella with social constraints, in particular those constraints placed on women, Corinna the artist ultimately fails seriously to challenge or move beyond them. Rather, she collaborates in her own framing—although the reader might justly wonder whether her story could have any other outcome, overdetermined as it is by the narrative frames of the three men who tell it.

While Corinna's tragedy plays out the cliché of woman as art, the comedy *Emma* overturns the no less powerful cliché of woman as mystery. "Whereas most male-authored texts," Andrew contends, "have the very purpose of showing that woman is enigma,"[74] Krichevskaya's novella presents Major L., Emma's future husband, as the real mystery. Although Emma is melancholic and solitary, like the Major, the reader learns very early on in the narrative the exact reason for Emma's sadness—the untimely death of her first love and fiancé— while the Major's sorrow is much more abstract and bears a closer resemblance to the inchoate romantic longings of Russian heroines in the tradition of Pushkin's Tatiana. In fact, the Major, like a romantic schoolgirl, pours out his emotions in a notebook, which Emma finds and reads. There, he gives vent to his desire for a soul mate: "What gloom! To cross this wide world in vain search of a heart that will beat in time with mine, to stretch out my hand in vain, hoping to feel true love strike! O, dear creature, about whom I've dreamed for so long! Appear before me and light up my soul with a ray of happiness!" Emma is eventually successful in curing the Major of his melancholy and leading him back into society; he even retires from the army without the slightest regret so as to spend all his time with Emma in their domestic paradise in the countryside.

Although sentimental archetypes are evident throughout Krichevskaya's oeuvre, one can nevertheless trace the evolution of a more sophisticated and nuanced representation of good and evil in her prose fiction in the 1820s–1830s, clearly influenced by literary realism. Compare, for example, Krichevskaya's first drama, *Blind Mother*, to her later and more popular drama, *No Good without Reward*. Fully within the tradition of the *drame larmoyante*, or lachrymose drama, *Blind Mother* is almost entirely devoid of humor, except for

74. Andrew, *Narrative and Desire in Russian Literature, 1822–49*, 97.

some good-natured ribbing of the lovesick hero by his friend Victor, while in *No Good without Reward* one encounters one of the more interesting and complex characters in Krichevskaya's fiction: Countess Pustilgina, whose surname alludes phonetically to the word *pustel'ga*, "bird of prey," which can also be used to designate a vacuous person. Although the Countess is devoted to society life, she nevertheless demonstrates a genuinely moral character, unlike her utterly frivolous society counterpart Bibi in *Count Gorsky*. First, she fully appreciates Aurora, the heroine, not only for her beauty but also for her virtue. In fact, she tells Aurora that if she could choose a different character for herself, she would choose Aurora's. Second, she understands the Count, Aurora's fiancé, to be utterly insincere, and lets him know it in the wittiest repartee in all of Krichevskaya's writing. Third, although unwillingly, she keeps the Count's secret—that he is marrying Aurora only for her inheritance—because she has given him her word to do so, distinguishing herself from the loose-tongued gossips who populate the genre of the society tale. Finally, at the end of the play, she asks Aurora if she might continue to live in her house: "Accept me into your family; I feel the only place I'll find pleasure is in your company."[75] It appears that the Countess, like the weak-willed male characters in other works by Krichevskaya, is willing and able to be improved by the example of perfect female virtue.

At the same time, the Countess is distinguished from Krichevskaya's selfless heroines—first, by her joie de vivre, and, second, by her wit and humor, which inject some much-needed comic relief into the melodrama. Situated somewhere between virtue and frivolity, the Countess is unique in Krichevskaya's fiction and points to the beginning of an evolution beyond the absolute categories and archetypes of sentimental literature toward the more complex characters and greater moral ambiguity of literary realism. In *Count Gorsky* Krichevskaya goes so far as to embed what might be described as a metaliterary joke, when the Count tells his friend, Aleksander Lvov, that he must go to the city of Kh——, which is known for the beauty of its women. This is likely an encoded compliment to the women of Krichevskaya's native city of Kharkov and to Krichevskaya herself. In any case, the lack of success of the largely sentimental novel *Count*

75. Krichevskaia, *No Good without Reward*, 57.

Gorsky suggests that Krichevskaya was ultimately unable to keep up with changing literary tastes. Nevertheless, the values expressed in the kind of sentimental fiction Krichevskaya produced—especially the association of women with a certain moral authority and emotional directness—lived on in Russian letters, most notably in the works of Fyodor Dostoyevsky.

Conclusion

One of the most intriguing and valuable aspects of Krichevskaya's writing, and especially her fiction, is the simultaneous presence of various literary tendencies from various epochs, a quality that distinguishes her work from that of her fellow writers, male and female alike, and makes her work especially representative of "the hybridization of genres and the experimental mode typical of the early nineteenth century."[76] As mentioned above, she favors the eighteenth-century moralistic practice of endowing characters with "speaking" or tag names, such as Dobroliubova, or "lover of goodness," and of crediting the capacity of moral education to instill ethical principles in the wayward. Despite the declarations of love, swoons, frenzy, among other things, her prose focuses on virtue, a quality that may be inherent—and more often in women than men—but that also can and should be imbibed and cultivated via contact with paragons such as Countess Gorskaya. Krichevskaya certainly attributes to women the capacity to inspire, reform, and elevate men by the sheer example of their passive piety (recall Samuel Richardson's *Pamela* and *Clarissa*). And the author follows sentimental practices by trumpeting spiritual purity, yet insisting on qualities like the woman's extraordinary beauty or shapely figure (a sleight of hand exposed by the satirical *Shamela*, Henry Fielding's parody of Richardson's novel). The epistolary form, the obsession with endlessly discussed feelings (for spouses, parents, offspring, friends, servants and mistresses, neighbors, etc.)—often in place of action—the consolation of tears, and the blind, dead, or sick parent (in *Count Gorsky*, virtually everyone falls ill from embattled sensitivity, sadness, or insult and does so in a matter of minutes!) are also part and parcel of sentimental topoi. At the same time, romantic elements

---

76. Tosi, *Waiting for Pushkin*, 370.

intrude, particularly in Krichevskaya's prose of the 1820s and 1830s: the volatile hero, uncontrollable passion, wild rides at night, and the central plot of a love thwarted by circumstance. Furthermore, German idealism, which exerted a weighty impact on Russian intellectual circles of the 1830s, conceived of women as the embodiment of both virtue and maternity, and of love as an all-embracing metaphysical phenomenon, which is also reflected in Krichevskaya's work. Finally, as mentioned above, Krichevskaya's depictions of life on the Russian country estate anticipate Russian realist authors' fascination with this site. Another important realist element that appears in Krichevskaya's prose fiction is the exploration of characters' psychology, something often absent in sentimental literature, especially in regard to the sentimental heroine. Particularly striking in *Count Gorsky*, for example, is miscommunication between the characters, their misinterpretation of what is said and, more importantly, of what is not said, something that will become a hallmark of the nineteenth-century realist prose of authors such as Anton Chekhov and Henry James. Of course, true to the syncretic nature of Krichevskaya's work, these realist elements appear in an epistolary novel, a genre that was once a staple of sentimental writers but by 1837 was long outmoded.

Analysis of Krichevskaya's work reveals the author, who preceded better-known woman writers, such as Elena Gan (1814–1842), Evdokia Rostophchina (1811–1858), and Maria Zhukova (1804–1855), who worked within a more preromantic and romantic paradigm, to be a pivotal figure in the development of Russian woman's literature. Moreover, Krichevskaya was precocious, publishing her first poem at the age of fifteen or sixteen, while the others did not appear in print until they were in their twenties or thirties. What distinguishes Krichevskaya's prose from that of those other women writers is her dogged insistence on happy endings—with the exception of *Corinna*—that seek to demonstrate the beatific power of "virtue in distress," presented in a moralistic key. Whereas in Krichevskaya "All's well that ends well," the overwhelming majority of society tales end with the doom of one or both young protagonists.[77] Krichevskaya

---

77. See the above-mentioned collection edited by Andrew, *Russian Women's Shorter Fiction*, and Rostopchina's "Money and Rank," in the anthology *Russian and Polish Women's Fiction*, ed. Helena Goscilo (Knoxville: University of Tennessee Press, 1985), 15–84.

swims against the current in positing the ability of unwavering probity to solve all dilemmas. That faith, however desperate, which installs boundless, exclamation-mark-rich happiness at work's end, allows Krichevskaya in the rest of the narrative to dwell at considerable length on the sufferings and trials (a diminished parallel to Christ's trajectory) besetting her protagonists. One might conjecture that Krichevskaya, unmarried and stuck in the outskirts of Kharkov, was more personally invested in the story of salvation through feminine virtue than her fellow women writers listed above, all of whom married—although none of them happily—and lived at some point in St. Petersburg and/or Moscow. Ultimately, Krichevskaya's fiction and poetry are of interest because they illustrate not simply the transition in Russian literature from sentimentalism to romanticism and realism, or the syncretism of the period, but one woman's valiant attempt to make sense of her life and to imagine some form of agency for herself through the various literary topoi available to her.

Liubov Krichevskaya's life and work reflect a pivotal moment in the construction of modern gender roles and expectations. Arguing against arranged marriages, on the one hand, Krichevskaya nevertheless lived in a time when the presence or absence of a dowry largely determined a young woman's fate. Therefore, I tempered the urge to update Krichevskaya's work in order to make it speak more directly to the contemporary reader, since the predicaments in which Krichevskaya's heroines find themselves are so historically specific, typically involving either differences in class or economic standing and highlighting the few options available to unmarried women at that time. I also chose to follow some of the stylistic conventions of Krichevskaya's time, capitalizing aristocratic and military titles that appear without a surname—e.g., the Major, the Count—to remind the reader of the centrality of rank and station. To a great extent they defined a person's identity and life options.

   I also chose to retain certain historically bound concepts that I felt reflected the largely sentimental worldview reflected in Krichevskaya's work. For example, the concept of "postoianstvo" in respect to emotions appears throughout Krichevskaya's work and corresponds very closely to the English term "constancy." While the word undoubtedly sounds quaint to the contemporary English reader, it opens a tiny window onto sentimentalism. Unlike more contemporary terms that imply personal responsibility, such as "loyalty," "constancy" can refer to either an individual or that individual's emotions. Constancy, then, reflects the fact that in sentimentalism, individual agency is circumscribed by the enormous power of emotions, which sentimental characters often find impossible to govern. For example, when the eponymous heroine of Krichevskaya's novella *Corinna* is publicly humiliated, the shame causes her literally to waste away and die.

   In translating Krichevskaya's verse, I faced the enormous challenge of finding some accommodation between form and meaning. In many instances, if I were to remove altogether the formal poetic elements, that is, rhyme and meter, I would be left with only sentimental commonplaces, clichés. Moreover, Krichevskaya's youthful verse often displays rather primitive rhyme and metric schemes, which, I felt, gave me some leeway. I, therefore, made selective use of rhyme and meter to render some of the charm of Krichevskaya's observations, as in the poem "To Rtishchev" (1817): "A robin won't take the sweeter song/That to the nightingale belongs." I also attempted to preserve the rhymes in the ending couplets of her verse, as the rhyming couplet was a favorite device of Krichevskaya, in which she often displayed great playfulness and wit. Of course, a little rhyme goes a long way in English, and in general I followed Vladimir Nabokov in sacrificing form to semantic content whenever necessary. I went against the reigning norms for the translation of poetry into English, however, when it came to Krichevskaya's four-line verses, or *chetverostish'e*, a popular Russian verse form. I maintained rhyme—however clumsy— in these poems, for in my opinion all the poignancy of this verse form derives from the tension between its formal restraint and its often very emotional content. The poems are arranged thematically, beginning with Krichevskaya's more optimistic poems, about art and poetry ("To Rtishchev," "To a Frame without a Picture," "A White Sheet of Paper," "On the Militia of 1812"), to her sentimental verses that thematize *toska*, or "yearning" ("To Gr——ry F——ch Kv——ka," "The Dniepr"), ending with her most poignant verses, which give voice to her despair ("Truth," "In Answer to the Question: Why Do I Sleep So Much?" "Another Song," and "From the Banks of the Ternovka").

I used a modified Library of Congress transliteration system to transcribe characters' names, rendering the final masculine suffix -skii in many surnames as -sky, and eliminating the apostrophe that indicates the presence of a soft sign in the original Russian so as not to make the names unduly confusing. Therefore, Countess Pustil'gina becomes Countess Pustilgina. According to the same principle, I transliterated the name Korinna as Corinna, thereby rendering the possible allusion to Madame de Staël's novel *Corinne* more obvious to readers. I resisted the temptation to overly domesticate the characters' first names, and so, while I rendered Aleksandr as Alexander, I rendered Iulii as Yulia, not as Julia, and Sofiia as Sofia, not as Sophia. Moreover, I decided to keep the gendered suffixes of Russian surnames, that is, Count Gorsky, Countess Gorskaya, but the Gorskys, in order to show the inescapability of gender in the Russian language. The English reader, however, should understand that these suffixes are obligatory in Russian and therefore stylistically neutral. At the same time, I chose to retain in my translations the full variety of Russian diminutive forms, which are stylistically inflected, reflecting often subtle shifts in tone. The widest variety of diminutive forms appears in the epistolary novel *Count Gorsky*. For example, Mrs. Liubskaya is Sofia, Sonya or Sonechka, depending on the context. The forms ending in –ka (Liubinka, Sonechka, Volodenka) are affectionate diminutives used most commonly among female friends and with children. Although the variety of Russian names is often confusing for the English reader, the fact that Krichevskaya's novel is epistolary makes the interlocutors clear and the diminutive forms therefore easy to attribute.

My most blatant intervention involved the presentation of dialogue, which often appears in Krichevskaya's text in dense paragraphs without attribution, making it at times difficult to follow. In several cases, I unpacked these paragraphs, arranging the dialogues according to contemporary English convention, indenting each speaker's contribution. Russianists may be interested to know that Krichevskaya uses quotation marks, perhaps under the influence of French, rather than the dash, which typically introduces direct speech in contemporary Russian.

In general, Krichevskaya's work may interest the modern reader both for its historically specific elements and its timeless expression of human joys and sorrows. I sought in my translation to accommodate both aspects of her work.

BRIAN JAMES BAER

To My Readers *[Foreword to* My Moments of Leisure*]*

They say that gratitude is a sign of a good heart. What a pleasant thought for me! Wishing to restrain my reader's confidence in me, I appear before him with gratitude as he, having entrusted himself to my hasty decision to publish *My Moments of Leisure*, takes it in his hands with the hope of enjoying at least one hour of pleasure. No! I do not delude myself with that sweet dream. Neither the voice of vanity nor the requests and approval of my friends could compel me to assume such boldness as to hope that I might provide my readers with some moments of pleasure. I know that friendship is the most partial censor and so in this case must not be trusted.

Knowledge and learning did not tune my lyre; and even the common expression "I studied to make a penny" does not apply to me, for I did not study for that. My entire education consists of the abridged catechism taught to me by my gentle, good-hearted mother. Thank God! I feel that this is enough for a truly Christian life. But how little it is for one who wishes to adopt the lofty title of writer.

And so, respected reader, I do not promise you anything with my moments of leisure. I do not publish them for fame. A much loftier sentiment led me to do it and, having forgotten my faults, I hope you will show me your patience. Could I have imagined that these pages, which I wrote to pass the time, would provide me, and me alone, with that incomprehensible satisfaction produced by the hope that I might in some way encourage the respected Public to grant new favor to the orphans cared for by the Kharkov Beneficent Society, to which my heart dedicates these frail works? Sensitive hearts! Marvel at my craftiness in finding a way to be read by you. Who among you would refuse to be a benefactor to humanity in need? Ah! Blessed is the moment when I moved my pen from my book of expenditures to these pages.

Several Excerpts from a Journal Dedicated to My Friends

June 1. Early morning. Everyone is sleeping, and I, with my sadness and with pen and paper in hand, go into the garden. I sit down in a covered walkway to write to you. Not far from me there's music playing, and my soul is transported to you. God! What sorrowfully sweet moments You send us!

Now I'm writing from beneath a beautiful pear tree. Not far away a spacious meadow opens up before me, and there some seventy Russian peasants are cutting hay. There's a village beautifully situated beyond the river. But I'll describe to you a scene that's even closer and more astonishing. Behind the plum tree there sits a young girl. The same emotion has led the two of us to go out walking so early in the morning. For me, it was love for you. For her, it was love for a young gardener. But she's the winner. They're together, while I'm alone! Perhaps you're still sleeping, my dears! And your guardian angel—is he carrying my sigh to you? I say "your guardian angel" because my sigh is so pure. I go over to a rose bush that beckons me: a sweet flower bends toward me! But cruel fate has declared: "Foolish one! That flower isn't for you!" My dears! I was made to share my soul with you, but we are separated by an abyss!

A girl and a rose cannot be concealed. This is so, my friends! My observation is amusing, but true. This is my proof: I went over to a rose bush and kissed the finest rose, imagining that I was kissing you. I then decided to pick it so that when I read you this I could say, "There it is!" I took hold of its stem, but cursed etiquette whispered in my ear, "You can't pick flowers without the hostess's permission." And the stem fell from my hands! I walked away, then stopped and looked at the rose, thinking, "I feel sorry for you ... No, no! I won't be separated from you. Who would bother me if, after I picked you, I hid you—and no one knew you existed." And so I picked the rose and hid it in my reticule; I then walked into the parlor. The hostess sat me down next to her and spoke to me of this and that until at last the conversation turned to the topic of young ladies. "How nice it is," the hostess said, "when a young lady behaves herself well ... Do you smell that, my dear? Don't you smell a rose? Where could it be?" I smiled and answered: "Indeed, Madame. In my opinion, no matter how hard a good girl tries to hide herself, her principles and talents will reveal her." And as if to confirm it, the rose spread its fragrance throughout the room and the hostess tried to find out where it was. A girl and a rose cannot be concealed!

You, my dear ones! You do not shine in society, but there are many who love you, praise you, and admire you!

June 2. I'm on the Dniepr, my friends! Now seated by the window, I see how proudly this magnificent river flows! I can see the Nenasytinsky Rapids, which produce a wild and deafening noise; I see the planks of dilapidated wooden barges sail by. I look at the rocky hills on the other shore of the Dniepr and at the buildings of Mr. S.'s estate, beautifully scattered across those hills. A stone church with a garden surrounded by small trees adds even more charm to this picture. But you are far away from me, my friends! You're not looking at these sights. Perhaps you're sitting next to one another at this very minute, remembering me—and the picture that sadness has painted in my heart? There you can see the same turbulence as on the Dniepr; and there you feel the same pounding as the boats against the rapids! The desire to see you cannot be interrupted by severe weather or by the gloom that surrounds me! Often toward evening I travel to you in my thoughts. I imagine that I'm wandering with you in K. I stop beside a lime tree and read the initials and hieroglyphs engraved upon it. And you are with me; you understand me! Ah! What a burden for the heart when we look around us and do not meet with a single familiar glance, a glance that would penetrate our heart and restrain its yearning with sympathy! Why this multitude of people! One person who is dear to us is enough to make things seem beautiful. And this clear moon, reflected in the Dniepr in a thousand beams, would instill such sadness in me if not for your sweet face in my imagination. It's time to sleep. May your guardian angels be with you! My eyes are very sleepy, but this paper is as much a magnet for my pen as you are for my heart. Perhaps you're imagining now that your friend is talking with you, and then pressing you to her heart, saying, "It's time to sleep!"

June 3. Today we got up early and left. I must confess I'll miss the Dniepr! Although the road was beautiful, we sat in silence. Now I'm writing to you from the estate of K. He's not at home so I'm writing to you from his study, from his writing desk, with his pen. Before me lie several books. I open one and see the verse, "The Tear of a Friend on a Foreign Shore!"

> How long until I see
> The sweet land of my birth?
> How long until I feel,
> My friend, your tender gaze?

I pictured myself here. I cannot imagine how strange man is! My separation from you oppresses me, but at the same time I find a certain joy in being far from you. This is my school! Through this separation, I come to know myself, which is something truly difficult. During that happy and, one might say, blessed time we spend together, my dear ones, tenderness alone fills my heart. My mind forgets itself and is occupied with you. But here, it is occupied with you and me. To know a person is very difficult! No matter how good a camera obscura may be, it's always more difficult to picture something in it when there's no illumination from the sun. In the same way, no matter how intelligent a person may be, without a ray of knowledge, one cannot penetrate him. When you look at a flower—let's say, a purple one, a violet—it's sometimes darker and sometimes lighter, sometimes fresh and sometimes wilted. Ah! That's an image of ourselves! We can never say, even about the most virtuous man, "He is always the same!" No, my friends! Good will be good. But it is impossible to be so for even a few minutes if the seed of evil or thoughtlessness has been planted in his heart! Is it not true that you, my friends, whose hearts overflow at the slightest tenderness, are sometimes worse and sometimes better?

My Comments

In my youth I had the habit of copying down excerpts from every book I read. Without delving into the precise study of a well-turned phrase, I would write them down with pleasure and at times laugh at the contradictory thoughts that give the true picture of our lives. Often in my excerpts, the very same writer, on the very same page, with equal eloquence tries to convince us to love and to loath. Recently, while looking over these excerpts, I was unexpectedly touched when I came across the words, "One who's never seen the rising sun cannot sense God's majesty!" I underlined these words on the paper but not in my heart, which will never stop sensing that the infinite Being appears to us with equal majesty in the smallest blade of grass no less than in the stars that illuminate us! When we seek that great God, how close He is to us! Our will is an impediment that prevents us from seeing His incomprehensible majesty in everything. If a single sunrise portrays Him to us, then how pitiful are those who, out of innocent carelessness, sleep through half the day, let alone the sunrise. And can it be that God in His majesty will, for this sin alone, without taking into account all their goodness, refuse to shine upon them? No! This thought shouldn't frighten men! Can only that which blinds us represent God, who condescends to us with meekness and humility, God who lives not in a king's palace, but among the wretched and the poor, among those who are sick in body and soul, and those who are in need of happiness in this life. He didn't let Himself be known in a shining flash of light reaching to the ends of the earth or in the majesty of the Creator, the sight of which makes holy men tremble. He let Himself be known through mercy, that immeasurable representation of godliness, which brings God closer to man, and man to that Great God, who alone can fully allow every heart to feel God's majesty.

In the full brilliance of the rising sun, an evildoer flees his vice, racing into impenetrable thickets to hide his crime. Does he feel God's majesty? Does he see it? Does he perceive it? Why would he? To curse the heavenly sphere that halted his cruelty? The sun, halfway through its path, also shames the idler who, having no wish to part with his pleasant dreams, enjoys his rest in bed without opening an eye. But the sweetest rest, this happy carelessness, cannot shut his heart to the voice of the suffering. No sooner is his ear struck by a sickly cry than he rushes toward it without a second thought. He wipes away tears and presses every unfortunate one to his heart. He gives them everything and is even ready to sacrifice his bed, which only an hour before was the sweetest thing in the world to him. The mother of that poor family, on her knees, lifting her arms and begging the Creator to bestow happiness on the benefactor who, carried away by his emotions and enlightened by a ray of inexplicable beatitude, is such a spectacle that no one could look at him without flying to God in his thoughts. I believe that the evildoer himself, the one for whom the rising sun inspired only indignation or failed to make him notice it at all, this evildoer would tremble in his soul at this, and in that moment would know God, who gives to man the joy of the angels.

We often see people through the weaknesses of our hearts, immersed as they are in all the misfortunes of this world. The evildoer is indifferent to the rising and setting of the sun, day and night, and even the passing years. He would disappear in this life and in life eternal if God in His mercy, as a demonstration of His majesty, didn't send him a kind, gentle, and indulgent friend, who doesn't reproach him, but sympathizes with him, who doesn't frighten him with the wrath of God, but together with him falls before the Lord and with his heart's emotion begs His mercy. Oh! Is not such a friend, such a priceless gift from God, capable of convincing every soul of the greatness of God!

Man! Made in the image of that God! Once you grasp the will of the Creator, can you accept with indifference that the sun—or anything else— could represent more than you yourself the majesty for which you alone were destined? The finest aim of God's works is our heart, which is so darkened by our delusions that it cannot reflect God's incomprehensible majesty.

A Plan for a Temple of Love in the Heart

The great Architect who built our hearts arranged them very simply. The best part He gave to love, which decorated it according to its wonderful taste.

The large hall of love has three entrances and several more secret doors. The interior of the temple is white, the ceiling is a heavenly color, and the throne of love is pink with a white pedestal. Vases with myrtle, roses, and other fragrant flowers, placed around the throne, fill the entire temple with an indescribable aroma! The first entrance into the temple of love is a direct path from the myrtle and roses; Sentiment stands guard at this entrance and hands the visitor over to Hope, who leads him to the throne of love. Directly opposite is Love, sitting upon her beautiful throne. How majestic she is in her white garments!

A garland of jasmine adorns her head. How beautifully she smiles at the visitor and with what pleasure she offers him her hand!

A winding path leading to the second entrance to the temple is planted with cypress and curved bluebells—an emblem of the individual burdened by sorrow. Here Impatience stands guard and passes the visitor on to Sympathy, who leads him to the temple of love. But, alas! Love is not facing this entrance, and so, poor visitor, you must imagine her charms, for you cannot enjoy them. However, remember that you were led there by Sympathy and Patience. And how tender and pleasing are the looks given to you by Love, who turns toward you from time to time!

The third path to the temple of love leads through a walkway lined with oaks. Beautiful forget-me-nots appear between the sturdy oaks. Respect guards this entrance and hands the visitor over to Friendship, who greets him and leads him to the throne. Love is visible to him only in profile, but not a single smile from her escapes his gaze. The secret doors of the temple are guarded by Chance, Absent-mindedness, Vanity, and other such things.

Thoughts

Distrust! What could be more horrible? Under its sway, the kindest heart grows stern.

One who crushes a violet underfoot does not ask, "Why has it wilted?" He will either toss it away so as not to be oppressed by it or place it against his heart so that its warmth will revive the flower.

The heart is a secret lock. When sorrow depresses the spring of that lock, it opens in order to allow in the tenderest and finest sensations.

There is sorrow that for no particular reason oppresses our soul. Our heart is constricted and, it seems, no sigh could relieve it. There is no thought that is pleasing, and even in your favorite imaginings you find something gloomy, something that crushes us. But at the same time, no tear appears in your eyes. Ah! What could be more horrible than such a state? If there is not strong pressure on our heart, we cannot say that we exist!

Sometimes I think there is no evil in the world. We are happy and unhappy, we suffer or rejoice in a cheerful spirit according to the disposition of our emotions. When we look at things with trust, everywhere we encounter good people; everyone seems disposed toward us with all his heart. When we don the glasses of sorrow, everywhere we see disappointments that resemble malice. Ah! Our hearts contain both heaven and hell! But there is more of the latter because we make no attempt to regulate our emotions.

Fortunate ones! Enjoy this happy time! It flies by so quickly, and there is no other time like it. In nature one April resembles another, while in our hearts, two Aprils may contain such different things!

Blind Mother, or The Reward of Virtue Tested; A Drama in Three Acts

DRAMATIS PERSONAE
Count Priamov[1]
Modest, his son
Victor, Modest's friend
Doctor Merl[2]
Mrs. Liubomirova, a blind woman[3]
Sofia, her daughter[4]
Maria, the old servant of Mrs. Liubomirova

ACT I
SCENE I
VICTOR AND MODEST

A room in the home of Count Priamov. Modest in a dressing gown is writing; after a short pause, Victor enters wearing a uniform.

VICTOR: If you're at your desk, then today must be mail day for Amour?

MODEST (*turning*): Ah! My friend, you've come just at the right time! I've been gloomy all morning.

VICTOR: And so you're writing a sad elegy? Will you be crying long? Pathetic fellow! Is it fitting for a soldier to fear a barricade erected by love?

---

1. *Priamov* is formed from the Russian word *priamoi*, meaning "straight."

2. *Merl* is taken from the French word *merle*, meaning "blackbird," which can also be used to describe people, as in the expression *vilain merle*, "an unpleasant person."

3. *Liubomirova* means "lover of peace" in Russian.

4. Sofia means "holy wisdom."

MODEST (*rising*): But where is the weapon capable of defeating her?

VICTOR: Weapon? Love herself, my friend, has selected the weapon to be used against her. Flatter, pet, and repeat the magic words "I love you!" and the myrtle wreath will blossom upon your head.

MODEST: It's clear you've never been in love. Flatter and pet, you say, as if one has the time to invent endearments when one's truly in love.

VICTOR: Guilty! I forgot that those of you in love never have any time. You're always preoccupied, always in a hurry and fidgeting; and you have time for nothing, although you spend most of your time in empty sighs.

MODEST (*smiling*): Can you, with such a stony heart, paint a picture of love? Can your crude brush portray all its hues, all its pleasing aspects?

VICTOR: Why are you always weeping if love is smiling upon you? You have to be very simple indeed if you can be so deeply in love without any hope of being loved in return. It's impossible!

MODEST: Who told you I'm not loved? But is it possible for a heart to be happy when the object of its love is suffering?

VICTOR: What prevents you from alleviating the misfortune of your love object?

MODEST: First, teach me how to do that. No! You don't know the nobility of my Sofia's soul! Would she wish to accept charity?

VICTOR: Nobility of soul may be called excessive pride when it refuses help from a true friend.

MODEST: Is it possible she can't read what's in my heart? Wouldn't she detect deception in one she understands all too well and who on every occasion shows her not friendship but the tenderest love? She spurns everything without any right to do so.

VICTOR: So offer her your hand.

MODEST: Finally you've said something intelligent. But to my misfortune, the answer to that will be, "Impossible."

VICTOR: Why is it impossible when you love her and she loves you?

MODEST: Have you truly forgotten that I have a father and wealth, while my Sofia is poor?

VICTOR: What does that mean?

MODEST: That my father will never agree to it. "She's poor," he says, and doesn't care to know that her rich heart more than compensates for her poverty! (*growing thoughtful*) My friend, what power can his opposition have over my love? According to his desire, I will not belong to Sofia. But no power, no wealth can hinder me from loving her alone for all eternity, which is all my happiness requires. Wealth and power hold no sway over heartfelt emotions!

VICTOR: No, Modest! Your duty is not restricted to your eternal love for Sofia. You dispose of yourself as if you belonged to yourself alone. Didn't you seek Sofia's love in return? Didn't you cause her to suffer more than before? Modest! You must find the means to make her happy, and not by your true love alone. You must be able to look at her and say, "I did not destroy her well-being; I increased it."

MODEST (*embracing Victor*): Victor! Victor! My heart understands you! I swear that even if I loved that supremely good creature less, I'd dedicate my entire life to providing her with happiness, if I knew I could.

VICTOR (*pressing Modest's hand with feeling*): I've long been convinced that you're a truly noble person. Didn't you show her tenderness and seek to be loved by her? If not, her sensitive heart would never have cultivated an inclination toward someone who, although worthy of all her tenderness, is above her in title and wealth. Don't play with a heart if you aren't sure you can provide it with happiness. Can it be guilty of anything if love is destined by nature? But do you really know that Sofia loves you? Did she tell you that?

MODEST: No. She hasn't said it. But is that necessary, Victor? True love is so discerning that even a hint of mutual affection cannot hide from it. With every visit I see new evidence of Sofia's tenderness toward me.

VICTOR: But is she revealing her attachment only to strengthen yours?

MODEST: Don't insult her, my friend, with the thought. Although she cannot tolerate deception, she conceals her feelings with surprising vigilance. Oh Victor! What charm fills the heart of the one who's the object of those feelings! With what patience she bears all domestic want, and with what tender solicitude she cares for her blind mother!

VICTOR: So you need to think of some way to convince your father.

MODEST: If only he'd agree to see Sofia, he'd certainly love her.

VICTOR (*smiling*): Be careful it doesn't spoil things more. Sofia is lovely, and beauty and loveliness have the same effect on old men as they do on the young. Incidentally, it seems to me he'd agree to see her if you gave him your word to obey his will. If after that he still opposes your wish …

MODEST: Better to say my happiness! But I don't know. I have a sense of foreboding …

VICTOR: What use do I have for your foreboding? It's good that I'm not in love—I'd have to have sentiments and presentiments, and God knows what else! Has Sofia's mother been blind long?

MODEST: Three years. Doctor Merl found nothing on her eyes but some insignificant growths, which are very easy to remove. After an urgent request from me, he's agreed to do the operation today.

VICTOR: What a reward for this poor mother's patience if the first thing she sees is her dear daughter's happiness! We mustn't waste any time. Let's go to your father.

MODEST (*sorrowfully*): You don't know how categorically he denied my request! Although it pains my heart to postpone disposing of my happiness, I can't undertake anything without Sofia's consent.

VICTOR: That's true. A soldier mustn't undertake anything without the permission of his Superior. But please tell me what you were writing.

MODEST: Some account. Father gave it to me to break the chain of my thoughts, as they say. And, I think, to remind me of the income that's stopping me on the path to my happiness.

VICTOR: Abandon that sad thought, my friend. It's better to act than to sigh. I've heard from your love-sick brothers that hope always accompanies love. So why do you despair?

SCENE II
MODEST, VICTOR, AND COUNT PRIAMOV

Count Priamov exchanges bows with Victor.

MODEST (*handing the account to the Count*): Father! I fulfilled your command.

COUNT: Thank you, my friend! Victor! Have you forgotten us?

VICTOR: One who wears the uniform must conceal his own wishes in his heart. You know when you're in military service you can't always dispose of your own time. Last week I was on duty.

COUNT: Now that's another matter. It seemed to me you didn't like us anymore.

VICTOR: Your goodwill toward me and my friendship with Modest wouldn't allow that to happen. Moreover, I don't believe true feelings can ever change.

COUNT: They can change very much.

MODEST: Impossible!

COUNT: All you young people think like that. It's as difficult to convince you otherwise as it is to convince a bad writer that his works are worthless.

MODEST: Leave us with our delusion. We don't envy those experts in living life in society. We only want our lives to be sweetened by love and friendship.

COUNT: For how long, my friend? Trust my experience. Everything passes.

MODEST: Father, what would it be like in the world if people knew there was nothing permanent and spent every moment thinking of it?

COUNT: What would it be like? People would be smarter and wouldn't waste time with empty sighs but would spend their time on useful things.

MODEST: Do we encounter so few of those people nowadays?

COUNT: But the vast majority of us are sighers. Nowadays it's become the custom for a person to be incapable of living without sighing his youth away. Before being able to understand anything, he risks making a choice, taking the most important step in his life, at the pleasure of his fickle mind. To love is a necessity for them—the only thing we're born on this earth to do. I agree that every man must have an attachment to some object. However, he needn't turn a deaf ear to the advice of reason, or against that advice give his love to whoever crosses his path. A young man of noble family who is captivated by the pretty face of the poorest girl thinks his father is wrong to say to him, "Be careful! Beauty's not eternal, and it fades even more quickly in poverty."

MODEST: And if this young man has enough to make that poor girl rich, then why can't he indulge his feelings?

COUNT: Because their stations are different. Good sense would never approve such a union.

MODEST: And so, according to you, Father, a rich man must forget he has a heart and a poor girl must renounce the hope of happiness?

COUNT: Absolutely not! But you say that a poor girl must find happiness with a rich man. Why can she only find it with a rich man?

MODEST: Father, you didn't understand my words properly. I spoke of a girl who felt an inclination toward a man. According to your words, she mustn't even consider the happiness of belonging to him simply because capricious fortune placed her in a lower station.

COUNT: But who's to say that financial interest isn't propelling her love?

MODEST: The honest principles of that young lady.

COUNT: You rarely look at them. But shouldn't we end this conversation? There's too great a distance between youth and old age. I only know that no one can dislodge my opinions. (*To Victor, who is lost in thought*) Why have you become so pensive, Victor?

VICTOR: I was thinking about our conversation and found that you were right. But the way I see it, a father who's confident in the good heart and fundamental principles of his son can give him the freedom to choose his own spouse.

COUNT: Excellent! Even if my son would be unhappy?

VICTOR: I think it would be more distressing for you to see your son unhappy because of you than because of his youth. In the latter case, he would try not to hide it from you and would seek out means to lessen his unhappiness. In the former case, regardless of how tender his affection was toward you, you'd see his unwitting reproach in everything. Admit it, we experience a small misfortune caused by others more acutely than one we bring upon ourselves.

COUNT (*moved*): Your arguments are just. Knowing Modest's feelings, it would be inexcusable of me to appear not to understand the aim of your comments. But listen, Victor. Are you saying that I shouldn't consider the thorns along my son's path? When I see ruts in the road, shouldn't I level them so that he encounters no difficulties in his travels?

MODEST (*taking the Count's hand and placing it to his heart*): Father! I give myself over entirely to your will.

COUNT: And so my will is that you never raise this conversation again. (*He raises his voice slightly.*) I know what I'm doing. I detest that emotion that deprives me of my gentle Modest's obedience.

MODEST: Oh! No, Father! There's no emotion that could make me forget my duty. (*He becomes pensive.*)

COUNT (*to Victor*): You have a new colonel and from what I hear he's a man of great talents.

VICTOR: That's true! And best of all, he's good and knows his responsibilities. He's cordial in his interactions with us and exacting toward those who are negligent in their duties.

COUNT: For that he's rewarded with the love of his subordinates. Modest, I'd like you to visit him with Victor. At your age, you mustn't overlook a good acquaintance.

MODEST: Very good, Father! Let's go, Victor.

VICTOR: You're not dressed.

MODEST: Well then, let's go to my room. Good-bye, Father. (*Leaves by the side door.*)

COUNT: I'll expect you at lunch.

SCENE III

COUNT (*alone*): Everywhere you cast an eye you encounter people with romantic delusions. The values of sensibility have settled in every mind. Often those who don't understand them learn them by rote in order to give themselves a fashionable air. Oh, people! When a father watches with concern the steps taken by his son and, foreseeing a fall, tries to stop him—doesn't this belong to the realm of sentiment? (*He grows pensive.*) But what if this Sofia truly possesses all the qualities capable of bringing happiness to my Modest, and loves him and not his wealth? No! Before I refuse consent to their union, I should get to know her personally or through someone who's worthy and devoted to me. Modest! You shouldn't judge your father so severely.

SCENE IV
THE COUNT AND DOCTOR MERL

COUNT: Hello, my good Doctor! How are you doing?

DOCTOR: Very well, Your Excellency!

COUNT: Where were you just now?

DOCTOR: At poor Mrs. Liubomirova's.

COUNT: At Mrs. Liubovirova's? I've heard something about her.

DOCTOR: Surely, only good things. She's a most virtuous soul! And her daughter! One would have to be very stoic indeed to have no desire to earn her affection.

COUNT (*smiling*): It seems you haven't despaired of success.

DOCTOR: Pardon me, Your Excellency, but I don't wish it so much for myself. Truly, I'm satisfied with my whole heart when the meek Sofia, with the frankness of a friend, relates to me her fears regarding her mother's illness.

COUNT (*surprised*): Her name is Sofia? (*quickly*) And she is kind?

DOCTOR: Kind? From that ordinary word it's clear you don't know her. She's an angel in human form, and in such a form that everyone who gazes upon her wishes to be useful to her in some way. It's only too bad this dear young lady is so unhappy!

COUNT: How have you determined that?

DOCTOR: I have eyes. I have a heart. When I see another's sorrow, I feel it.

COUNT: How did you become acquainted with this family?

DOCTOR: You know my responsibilities. Where there's a suffering body, I must treat it with my art. Where there's a suffering heart, I must treat it with compassion, which serves as support if not as medicine.

COUNT: And so, you are perfect, Doctor?

DOCTOR: It is a principle of mine, Your Excellency, to be as useful as I can be to everyone.

COUNT: A fine principle! But we sometimes make mistakes. When we think we're supporting someone, we knock him to the ground.

DOCTOR: In that case, it's not we who are to blame, but chance. It would be far worse to see a person dying of thirst and refuse to give him anything to drink only because too much could be harmful to him.

COUNT: No, my friend! It doesn't always work to say, "Don't drink anymore." A drop can embolden a person and restore his strength so that he'll grab the cup from your hands and, before you can prevent him, drink it to the bottom. Then you'll reproach yourself for having caused his death, but it will be too late!

DOCTOR: Such a thing might occur with a single individual—and for that, thousands must die?

COUNT: I'm very interested in getting to know this Mrs. Liubomirova. What illness is she suffering from?

DOCTOR: Hers is the most severe illness in the world: she cannot see her only daughter.

COUNT: To put it more simply—is she blind?

DOCTOR: Precisely. Three years ago she lost her good husband, which left her in poverty. Unable to put her small household in order, she lost her sight. Imagine poor Sofia's state! Two losses at almost the same time—the one more distressing than the other.

COUNT: An unenviable situation! And so she's poor?

DOCTOR: Isn't a virtuous soul capable of suppressing its own grief in order to bring peace to others? She firmly resolved that her mother should remain unaware of their difficult situation, and she's fulfilled that intention perfectly.

COUNT (*with surprise*): What a noble soul!

DOCTOR: Oh, Your Excellency! You wouldn't be so surprised if you had even a brief acquaintance with this young lady! In addition to the unparalleled care she provides her mother, she gives solace to everyone who comes to her in need. What am I saying? Everyone who comes to her—no! She seeks out the poor and helpless and shares with them all she has. When you see her and speak with her, it seems she doesn't belong to this world. She hasn't a single desire, a single intention for herself alone.

COUNT: What a lovely portrait, my good Doctor!

DOCTOR: I swear to you, Your Excellency, it isn't far from the original. When you see someone down on his luck, ask him, "Who comforts you?" His answer will surely be, Sofia!

COUNT: Well, my good man, what's wrong with her mother's eyes?

DOCTOR: I examined them and found that she could be helped.

COUNT: What did Sofia do then?

DOCTOR: Sofia fell on her knees before me and cried, "Help her, and my gratitude will be eternal. Take everything we have and return the gift of sight to my beloved mother!" That voice, Your Excellency, is capable of making a monster into the most virtuous of men.

COUNT (*surreptitiously wiping away a tear*): The voice of a charming girl has special qualities.

DOCTOR: You can't call Sofia charming. All that charms is pleasing to the eye, but she's more pleasing to the heart.

COUNT: Is she suffering from any illness?

DOCTOR: I don't know. At least she's never complained of anything.

COUNT: Is her pulse strong or not?

DOCTOR: I don't know that either. Sofia is very poor, and can a poor girl give vent to her emotions? She dares to open her heart to God alone, not to people under any pretense—they can be more cruel than fate itself. Although Sofia possesses every virtue and merit combined together, would some rich man agree to call her his daughter only because she loves his son?

COUNT (*pausing in thought and then extending his hand to the Doctor*): Tell me frankly, my good Doctor! What was your motive in saying so many good things about this young lady?

DOCTOR (*surprised*): My motive? (*reproachfully*) I assure you, Your Excellency, that any honest man who knows Sofia well and speaks of her perfections can have no ulterior motive. You should know me well enough, Count! Flattery and deception have always been and will always be antithetical to my principles.

COUNT (*shaking his hand*): Forgive me, my friend! I've offended you in all innocence, but I thought perhaps my son had spoken to you about this.

DOCTOR: Now I see the source of your suspicion. I swear your suspicion is unjustified! And so as not to leave you with the slightest doubt, I must break my word.

COUNT: No, please don't do that.

DOCTOR: I'm not afraid to break a promise if it will vindicate Modest and give some pleasure to your parental heart. With the request that I not tell anyone, not even you, Modest, in the goodness of his heart, has commissioned me many times to treat the sick at his expense. And so, judge for yourself, whether I could conclude anything from his wish that I help Mrs. Liubomirova. I'm guilty before Modest as I didn't even imagine that his heart could be so noble! To love Sofia is to love virtue!

COUNT (*embracing him*): After offending you, I don't dare tell you how grateful I am. (*He pauses.*) Tell me, what are you planning to do for this poor woman's eyes?

DOCTOR: I hope to successfully complete the operation today.

COUNT: Today? And your fee?

DOCTOR: Sofia's eternal gratitude.

COUNT (*taking the Doctor by the arm*): That's enough, my good Doctor. I intend to make you an important confidant. Let's go to my study. (*They exit.*)

END OF ACT I

ACT II
SCENE I
SOFIA

A room in the house of Mrs. Liubomirova; it is clean and tidy. Sofia, alone, places a large, old chair in the middle of the room. She dusts it off, then examines it.

SOFIA: Honored chair! There was a time when Sofia was so small, you were her bed. She fell asleep in your arms and woke up with a joyful smile! That smile disappeared long ago. And now when I place you here in the hope of witnessing my dearest mother take her first gaze while sitting upon you, a dark foreboding settles in my heart. Isn't it true that happiness and unhappiness are so closely bound together that it's impossible to enjoy one without being touched by the other? What will I lack when my mother's health is restored? (*Pauses in thought; the old wall clock chimes; Sofia counts quietly.*) Twelve o'clock and the doctor isn't here yet. Let me see what mother's doing. (*Approaches the door of her mother's room and quietly looks inside.*) She's fallen asleep. My dear friend! Why can't I offer up to your first gaze everything that's dearest to your heart? Even in your Sofia you won't find the peace you once saw and that once comforted you.

SCENE II
SOFIA AND MARIA

(Maria hands Sofia a letter.)

SOFIA: Who's it from?

MARIA: Doctor Merl. The messenger's waiting for your reply.

SOFIA: All right. (*She takes the letter.*) Dear Maria! Go to mother and wait there until I call you. If she wakes up, don't mention the letter. I'm afraid he's postponing our happiness. (*Maria exits.*)

SCENE III

SOFIA (*walks downstage and reads the letter aloud*): "Charming Sofia! I've finally resolved to tell you that the restoration of your mother's sight depends on you alone. You offered me your estate as payment for my skill. I demand lovely Sofia's hand—I need no other payment. If you esteem your mother, consent, and the happy Doctor Merl will appear this very moment." (*The letter falls from Sofia's hands; she stands motionless, then clasping her hands together she cries out.*) Good God! What's he demanding of me? (*She paces back and forth across the stage and stops downstage.*) If I esteem my mother, then I must consent. Can there be a more horrible test! (*She wrings her hands.*) Sofia, Sofia! What will you do? Is there a person in this world to whom you'd dare to open your heart or to ask for help—and who, upon seeing into my heart, wouldn't say, "You evil person! Don't demand that. She cannot possibly do it!" (*She shudders.*) But my mother is blind! Must her sweetest hope be crushed? Especially now, when its fulfillment depends entirely on me! Won't every look I give you be an agonizing reproach to my heart? (*She raises her hands to heaven.*) God, strengthen me! Cure the acute illness of my soul! Erase that feeling that hopelessly fills my heart. That feeling alone can bring me happiness, but it cannot be fulfilled! And so it isn't hard for me to forsake all happiness on earth! (*She turns toward her mother's room.*) Sleep peacefully, dearest mother! Your guardian angel will illuminate the soul of your daughter, and she'll do everything for you. Your gentle gaze—purchased at such a price—will bring me peace! I must conclude this soon while I still have the strength. (*She picks up the doctor's note, sits down at the desk and writes; she then calls out.*) Maria! Maria!

SCENE IV
SOFIA AND MARIA

Maria enters, then steps back.

MARIA: My God! What has happened to you?

SOFIA (*smiling bitterly*): Nothing, dear Maria! Here is my answer for the doctor's messenger.

MARIA: Is he refusing to help my mistress?

SOFIA: No.

MARIA: Then is he asking for much in payment?

SOFIA (*forgetting herself in her emotions*): Too much, dear Maria!

MARIA (*shaking her head*): Who would have thought it of such a person? He was always so friendly, so good ...

SOFIA: Send the messenger off soon.

MARIA: Immediately, Miss! (*She exits.*)

SCENE V
SOFIA

Now alone, she throws herself onto the chair and covers her eyes with her hands.

SOFIA: Was that truly the right thing? Didn't I act too hastily, without the advice and consent of my mother? I can still turn back. (*She gets up and then sits back down.*) No! The Lord Himself put the thought in my mind. Dear mother! You would've never agreed to this proposal. You would've denied me the ultimate solace of using my life to fulfill the sweet duty of my heart.

SCENE VI
SOFIA AND MARIA

MARIA: Don't be distressed, dear Miss! I've thought of a way to fix this misfortunate. Hasn't good Count Priamov always offered us his assistance?

SOFIA (*interrupting her*): Dear Maria, for God's sake, be quiet!

MARIA: What else can be done, Miss? Truly, doesn't one need to be without a heart to deny my mistress her hope?

SOFIA: She will see. This very day, she will see. Go to her and do me the kindness of saying nothing.

MARIA: Of course, Miss! (*She exits, going into Mrs. Liubomirova's room.*)

SCENE VII
SOFIA (ALONE)

SOFIA: Good Maria! But it's not money that's demanded here, it's my life! (*She pauses in thought, then rises with a calm expression on her face.*) Sofia! Doesn't the reward you're about to receive bring you joy? It's not all of God's children who are sent the means of fulfilling their duty—of showing their mother that a child's heart can transcend itself and show tenderness. I'm satisfied with myself.

SCENE VIII
SOFIA AND MODEST

SOFIA (*as an aside*): Now, Sofia, you need to be strong! (*to Modest*) Count!

MODEST: You're pale, Sofia! Could it be that my arrival has frightened you?

SOFIA (*trying to regain her composure*): Oh, no! I thought that it was Doctor Merl. You still don't know, Count, that he's undertaken to operate on my mother's eyes, and he's sure of his success.

MODEST: Happy fellow! He was allowed to be of use to Sofia! There are some people who would have agreed to give their life for one such wonderful moment. But Sofia refuses them and tries not to look into their heart.

SOFIA (*clasping her hands and making a great effort to hold back tears*): What have I done to you, Count? Have mercy on me in this difficult moment.

MODEST (*moved*): Are you unwell? A terrible change has come over your face—you're suffering! Sofia! Can't I share it with you? If you don't want me to, I'll keep quiet about the other feelings in my heart—

but at least allow a friend to offer you help. Your sorrow is unbearable to me.

SOFIA: Calm yourself, Count! I'm not well, it's true. Thinking that my mother would be able to see me today, I couldn't fall asleep for most of the night.

MODEST (*taking her by the hand*): Oh, Sofia! With what obedience my heart calms itself when you wish it! I agree that the expectation of happiness can disturb you—only I dare not expect anything so pleasing for myself.

SOFIA: Your kind heart will find pleasure in the happiness you provide for others.

MODEST: A vain conviction, my dear Sofia! No! No feeling of goodness can satisfy a heart that demands happiness from something that is denied it. If I could provide someone with happiness, I'd be glad, but I wouldn't stop desiring it for myself. And if I didn't find it, my heart would grieve amid all its blessings. Ah! I know from experience that in pleasing moments we're drawn closer in our thoughts to that one thing that constitutes all the good in our lives and from which fate has separated us. And so, can a person in love ever be at peace? Only one thing, dear Sofia, can lessen his sorrow—the priceless assurance that he is loved.

Sofia, embarrassed, looks down at the ground.

MODEST: Without that sweet hope, life for me is a burden! For example, will a man who's dependent on his father dare to ask permission to wed his beloved when he doesn't know if that will be pleasing to her? Doesn't his father have the right to say, "You're only requesting your own happiness, not hers." What are your thoughts on that, Sofia?

SOFIA (*taking his hands in hers*): With what joy I would consent to think and feel no more!

MODEST: What a cruel wish! For you to be without feelings? Then where would the man who's placed all his happiness in those feelings find comfort? Your gentle heart, which is prepared to sacrifice itself for others—does it wish to see my death?!

SOFIA: Prepared to sacrifice itself for others? Modest!

MODEST: No, no! You bear a sorrow I must know! I can't bear the thought of you suffering. Sofia! (*He takes her hand.*) For God's sake, open your heart to me! If you love me, even a little, then allow me to share your sadness. Don't be frightened by my father's refusal. Today he opposed my requests in a more condescending manner. If he saw you, he'd surely consent to my happiness.

SOFIA (*indecisively*): Modest! (*She hears her mother's voice from behind the scenery; she shudders, then falls semiconscious into the chair.*)

MODEST (*frightened, he rushes toward her*): My God! What's happened to you?

SOFIA (*covering her eyes with her hands*): My good mother! Hurry to my aid.

MODEST (*surprised and troubled, he looks at Sofia*): I don't understand anything! And who will explain it to me?

SOFIA (*soon rises with a sorrowful but calm expression*): Listen, Count! You will learn everything tomorrow, but today, I beg you, do me the kindness of leaving me alone!

MODEST: I beg your pardon! (*As he exits, he looks back, while Sofia stands motionless.*)

SCENE IX

SOFIA (*alone, looking sorrowfully at the door*): Unhappy Modest! What torture Sofia is preparing for you! My God! Can I bear his suffering alone?! No! I must tell the doctor my heart isn't under my control. Won't my perpetual sadness give me away? Oh, people, people! I would beg for your sympathy if it could relieve my heart! What heaviness there is here (*pointing to her heart*), and how much more must I endure! (*She walks toward the door of her mother's room.*) I'll go look for strength in my terrible predicament. (*She opens the door.*)

SCENE X
DOCTOR MERL AND SOFIA

Sofia clutches the chair and holds on to it.

DOCTOR (*confused after noticing this*): When I received your note, I rushed to convince myself of my happiness!

SOFIA: Ah, Doctor! I didn't promise you happiness. I feel strongly I'm in no condition to provide you with that.

DOCTOR: You, Sofia? Who possesses this gift if not you? And what more can he desire, this mortal who's been deemed worthy to possess your heart?

SOFIA: My heart? (*She takes the Doctor by the hand.*) Listen, my dear Doctor! Nothing on earth could force me to deceive you. And so I'm not afraid to tell you I haven't the power to dispose of my heart. But if you could be satisfied with sincere friendship and obligations sacredly kept, then I'm ready to belong to you.

DOCTOR (*kissing her hand*): Dare I ask you to turn your love toward me? Time and circumstances easily alter our feelings!

SOFIA (*sorrowfully*): How I envy the one who could think that!

DOCTOR: And so, will you allow me to see your mother? We mustn't waste any time.

SOFIA (*with a feeling of intense joy*): My God! How could I forget this priceless reward. (*She exits.*)

SCENE XI
DOCTOR MERL (ALONE)

DOCTOR: What has it cost me to see this angel in such a state? I'm amazed at those people who can look with indifference on the suffering of their fellow man—suffering which they themselves have caused. (*He prepares his instruments.*)

SCENE XII
DOCTOR MERL AND SOFIA

(*Sofia leads Mrs. Liubomirova onstage and sets her in the chair; Maria assists her.*)

SOFIA (*wiping away tears, kneels beside the chair*): Mother, my friend! Be calm! Heavenly angels will protect you!

MRS. LIUBOMIROVA: Oh! I'm calm! The hope of seeing my Sofia gives me strength. Doctor! I'm ready.

(*Doctor Merl lifts his eyes heavenward as if asking for help; he then picks up instruments and performs the operation; wringing her hands, Sofia looks at her mother, while Maria cries in the corner.*)

DOCTOR (*joyfully*): Congratulations, Madam! It's all over. You can see!

MRS. LIUBOMIROVA (*looks about and almost in a stupor embraces Sofia*): Good God! I can see my daughter!

SOFIA (*still kneeling, embraces her*): Oh, Mama! What a sight! Look again at your Sofia! (*She presses her mother's hands to her heart.*) My God! Extend this divine moment for my heart.

MRS. LIUBOMIROVA (*looking at Sofia with sorrow and tenderness*): Sofia! Sofia! (*She straightens Sofia's hair and kisses her forehead.*) How lovely you are! Good Doctor! How great is your good deed! Every look I give my Sofia will help convince my heart of my eternal gratitude.

DOCTOR: I assure you, Madam, that never has any doctor received so much satisfaction from his art as I have now. However, as pleasant as this indescribable scene of your happiness is to me, allow me to remind you, Madam, that great strain can be harmful to your sight. You must cover your eyes.

SOFIA (*grabbing her mother's hand*): Oh, no! No!

MRS. LIUBOMIROVA: Don't take away from me the pleasure of seeing my Sofia!

DOCTOR: I'm sure Sofia wouldn't want the pleasure of seeing her to have negative consequences for you—consequences that neither my art nor the most heartfelt desire would be capable of alleviating.

MRS. LIUBOMIROVA: I beg your pardon, dear Doctor! One more look at Sofia and I'll be ready! (*She looks at Sofia, who is embracing her about the knees, then the doctor folds a scarf in two.*)

MARIA (*approaches with tears in her eyes*): Madam, look at your Maria.

MRS. LIUBOMIROVA: I'm sorry, my friend, that I didn't notice you before. Embrace me. (*Maria kisses her hand.*)

DOCTOR (*covering Mrs. Liubomirova's eyes with the scarf*): Keep this on for two days, Madam!

MRS. LIUBOMIROVA: May I look at my Sofia at least once a day?

DOCTOR: You may.

SOFIA (*embracing her mother*): Mama! My friend! How happy your Sofia would be if your eyes could see only pleasant things.

DOCTOR: Now, Madam, you must rest.

MRS. LIUBOMIROVA: Whatever you wish, my good Doctor! Even with my eyes covered I can see Sofia. You've given me such happiness. May God reward you! For such a good deed He'll send you a reward that I'm unable to give.

(*Doctor Merl and Sofia are embarrassed by these words.*)

SOFIA: Let's go, Mama! (*Quietly to Doctor Merl*) Please visit us in about two hours. I'm so upset I can't express my gratitude to you. (*She leads her mother out and Maria follows behind them.*)

SCENE XIII

DOCTOR (*alone, putting away his instruments*): Thank God! I feel better now! It seems as if my good deed has redeemed my heart's unworthy deception and has washed away the tears I forced the unfortunate Sofia to shed. How I hope that this deception will serve the cause of her happiness. And who can resist the pleasant desire to earn her gratitude? Happy Modest! To be so loved? I would envy you if I didn't feel that you alone were made for Sofia! No, my good Count! I'm incapable of deceiving Sofia for long. And if you don't come during my appointed rendezvous with her, then I'll tell her everything. But will Modest, to whom I owe so much, forgive me?

END OF ACT II

ACT III
SCENE I
SOFIA AND DOCTOR MERL

The same room; they enter at the same time.

DOCTOR: How's your mother?

SOFIA: She's healthy, but feels very weak. I assume it's from so much excitement.

DOCTOR: Of course, Miss! Can I see her?

SOFIA: She asked you to wait a bit. Would you like to sit down? (*She offers him a chair then sits down herself; silence.*) Do forgive me, Doctor! I didn't have the time before to say a single word of thanks to you. (*lowering her eyes*) You've reconciled me with my heart's joy and given me new strength to fulfill the promise I gave you.

DOCTOR (*delighted*): And you also said, Sofia, that it wasn't in your power to provide me with happiness when your charming voice alone, penetrating the depths of my heart, assures me of the happiness I hope soon to enjoy! I'll try to show you, Miss, how greatly I respect your merits.

SOFIA: Happy the man whose voice inspires trust in good hearts and disposes them to sympathy. On the other hand, how poor is the man who casts his eye in all directions but doesn't meet with a single soul that understands his grief.

DOCTOR: What a gloomy thought! Are there really so few good people on earth? It seems to me that anyone who wishes to look for a friend can find one easily in this wide world.

SOFIA: Does it seem that way to you? Could it be you've forgotten those iron chains the world imposes on us with its prejudices. No, good Doctor! We see few people who are brought together by chance.

It seems the gaze of one penetrates the soul of the other, but cold decency places a barrier of darkness that keeps them from one another.

DOCTOR: You're right. I have a convincing example of that. It seems you know Count Modest?

SOFIA (*confused*): Yes! He is a frequent visitor to our home.

DOCTOR: He's a wonderful young man! I am his family doctor and only yesterday learned that he's in love with a virtuous young lady of limited means. I don't know her name, but assume her merits surpass everything if she was able to instill such an unprecedented feeling in the heart of Count Modest. I don't know how to tell you, Miss, with what tenderness he begged his father to agree to their happiness. And it seems the old man is wavering in giving his consent. What joy this noble young man will feel! I can say without a doubt that his beloved will be the happiest of women.

SOFIA (*leaning her head on her hand*): Ah!

DOCTOR: What's wrong, Sofia? Are you unwell? Allow me to take your pulse.

SOFIA (*looking mournfully in his eyes*): No, good Doctor! No one can relieve Sofia's illness!

DOCTOR (*as if not understanding her*): Why do you think that, Miss? You've just seen an example of it. What illness could compare with that of your mother, but my strong desire to help her met with the greatest success.

SOFIA: Ah! Good Doctor! Don't reproach me so cruelly! If it were only in my power to make myself healthy this very minute—but I can't. By God, I can't!

DOCTOR: Sofia! You must calm down or you'll fall seriously ill. (*Silence.*)

SOFIA: Allow me to ask you to do me a kindness: leave aside your demand until my mother has recovered. I gave you my word and it's sacred to me.

DOCTOR: I wouldn't have dared to think otherwise. Obviously, you haven't spoken to her yet of your promise?

SOFIA: Not yet.

DOCTOR (*joyfully*): All the better.

SOFIA: Why do you say that?

DOCTOR: Because it would be harmful to excite her in any way now. And you know that a mother can't be indifferent to the resolution of her daughter's fate.

SCENE II
SOFIA, DOCTOR MERL, AND OLD COUNT PRIAMOV

COUNT (*to Sofia, gazing at her in surprise*): Am I mistaken, Miss, in taking this for the home of Mrs. Liubomirova?

SOFIA: Not at all, sir. This is my mother's home.

COUNT: And so you are her daughter?

SOFIA (*bowing*): I am.

COUNT: May I see your mother, Miss?

SOFIA: She's not terribly well and so I don't dare promise that you can. However, I'll ask her if you order me to. But may I know who would like to see her?

COUNT: I'm Count Priamov.

SOFIA (*turns pale and bows*): Won't you sit down? (She throws herself into a chair before the others.)

COUNT (*sits down and fixes his gaze on Sofia*): Don't bother your mother. It will be very pleasant to pass the time with you while she rests. Doctor Merl is, no doubt, attending her

DOCTOR: Exactly so, Your Excellency!

SOFIA (*coming to her senses*): Doctor Merl, with the help of his art, has accomplished a magnificent deed. My mother has been deprived of her sight for two years, and he has returned it to her.

COUNT (*looking at Sofia with sympathy throughout the rest of the conversation*): May it do him good, Miss. Not every person in the world uses his talents in accordance with the will of God. Not every person finds joy in being useful to mankind. We all love goodness but take an interest in it only when it appears before us in a pleasing form. We make no attempt to find it when it's hidden beneath modesty.

SOFIA: True goodness, in my opinion, Your Excellency, gives little value to society's judgment. It doesn't even try to hide itself beneath a veil of modesty, knowing that it would be too obvious to those who are the object of its deeds.

COUNT: What a lovely thought! The individual who knows how to value virtue as you do surpasses every price on earth. Of course, what does such a person need with the judgment of people who lock their judge in their hearts. And so our good Doctor has been rewarded in abundance by being not only a witness to but also the cause of the first reunion of a tender mother with her incomparable daughter—the kind of daughter passers-by cannot look upon without being moved.

SOFIA (*bowing*): You are gracious.

COUNT: Not everyone is like you with those who need your help.

SOFIA: My help, Your Excellency? Unfortunately, everything surrounding me could serve as evidence to the contrary.

COUNT (*looking about*): The first time I entered your home I looked at everything surrounding you until my whole attention was absorbed by such riches that only a portion would be enough to satisfy all the needs of the heart. Having a sacred responsibility, I got to know you thoroughly, Miss, although I'd never had the pleasure of seeing you.

SOFIA: People are often mistaken, Your Excellency! Removed from society and denying myself all its desires while following the advice and example of the finest of mothers, I couldn't be accused of anything. However, I wouldn't dare assume all the virtues that sensitive hearts have attributed to me.

COUNT: You don't want to assume them because it's not with words but with deeds that you prove the opinion you expressed to us: that true goodness pays no heed to human praise—but at least it doesn't forbid people from being astonished by it. Who better than you, Miss, fulfills her obligations to her mother?

SOFIA: Can fulfilling such a sacred obligation truly astonish anyone? Oh, Your Excellency! How pitiful are those children who forget God's commandment! Can their hearts feel true comfort? No! Words of praise touch me least of all. Don't the sweet words of my mother surpass them: "I am pleased with you, Sofia."

COUNT: Who would not be pleased with you, Miss, and grateful to you for that heartfelt satisfaction that one cannot feel by listening to words of truth alone.

SOFIA (*lowering her eyes*): Is this why you rarely speak with Count Modest?

COUNT (*delighted*): With my son? No, Sofia! I heard him out this very day. I listened to him swear that you possess every merit, but I was too blind to believe him. Now I see that his words were true. I see that and ask you to forgive me.

SOFIA: Oh! My God! What should I forgive you for? Must everyone know Sofia?

COUNT: Every father must facilitate the happiness of his son. I should have tried a long time ago to get to know you personally. Knowing of Modest's feelings for you, I dared to think that a union with a young lady of limited means would demean him. I never imagined that her merits and intelligence could elevate him, and even more, make him happy. I'm pleased, Miss, to acknowledge my guilt before you in the hope of expiating it. Sofia, will you allow me to tell you frankly why I came here?

SOFIA (*with a start*): I'm happy to hear whatever you have to say.

COUNT: I assume I can speak of everything in the presence of our good Doctor? He's received in my home like a member of the family.

SOFIA: The good deed he's done for us gives him the same position in our home.

COUNT: And so, Sofia, I ask you to hear me out. My son, Modest, loves you with all the strength of a heartfelt attachment. But I was ill disposed to his impassioned entreaties for me to consent to your mutual happiness. Finally, a fortunate incident opened my eyes. From every side I heard flattering descriptions of you. Everywhere people were saying that you were God's finest creation. My Modest uttered your name with heartfelt respect. Tell me, could I then refuse to agree to his one condition—that I see you for myself. And if you were—forgive me for this test—what they said you were, to offer you my son's hand and to ask you to complete his happiness. Sofia! Now I ask this favor of you.

SOFIA (*jumping from her chair*): Oh! Kindest of men! What poison your words have poured into Sofia's heart! To complete Modest's happiness? My God! Where will I find the strength to refuse?

DOCTOR (*with noticeable self-restraint*): Sofia! What about your promise?

SOFIA: Ah! I feel it too strongly! (*She approaches the Count.*) My God! What must I explain to you? Unable to gaze any longer at that happiness my heart imagined for itself together with Modest, and having no hope of relieving the burden of my existence, I undertook to sacrifice my feelings for the responsibility God had placed upon me. Doctor Merl requested my hand as a reward for his skills. I agreed. My mother can see, and I am his!

DOCTOR: Sofia! I expected that from your noble heart.

SOFIA: Oh, if you could only feel what it cost me! It's the limit of my grief. Nothing can surpass it! Honored gentleman! I beg you to force Modest with your fatherly advice to banish the unfortunate Sofia from his heart. Let her mourn her happiness alone. Oh, God! I dare to ask you to grant peace to the noble Modest! Farewell, Count, and pass on my final farewell to your son! Are you satisfied, Doctor? (*She walks toward the doors of her mother's room but falls to the ground in a dead faint.*)

COUNT (*rushing with the doctor to Sofia's side*): What have I done? Help her! Help her!

SCENE III
SOFIA, DOCTOR MERL, COUNT PRIAMOV, MODEST, AND VICTOR

MODEST (*not seeing Sofia*): Victor? Am I seeing things? It's my father! What's he doing here? (*Moving closer, he sees Sofia unconscious and rushes to her side to help.*) Good God! Who brought her to this state?

COUNT: Forgive your old father, Modest! I'm the cause of this.

MODEST: Oh, Father! What has this angel done to you? Hasn't your distrust of your Modest caused enough sorrow? Oh, my God! Help her!

COUNT: Not knowing the real reason for my visit, you're accusing me for nothing, my friend.

MODEST (*not listening to his father, bends over Sofia*): Sofia! Sofia! Open your sweet eyes! (*To Doctor Merl*) I beg you to help her. (*They all lift Sofia and place her in the chair; Modest takes her hands and kisses them without stopping.*) There's no power on earth that could tear Modest away from Sofia. Your opposition, Father, can't prevent me from dying at her feet. (*Sofia regains consciousness; Modest notices this and throws himself on his knees before her.*) Sofia! Sofia!

SOFIA (*opening her eyes and seeing Modest, she looks around her*): Mama! Where's Mama?

MODEST: What's happened to you, Sofia? Why did you faint like that?

COUNT: Didn't I tell you, Modest, that I was the cause of it! Listen to what happened and then judge your father.

MODEST (*impatiently*): Please continue. I'm listening.

COUNT: Hearing over and over from you one and the same thing— that you loved Sofia—I wanted to get to know her quickly. The doctor revealed to me that he was attending Mrs. Liubomirova at your request and that he hoped to help her. It took great effort on my part to convince him to test Sofia. Finally, he promised me he would act as if he wouldn't agree to help her mother unless he received her solemn word that she'd be his.

MODEST: I sense that she agreed. Oh, Sofia! You didn't foresee what a blow to my heart you were preparing! Who could take you away from Modest?

COUNT: It was a ruse.

SOFIA (*leaping from the chair*): A ruse? Thank God, it was a ruse!

MODEST: Innocent soul! Who could have doubted your virtue? You see, Father, how much good there is in this sweet creature! In a moment of joy, she forgot all the weight of her sorrow. (*He gives his hand to Sofia.*) Sofia! Sweet Sofia! And so you haven't rejected my heart?

SOFIA (*in tears, releases his hand*): Can someone refuse possession of something that is the finest thing on earth? Ah, what a wonderful heart!

MODEST (*kissing her hand*): Father, Father!

COUNT (*wiping away tears*): Forgive me, Modest! I'm an old, distrustful fool and couldn't believe that the heart of a woman was filled with every virtue. Forgive me, my son! And you, the daughter of my heart, my Sofia! Embrace your father! (*Sofia and Modest rush to embrace him and in their exuberance fall on their knees; the Count places his hands on their heads.*) May God bless you, my children! Get up, get up! Embrace one another. Let my heart take joy in your happiness.

SOFIA: No, Modest! We've received a blessing only from your father— what about our gentle mother? She still doesn't know how happy her Sofia is. I'll go and get her.

MODEST: Oh, Sofia! You're incomparable in everything! (*Sofia exits into her mother's room.*)

SCENE IV
COUNT PRIAMOV, DOCTOR MERL, MODEST, AND VICTOR

MODEST (*kisses his father's hand*): Father, is there any way I can smooth over my behavior toward you? I dared to think you were opposing my happiness and reproached you for your cruelty. No matter how extreme my passion was for Sofia, I shouldn't have forgotten my filial obligations and your constant tenderness toward me.

COUNT: I hope that your happiness, my beloved Modest, will wipe from our memory all past regrets.

VICTOR (*shaking Modest's hand*): Now, my friend, accept my congratulations. Up until now I haven't wanted to disrupt this scene, so pleasing to the sensitive heart. I myself have enjoyed it.

MODEST (*embracing him*): Oh, my Victor! What a pity I don't possess at this moment your persuasive eloquence so that I could express my gratitude to you. What words might express my happiness?

DOCTOR (*to Modest*): Count! Forgive me the ruse that cost you so dearly.

MODEST (*embracing him*): My dear Doctor! Sofia is mine. She fills my heart, banishing all unpleasant memories. (*He shakes his hand.*) To the contrary, I'm obliged to you. Father could never have loved Sofia as much as he does now. I'll try to make her happiness the reward for the tears your ruse forced her to shed. Don't those priceless tears signify that she loves me?

VICTOR (*smiling as he gazes at Modest*): Dear Modest! How obvious it is you're happy. All your movements show it. How I hope to see you always in such spirits.

MODEST: My friend! My heart is so full that I never had such a desire to recount its emotions.

VICTOR: Oh! I never had such a desire to look at you, to listen to you. Every one of your words is infused with the ecstasy that fills your heart!

MODEST: Whose heart if not yours can share this ecstasy with me?

SCENE V
COUNT PRIAMOV, DOCTOR MERL, MODEST,
AND VICTOR

(Sofia leads Mrs. Liubomirova on stage, with bandaged eyes)

SOFIA: Doctor! Uncover her eyes. Let her see her happy Sofia.

DOCTOR: You may do it yourself, Miss.

SOFIA (*removes the kerchief from Mrs. Liubomirova's eyes and immediately embraces her*): Mama! Dear Mama! Thank God for your Sofia's happiness.

MRS. LIUBOMIROVA: My sweet friend! Doesn't His all-seeing gaze look deep inside our hearts? There lives the gratitude of those who esteem His mercy! (*Looking around her.*) Where's my Modest?

SOFIA (*taking Modest by the hand and leading him to Mrs. Liubomirova*): Can it be that you didn't recognize him? Who could be more sweet and handsome?

Mrs. Liubomirova embraces them in turn.

COUNT: These are our children, Madam! I blessed them with all my heart. Now it's your turn.

MRS. LIUBOMIROVA (*pressing Modest and Sofia to her heart, she raises her eyes skyward*): Almighty God! May their hearts nourish this pure love to the grave! I can now close my eyes with joy for all eternity.

SOFIA: That will be no time soon. (*She drops Modest's hand.*) Modest! Now I'm yours! (*They embrace one another.*)

Curtain.

No Good without Reward; A Comedy in Three Acts

DRAMATIS PERSONAE

Mrs. Dobrova[1]

Aurora, her daughter[2]

Count Vetrov, renting rooms in the home of Mrs. Dobrova[3]

Countess Pustilgina, also renting rooms in the home of
Mrs. Dobrova[4]

Stradaev[5]

Erast, Stradaev's son

Yulia, Stradaev's daughter

Pravdin, a rich merchant and the brother of Mrs. Dobrova[6]

Vsyskalov[7]

Boy, non-speaking part

ACT I
SCENE I

Mrs. Dobrova's room, poorly furnished, but tidy

AURORA (*alone, sewing*): If I provide my dear mother with peace of mind, will I ever have any for myself? Oh, no! A feeling of virtue can't make us happier if we separate ourselves—even in our thoughts— from belonging to our beloved. A certain philosopher once said in vain, "One must try to quiet the whispering of the heart; the more one sacrifices, the more pleasing the reward." What a wonderful convic-

---

1. *Dobrova* is derived from the Russian adjective *dobryi*, meaning "good" or "good-hearted."

2. *Aurora* is the Latin word for "dawn."

3. *Vetrov* is related to the word *veter*, "wind," the adjective for which, *vetrennyi*, can be used to describe a frivolous, inconstant person.

4. *Pustilgina* (Pustil'gina) alludes phonetically to the word *pustel'ga*, "bird of prey," which can also be used to designate a frivolous or vacuous person.

5. *Stradaev* is derived from the verb *stradat'*, "to suffer."

6. *Pravdin* is related to the noun *pravda*, "truth."

7. *Vzyskalov* is derived from the verb *vzyskazat'*, meaning "to force payment."

tion! But I'd like to ask this thinker how he would feel if he were in my place!

SCENE II
AURORA AND COUNTESS PUSTILGINA

COUNTESS: Good afternoon, Aurora! Allow me to rest here beside you. (*Throws herself into a chair.*) That ball has tired me to death. Has the Count arrived?

AURORA: I don't know. (*Looks at the Countess.*) Countess, you're terribly altered. Is it possible to take such little care of yourself?

COUNTESS: Altered? Why should it be so? I'm as accustomed to this tiring occupation as you are to your work. Two hours at my toilette will erase even the traces of that fatigue that so frightens you.

AURORA: Perhaps. But that lifestyle is incomprehensible to me.

COUNTESS: We'll see if you say that when you're the Count's wife. I'm sure that within a few days you'll be taking lessons from me in the art of passing the time. However, Aurora, you won't receive those lessons unless you promise not to use your dangerous charms to eclipse me.

AURORA: You're joking, Countess. Could you ever fear me? I'm accustomed to solitude or, better put, obscurity, and harbor no hopes of pleasing society. Society loves only those who can be of some use to it. It's tiresome to be someplace where we mean nothing to others and find nothing for ourselves.

COUNTESS: How is it possible to find no pleasure for yourself among so many people?

AURORA (*smiling*): People who confer their praise or criticism upon our outer appearance? People who one moment liken us to a goddess and the next fail to recognize us? And you want me to exchange my beloved corner for high society? No, Countess!

COUNTESS: But of course you've forgotten that you'll be dependent on your husband, who'd probably die if he had to spend two consecutive hours in your beloved corner.

AURORA (*downcast*): You're right, Countess! I must disregard my own will.

COUNTESS: That's the other extreme, my friend! You don't know the Count well if you think he'll deprive you of your will. Locking wives in towers has gone out of fashion. Today you're free to go anywhere—as long as you don't run into your husband. But tell me, Aurora, is it truly more pleasurable to sit with your head bent over your work than to be where we can see everyone, take an interest in everyone and, best of all, have everyone take an interest in us?

AURORA: That's pleasing only to someone who has prepared herself for life in society, whose desires are fulfilled by rushing to social functions, whereas my desires ... Ah! Shall we stop talking about this?

COUNTESS: With such an alluring face, with such talents—fie, my friend, it's a sin to be so unsociable. Does pleasure hold us in its grasp? No, we hold pleasure in ours!

AURORA: You're right, when we find it in our own hearts—but when it departs, we begin to search for it in vain in others; and we can't expect anything even from time itself, which, they say, heals all wounds; it carries our life along without making it any more pleasant.

COUNTESS: O my sweet Aurora! What gloomy thoughts! When I used to see you always so calm, I envied your happiness.

AURORA: My happiness? O Countess! You envied a poor man his empty purse!

COUNTESS: It's good the Count can't hear that.

AURORA: Do you think I've hidden from him how little my status will add to the brilliance of his social life? But he doesn't want to understand me, and I cannot grasp what has induced him to ask for my hand.

COUNTESS (*laughs*): What else if not true and passionate love.

AURORA: To give myself over to that thought would be a mark of excessive pride. I don't consider the Count capable of constant affection. It would be enough if he were governed by pity for our poverty, which would guarantee my future peace of mind.

COUNTESS: No one has ever remarked that the Count likes to sacrifice himself. But then, why lose the hope that your virtue will make of him a completely new man. I know personally the power of your alluring meekness, although I'm one step further removed than the Count from your perfection.

AURORA: Countess! You imagine that you're still at the ball, surrounded by people who take compliments for the truth.

COUNTESS: But that is the truth. Remember that I'm saying it to a woman, and I wouldn't have said such a thing in another place for anything. But I don't consider you, Aurora, an earthly creature. And I confess that if I could choose another character for myself, I would choose yours.

AURORA (*with emotion*): How kind you are, Countess. But perhaps it's not my character but my circumstances that have made me who I am.

COUNTESS: All the same. You only imagine that a happier lot would have made you different. (*Rises.*) Goodbye, dear! New conquests await me this very day. I must take advantage of them before you enter society.

SCENE III

AURORA (*alone*): It seems to me that this wide world is darker than a dungeon, and that my gaze will never find another who speaks to my heart. O Erast! If you've forgotten me, then why can't I know it before I have to renounce you forever? Forgotten—what a horrible word! Do I really want to hear it? Oh, that news, whether we want to hear it or not, always arrives too soon. It would be better, much better, while I still know nothing, to tear from my heart the priceless hope that has dwelled there until now and, clutching that incurable organ with these two hands, throw it without thinking into the abyss that opens up before me. Only those who have loved and have had to part with their beloved forever can understand my feelings!

SCENE IV
AURORA AND MRS. DOBROVA

AURORA (*approaches her mother*): Mama, aren't you feeling well?

MRS. DOBROVA: Don't worry, my dear! Perhaps a better future will give me strength.

AURORA (*brings her mother a chair and herself sits down to work*): You're so weak, you deny me any hope of finding joy in the future. You want to make my future bitter, not sweet.

MRS. DOBROVA: No, my dear! I wouldn't want to add to your sorrows, but I'm afraid the unbreakable chain of those sorrows will diminish your hope.

AURORA: Is it possible for a heart that trusts in God's boundless mercy to lose hope? No, Mama! No misfortune in the world can deprive me of hope. Didn't you always tell me that we are truly unhappy only when, in our confusion, we lose hope in the Creator's favor? When we rely on it, we are always and everywhere happy.

MRS. DOBROVA: That's right, my Aurora! May that faith always dwell in your heart! I'm also upset that I've had no news of my brother; I expected some word from him.

AURORA: Don't worry, Mama. Perhaps he'll show up soon.

MRS. DOBROVA: Perhaps! But then I won't need any human help; then the sorrow of seeing my daughter sacrifice her own happiness will have driven me to the grave.

AURORA: Isn't your peace of mind my happiness? O Mama! My heart never feels so much satisfaction as when it provides you with a single moment of pleasure.

MRS. DOBROVA: But there are also moments, my dear, when the most virtuous of us experiences extreme sorrow, and I wouldn't want to be the cause of sorrow for you.

AURORA: Dear Mama, what sorrow? When one has a heart that's always ready to do good, that loves all people as brothers, and does everything possible for them, can one be entirely miserable?

MRS. DOBROVA: And do people treat you in kind?

AURORA: That's their business, not mine. (*She embraces her mother.*) If everyone had a teacher like mine, they'd all act the same way toward me.

MRS. DOBROVA: Of course, my dear! It's better to be mistaken in people's gratitude than to shut your heart to them ... I've been waiting now for hours for Vzyskalov to come. Our promissory note comes due today, and I don't know what to do about it.

AURORA: Don't be distressed, Mama! Hasn't invisible help from heaven often delivered us from difficult situations at a time when my arms were still too weak to do anything for you, and my heart couldn't feel the full weight of your responsibility? I think the Count will pay what he owes us for the rental of his rooms.

MRS. DOBROVA: But won't it be difficult for you to ask him about it?

AURORA: If the Count has a noble heart, I'll need few words to convince him. Besides, we're only asking for what is ours.

MRS. DOBROVA: Aurora! When I imagine you spending your life beside this Count, my heart can't help but tremble. God sees whether I'm coolly sacrificing your welfare.

AURORA: How often this welfare is nothing but the fancy of our imagination! I hope that when I'm able to provide for you in your old age, it will disappear like the stars before the rising sun. The Count is just thoughtless, but when I see how well he treats you, I will of course love him.

MRS. DOBROVA: Love? O my child! That emotion isn't under our control. God forbid that I should ever see remorse on that sweet face!

AURORA: No! You will never see that, Mama! (*She hears a noise from behind the door.*)

MRS. DOBROVA: It seems the Count is here. I'll leave you two alone. Talk to him, my dear! (*She leaves.*)

AURORA: Alright, Mama!

SCENE V

AURORA (*alone, looking out the window*): The Count is leaving the courtyard. And now I have to wait until he returns with a thousand oaths of eternal faithfulness—and not a single one of them will touch my heart. O Mama! You'll tremble when you see me united to this man. Don't be afraid, my dear! I have enough strength to hide my tears from your penetrating gaze. And I'll suffer alone so that you might have peace of mind.

Exits.

ACT II
SCENE I
COUNT VETROV AND COUNTESS PUSTILGINA
(*the same room; the two enter from opposite sides of the stage*)

COUNT: It's you ... what a pleasant encounter!

COUNTESS (*taking a seat*): I doubt that it's your first this morning.

COUNT: You insult me if you think that my heart can take equal pleasure in every woman's gaze.

COUNTESS: God keep me from such a thought!

COUNT: Can anyone compare to you? At first sight my heart gave you the advantage over all the beauties of this world.

COUNTESS: If only over those to whom you've paid the same compliment, it would be enough.

COUNT: Are you unwilling to accept my amazement? Don't you understand the sighing of my heart? You—

COUNTESS: —Again with your heart! I assure you, Count, that I am as acquainted with your heart as I am with the stage sets for *Rusalka*.[8]

---

8. In Slavic mythology, a *rusalka* is a water sprite, a female ghost or mermaid-like demon that lives at the bottom of rivers. With songs, dancing and laughter, rusalkas would lure handsome men to the river bottom to live with them. Countess Pustilgina appears to be referring to the popular magical comic opera *Dneprovskaia rusalka* (The Water Sprite of the Dnieper), based on the German opera *Das Donauweibchen* by the Viennese composer Ferdinand Kauer, about a love affair between a rusalka and a prince. The rusalka later interferes

And I hereby release it forever from any raptures, amazement, torments and sighs, but I confess to you that I would like to have its complete trust.

COUNT: It's yours, Countess! Without limits. But dare I hope that in entrusting myself to you, I won't be betrayed?

COUNTESS: Don't worry! Although I may be a woman, I know how to hold my tongue.

COUNT: Oh! You were created to enchant people! I dream from time to time that our inclinations are the same and that you would approve of my intentions.

COUNTESS: I'm much honored, Your Excellency! But aren't you marrying Aurora?

COUNT: Yes! ... but that hasn't been entirely settled.

COUNTESS: No stammering, Count! No excuses. I know you're not afraid to assume the chains of matrimony, which will not tie you down in the slightest. But what do you hope to do as a gentle swain? Let's suppose Cupid, that fair and playful child, delivers the food of love to you on his little wings. What will your wife do? She could be included among the Graces, although, as you may recall, there's already a complete set.

COUNT: You're mistaken, Countess. I have prospects.

COUNTESS (*shaking her head*): It seems your prospects are not in perspective. Your painterly brush has, I suppose, unintentionally given

---

with the prince's marriage to a mortal woman. In Russia the opera was, as Simon Karlinsky puts it, "the biggest theatrical hit of the decade, perhaps even of the half-century" (*Russian Drama from Its Beginnings to the Age of Pushkin* [Berkeley: University of California Press, 1985], 186). Sequels, with music by Stepan Davydov, were also extremely popular until the 1840s, although "all serious playwrights and critics deplored the success of *The Water Sprite*" (187).

them the crudest shading. And although the heavenly dawn—Aurora—lights up the horizon of your life, can she continue to shine like that from beneath a blanket of poverty?

COUNT: I want to tell you about that.

COUNTESS: Tell me, tell me. I'm terribly anxious to know how a man of your principles suddenly makes himself sensitive and out of pity burdens himself with an entire family. It's a true riddle.

COUNT: Which for you, Countess, should be very simple to solve. Is it possible that you, with your perspicacity, have failed to find the source of my emotions, imagining me to be a complete fool? I am of course capable of losing my head, but only as a result of your coldness, charming Countess!

COUNTESS: What are these prospects of yours, Count?

COUNT: When I was in the capital, I happened to make the acquaintance of Aurora's rich uncle, who had just returned from a trip. In the course of our conversation, he gave me to understand that his niece would be his heir. As I was preparing to come here, I was still putting together my plan.

COUNTESS: In which the greatest mathematician could find no flaw.

COUNT: Naturally, Countess! Otherwise all my knowledge of society would mean nothing. Of course, I feigned true modesty and, having earned the trust of that simpleton, managed to wheedle out of him a letter and a huge sum of money to deliver to Mrs. Dobrova, which I …

COUNTESS: Don't tell me, Count, don't tell me. Now the breadth of your generosity has opened up before me. And the denouement to this interesting drama?

COUNT: The denouement is the nicest part! Aurora will weep, explode with anger, but all the same she will remain my rich wife. Her principles assure me that she will not want the one who has been joined to her to remain in despair. At the same time I will throw myself at her feet with all the signs of repentance and swear that it was only love and tenderness that induced me to employ this ruse, that I'll be her servant, her slave ... and ...

COUNTESS: Allow me to add the rest: her servant, her slave, and then, being the same thoughtless rake that you are now, you'll squander her money and forget she's still alive. O men! That's the true picture of your love!

COUNT: Why is there no exception, charming Countess! You alone are in a position to make any heart constant. Allow me to hope that you will not abandon this house.

COUNTESS: Although it's flattering, Your Excellency, to think that I could make of you a model of constancy, I'm afraid that your winged love, accustomed to fluttering from one object to another, would in a single moment destroy all my work. Moreover, Count, I cannot abide perfidy. I promised to hold my tongue and for that reason alone will keep my word, but a good wife may still make of you an honest man. (*Curtsies and exits.*)

SCENE II

COUNT (*alone, folds his arms as he watches the Countess depart*): Wonderful! Have I really been deceived by that cunning woman? It's the first time in my life this has happened. Clearly I'm now being punished for the thousand deceptions I've carried out! ... With such affectation she pronounced the words, "I cannot abide perfidy." Let's see, Madam, if you can outsmart me? In order to prevent the worst, I'll slander her to Aurora myself. I'll implore Aurora to beware of her as someone who once harbored a passion for me and now out of jealousy is determined to say spiteful things about me. It is, however, vexing.

SCENE III
THE COUNT AND AURORA

COUNT (*approaches Aurora and kisses her hand*): I swear to you, Aurora, your charms multiply with each passing day.

AURORA: I have always asked you, Count, to abandon flattery and speak to me in the language of sincerity.

COUNT When I see you, it's impossible to remember anything except that you're more beautiful than anything else on earth.

AURORA: It would be better if you told me how you enjoyed yesterday's ball.

COUNT: Exhausting! The dancing wore me out. You know that society is always a tyrant to those it favors with distinction, and I pay very dearly for the attention society pays me. Obliged to do everything that was demanded of me, I could rest only when my thoughts turned to you.

AURORA: Thank you, Count!

COUNT: Noticing my negligence and absentmindedness, many penetrated my secret; and it seems to me, my charming Aurora, that, although you have yet to enter society, you already have a number of enemies there.

AURORA: You don't please me with that, Count. In my peaceful life, I fear the word "enemy."

COUNT: That enmity will bring you fame. The fact that I keep you in my heart despite all temptation brings you even greater honor. (*Aurora bows.*) How is your dear mother?

AURORA: She becomes weaker every hour under the weight of need.

COUNT: How can she feel need when she has in her power such a priceless treasure as you, Aurora?

AURORA: In such circumstances as hers, giving oneself over to the dreams of a lively imagination could mean willingly increasing one's misfortune. No, Count! Her treasure is so small for her needs that she has instructed me to ask you for money. I'm ashamed to bother you with this.

COUNT: Oh, it's nothing, it's nothing, dear Aurora! It's a mere trifle, but it's a pity that at this time I have no money.

AURORA: But we have to make a payment today.

COUNT: What to do? I'm very foolish in regard to such matters. This very hour at the earnest request of a debtor, I extended the date of his repayment for quite some time. People have discovered my weakness and shamelessly take advantage of my kindness.

AURORA: Our lender doesn't have such feelings. He's demanding repayment immediately.

COUNT: Demanding? Would he dare to demand repayment when he finds out that your mother will soon be related to me? Tell him, Aurora!

AURORA: But I have yet to ask the Countess.

COUNT: As you wish. But as for the Countess, do you know, charming Aurora, that she despises your beauty and is determined to break up our future union?

AURORA (*smiling*): Is she thinking to frighten me with that?

COUNT: No, of course she won't succeed in that. However, by speaking ill of me, won't she force you to change your opinion of me?

AURORA: You have no reason to worry, Count! A single rumor cannot change my opinions.

COUNT: Then I'm at peace. Allow me to take my leave, dear Aurora! I promised to lunch with a friend—but I forget everything when I listen to you. (*Bows and exits.*)

SCENE IV

AURORA (*alone and pensive*): And that man is supposed to replace Erast in my heart? Oh! The more I look at him, the more I sense my happiness is destroyed forever. If only his prediction comes true and the Countess attempts to break up this burdensome union. Then with what joy I will work night and day to erase from my mother's memory all the hopes with which she deluded herself regarding my marriage to the Count.

SCENE V
AURORA AND VZYSKALOV

VZYSKALOV: Hello, darling girl! Are you the daughter of Mrs. Dobrova?

AURORA (*bows*): I am.

VZYSKALOV: How very pretty you are! It's a pity your mother's income wasn't growing along with you. I would have received my money sooner.

AURORA: Who's to know? Perhaps my mother's income was growing along with me. You must be Vzyskalov?

VZYSKALOV: Yes! And does that displease you?

AURORA: Why should it? You were a friend of my father, which is enough to warrant my respect. If you did wrong by a friend, it isn't his daughter but the friend himself who would accuse you.

VZYSKALOV: My friend himself? But he's dead!

AURORA: In my heart and in the conscience of every good man he's still alive.

VZYSKALOV (*looking at her with surprise*): My conscience is clear. I'm asking for what's mine. Here is the promissory note signed by your father's hand.

AURORA: I know that, but I'm hoping that you'll take pity on us and wait a little longer.

VZYSKALOV: I've waited long enough. Now I'm presenting that promissory note for repayment, which you will make whether you want to or not.

AURORA: Of course, a court of law will take all measures to ensure your satisfaction. And your friend's wife, having sold her home and all her belongings, will drag out her old age under another's roof. But there is a higher court! And I'm afraid that there you will have to repay that very same promissory note.

VZYSKALOV: Perhaps. But am I really taking everything away from someone who has an acquaintance with the Count and a daughter with such a face?

AURORA (*sadly*): You're doing it this very moment. Oh! Recognize that poor people can be honest. Of course, you have the right to demand what is yours, but that shouldn't give you grounds for destroying us.

VZYSKALOV (*with great surprise*): I see you're as intelligent as you are pretty. My friend, any admonition from your lips is pleasing, indeed.

AURORA: The best admonition regarding virtue is taught to us by the fate of the afflicted. And the ridicule of someone whose heart is silent at the sight has little effect on me.

VZYSKALOV (*trying to hide how touched he is*): Enough, enough, my dear! You'd better call your mother.

AURORA: No, I can't do that. If there's anything you'd like to say to her, I implore you, say it to me. Her spirits are so low, why should we force her to listen to her daughter's grievances. My mother is poor, but she has a heart that no rich man can buy with his money. I ask you to wait only until tomorrow, and I'll make every effort to pay back your loan. God will be my helpmate!

VZYSKALOV (*tears up the promissory note and gives it to Aurora*): Oh! Of course I don't have a treasure like the one your mother has. (*wiping away his tears*) Tell her that your virtue weighed more than my gold.

AURORA (*falls on her knees before him*): Forgive the heart of a daughter if I distressed you! If only for the good deed you did, forgive me!

VZYSKALOV (*lifting her up*): Forgive me! I distressed an innocent heart, and you tamed a cruel one.

AURORA: A man isn't evil if he can understand the unfortunate. My words may have been annoying to you, but they touched you.

VZYSKALOV: I came here without any emotions, without a heart, and entered the home of a friend, where everything should have been sacred to me! But I came as a villain, who for his own profit stops at nothing and seeks gold over the bones of his close friend. And now I'm a man. I am again your father's friend! Embrace me, my child! (*Embraces Aurora, wipes away his tears, and exits.*)

SCENE VI

AURORA (*alone*): God hasn't forsaken me yet. (*Picks up the torn promissory note.*) Father! If your shadow is flying over me now, it can be happy that the promissory note has been paid back in virtue alone! O Mama! I must cheer you up now and receive the kiss I deserve. (*She begins to exit but hears a voice from behind the scenery:* Do not deny aid to one who is suffering.)

AURORA (*looking out the window*): Oh, what a pitiful old man! His features and his voice are familiar, but I don't know where I've seen him. My heart is so contented now that I'm ready this very minute to give away everything I have. But what do I have? All my riches are in the purse Erast gave me while still a child as proof of his love. (*Thinks.*) Wait, old man! (*Exits via a side door and drops the purse out the window.*) Hey, friend! I'm giving you all the treasure I have.

VOICE OUTSIDE THE WINDOW: May the Lord be generous in granting you joy, kind soul!

AURORA: Thank you, but I ask you to pray also for Erast, for his kind soul, too, deserves joy. Oh! A good deed is no longer pleasing when we don't share it with our dear ones! (*Exits.*)

ACT III
SCENE I
A MISERABLE ROOM

YULIA (*alone, sewing in a lace-frame*): O happiness, where are you? Can it be that, just like people of the fashionable set, you only go to parties and never peek into the huts of the poor? (*pensive*) O God, the world is the work of your love! Why can't every pure love be happy? Who has more goodness than our Erast? And yet he suffers! Dear Erast! In order to provide us with peace of mind, you know neither sleep nor rest. Oh! I understand why Aurora loves you. (*Wipes away tears.*) Patience, Yulia. Someday the sun will shine, and it will light up your heart with joy. If that doesn't happen, you will know too well how to endure. (*Takes up her work again, but imperceptibly, bending over her lace-frame, falls asleep.*)

SCENE II
ERAST AND YULIA, WHO IS SLEEPING

ERAST (*enters and stops in front of Yulia*): Poor girl! Sleep, sleep. If only your whole life were like this sleep! You experienced sorrows early and didn't sleep at night so you could work more. But nature proved to be more stubborn than you. (*Sits.*) Aurora, Aurora! Will you be the Count's wife tomorrow? (*Smiles bitterly.*) Of course, that's much finer than being the wife of poor Erast, who sailed across the sea with his blind father to breathe the same air as you! (*Thinks.*) Perhaps she still loves me. But my silence forced her to doubt my fidelity. No, Aurora! The heart in which you live could never be inconstant. Your dear image accompanies my every action and now, when I would like to tear it from my heart, it lives on in my mind and deprives me of any peace. I feel like my head is spinning. I'm afraid I might be sick, I might die. Erast! Are you really afraid of dying? When the Countess hears of your death, she will pity you. Aurora! I don't deserve this!

YULIA (*waking up*): Ah, brother! Have you been back long? What a wonderful sleep I had! It's true what they say—for the unfortunate, sleep is like a second life.

ERAST: Where's our father?

YULIA (*just coming to her senses*): He went begging for alms.

ERAST (*putting his hands over his eyes*): For alms! My God! And I'm his son? Oh, how bitter my life is! (*Laughs bitterly.*) Alms! Where did he go to beg for them? People are mean, very mean. My poor father! If only I could give away my heart to satisfy your hunger!

YULIA (*jumping up*): Brother, dear brother! What's happened to you?

ERAST: Oh, give up on me, Yulia. Don't feel any sympathy for me, so my miserable existence might sooner end.

YULIA: Could I ever give up on you? Calm down, I beg you!

ERAST: I am calm, Yulia. One who's drunk the cup of sorrows to the bottom has grown used to its bitter taste. But drown those words in my heart: your father is begging for alms!

YULIA: You can't reproach yourself for that. What mortal has ever done for his father what you're doing for yours?

ERAST: But anyone would have the right to say to me: ignoble son! Why don't you tear apart the earth with your hands and from its depths provide bread for your father? So, Yulia! I haven't done everything. I remembered that I have a heart, a heart filled with love for one who is ungrateful! I've wasted time and money to travel here where she lives, thinking that, once near her, I would forget all my needs and her presence would strengthen me …

YULIA: Perhaps Aurora doesn't know we're here.

ERAST: She doesn't need to know. Today I rushed to their house. My imagination painted a charming picture of our meeting. But then I suddenly ran into an acquaintance and found out from him that Aurora is going to marry the rich Count! (*Bends his head over the table; Yulia cries.*)

ERAST (*lifting his head*): I envy you your tears, Yulia! What relief they'd bring to my heart. But I can't cry, even though my father is begging for alms and my beloved is marrying another. I still can't cry!

SCENE III
ERAST AND YULIA
(a boy leads onstage the blind Stradaev,
who is carrying the purse from Aurora)

ERAST (*looks at his father*): Aurora! Your hand gave alms to my father. Oh! I forgive you for all the evil you've subjected me to.

STRADAEV: I just begged for alms from a kind soul and she gave me, as she said, all she had.

YULIA (*bringing a chair, she sits her father down*): Sit down, Father. You're probably tired.

STRADAEV: No, my dear! Isn't Erast here yet?

YULIA: He's here, Father.

STRADAEV: Where is he? Why are you silent? Come to me, Erast! (*Erast, with a forceful gesture, kisses his father's hand.*) Erast! The money is mine, but the purse is yours. I hope to God that your fiancée's voice is as pleasing, as touching as that of the girl who gave this purse to me.

ERAST (*with feeling*): Father, Father!

STRADAEV: Her voice was as comforting as the voice of an angel calling us to eternity, to the end of our suffering. At that moment even I forgot my sorrows!

ERAST (*hiding the purse near his heart*): Aurora! Could I stop loving you? Ah! Why can't I forget my sorrows upon hearing your sweet voice? (*Exits in haste, and the boy follows him.*)

SCENE IV
STRADAEV AND YULIA

STRADAEV: Yulia! What are you saying? I don't understand anything. It seems he's upset.

YULIA: He's worried about you, Father!

STRADAEV: About me? (*Displeased with himself.*) About me!

YULIA: You've been begging for alms.

STRADAEV: And who drove me to that? Ah! My dear! The memory of that nasty affair humiliates me more than alms given to me out of compassion. I brought ruin on my children and felt no humiliation! I was depraved and didn't know it! So shouldn't I burn with humiliation now when my son has no peace of mind and my daughter works day and night?

YULIA (*embracing him*): Father! Would my life really be any happier if I spent my days in the useless merrymaking of high society? Fate has given me the very occupations I would have chosen for myself.

STRADAEV (*drawing her to his heart*): I'm blind, but my emotions see all too well what you are doing for your blind father. It seems that Erast knows the girl who gave me the purse.

YULIA: It was Aurora Dobrova.

STRADAEV: So, now I understand why her voice spoke to my heart. She's not a stranger to my son nor is she a stranger to me.

YULIA: Everyone is a stranger to the unfortunate. And what would have become of him if he hadn't been comforted by the hope that in every sorrow there is some benefit? Father, I recently read these beautiful words: "The tears shed by the suffering are not lost. Up above there is One who gathers them in order to wash away the smallest sins from our conscience. Love and mercy toward men are signs of God's glory."

STRADAEV: Very nice, my child, very nice. How I revere those great writers who remember the Creator in their work.

YULIA: Those who have experienced both good and evil are more likely to do so. And you know that the unfortunate are closer to God!

STRADAEV: Misfortune is a teacher to almost everyone, my dear. But it's only sorrow that brings us closer to God. Only the real tears of a suffering soul can wash our conscience clean! Pray, daughter, that the Lord will accept even my repentance.

YULIA: Father! Your soul, which has always honored virtue, can it not find hope in God's mercy?

STRADAEV: Even a scoundrel reveres virtue. And although he can't leave behind his wicked ways, he places virtue above them. And the heretic envies the good-hearted, who, in their sorrow, find comfort in their faith in the One who created them. And when I, Yulia, see in my children a model of the most striking virtue, how can I ignore it? How can I help but feel that virtue alone reconciles us with our conscience and places in our hearts a peace that no worldly misfortune can take away!

YULIA: Can it be that a single mistake weighs more than all the good deeds a person has done?

STRADAEV (*pointing to the sky*): Not there, of course, but here, daughter, among people. They are less likely to forgive those weaknesses to which they themselves are susceptible. To the shame of men, I must say, they haven't the strength to overcome the mockery of society. Not wishing to appear strange, I myself became depraved, even when my heart was filled with true love and I was surrounded by my dear children. Oh, how great Man's blindness can be! (*Falls silent.*) I don't remember ever seeing Erast in such a state. He was trembling, and his words were disconnected. Has he been here long?

YULIA: Not long. I was sleeping and when I woke up I noticed a strange sorrow in him, one that increased when he heard that you were begging for alms. When he saw Aurora's purse in your hands, he could barely stay standing and rushed off.

STRADAEV (*rises*): My poor son! Yulia, let's go and look for our Erast.

YULIA: Where, Father? Where shall we find him?

STRADAEV: Ah, my daughter! You don't know that a father's heart is the best guide. We'll find him! And God willing, before it's too late!

Yulia and Stradaev exit.

SCENE V
The same room as in the first act

COUNT (*alone*): Well, I can say that I have only to wish for something, and that very hour my wish is fulfilled. Not long ago I hadn't a single ruble, and now I'm a rich Count! Not long ago all homes were closed to me, and now all doors are opened wide at my arrival! Not long ago I had a reputation for infecting the morals of the young, and now I am meekness itself and a receptacle of good behavior! Finally, didn't women consider me unworthy of their attention? Now they all gaze upon me with pleasure. And what is the reason for this, you ask? Money and daring, daring and money—these are the elements that make up the human soul, and without which I would be groveling in nothingness, without which the most brilliant mind is often trampled beneath the weight of misfortune and the man who is virtue itself sees only foul weather in his life.

SCENE VI
COUNT AND ERAST
(*who enters wearing his hat*)

ERAST: Where can I find Count Vetrov?

COUNT (*surprised*): Here, sir! What would you like?

ERAST (*looking him over from head to toe*): Nothing more than to look at you.

COUNT: There's nothing out of the ordinary about me.

ERAST (*still looking him over*): I agree. The man for whom Aurora scorned my love, a love that was stronger and more pure than anything, that man ought to possess every perfection.

COUNT: Perhaps you'll find some of them in me.

ERAST (*sternly*): None. Although, now that I've been deceived by Aurora's angelic countenance, I distrust the outer appearance of everyone on earth.

COUNT: Might I know the purpose of your visit?

ERAST: It seems I told you I only wanted to see you in order to grasp the full measure of my misfortune. Be frank, Count, tell me: what induced Aurora to promise you her hand?

COUNT (*proudly*): Why do you ask this question, my good sir? Is it really so strange that a man who has found a woman's love should receive her hand?

ERAST: Of course it's not strange. But when a woman capable of distinguishing true merit chooses you as her partner for life—that is surprising news.

COUNT (*guffaws*): At least she is true to herself. Perhaps you have different tastes, and I seem more amiable to her than I do to you? That's amusing indeed!

ERAST (*pulls his hat down even more and moves closer to the Count*): There is nothing to laugh about here, Your Excellency! When all the blood rushes to a person's head and burns his insides, how dare someone else laugh? Or else! (He grabs the Count's hand and presses it tightly.) Or else—do you understand me?

COUNT (*pulls his hand away and moves away from Erast*): You are frightening, sir! You have clearly come here by mistake. I assure you, this isn't a madhouse.

ERAST: How dare you remind me whose house this is? Before you infected it with your breath, this house contained all my earthly joys! They're destroyed! But (*taking a pistol from his pocket*), but Aurora's love can't be taken from me any other way.

COUNT (*frightened*): What's this? You want a duel? No, no, I won't allow it until I know who you are.

ERAST: Who am I? Erast Stradaev, and although I'm not a count, my honor has not been sullied, and I wouldn't exchange it for Your Excellency's. I demand satisfaction.

COUNT: Here?! You have no respect for this house.

ERAST: I respect it in my very soul and so would not wish my dying moan to shock the one who has driven me from her heart too soon. Please get your pistols.

The Count leaves through the side door.

ERAST (*places the pistol on the table, falls into a chair, exhausted, then looks around the room*): O Aurora! Nothing is changed here but your heart! (*He leans his head on his hand and is lost in thought. At that moment Aurora enters.*)

AURORA (*looks at Erast with surprise and rushes to him*): Erast!

ERAST (*lifts his head, but doesn't have the strength to get up, so he extends his arms toward Aurora, but leans his head on the table*): Let me die, let me!

AURORA: Let you die? Oh, you will not die alone; Aurora will always be with you.

ERAST (*lifting his head, revealing a wild look in his eyes*): Do you really love me?

AURORA (*with tears in her eyes*): I love you, I've always loved you with the same devotion. (*At this moment the Count enters with his pistol.*)

ERAST (*pointing to the Count*): And him?

AURORA: Erast! My mother was in such dire straits; sorrow and depression were driving her to the grave. The only way to save her was to sacrifice myself. Erast! Tell me what your noble heart would do in that situation!

ERAST (*throwing himself at her feet*): I would do more than could be asked of a person. I would give you up, Aurora! But now?

AURORA (*lifting him*): I'm yours forever! (*They embrace one another.*)

COUNT (*still standing there, surprised*): Wonderful, sir! Remember she's my fiancée.

AURORA: Never, never!

COUNT: And your mother? Do you want to reduce her once again to poverty? (*He takes her by the hand and tries to lead her away from Erast.*)

ERAST (*pushing him aside*): Get away! Dear Aurora! Your love has returned to me the ability to act. Now I can work. Our parents won't have to suffer want. They'll find in me once more a son, a happy son! (*He embraces her.*)

COUNT: But tell me, sir, who do you take me for? Do you think that it will be so easy for you, after having insulted me and called for a duel, to take away my fiancée, to whom I paid the honor and good fortune of proposing marriage? And for all that, you want me to shake hands, bow, and leave you in peace? Of course, you assumed that I would be frightened by your proposal and run away at the sight of a pistol! No, my good man! I'll show you that fighting with me means bidding farewell to life. Take your pistol and assume your position! I'll comfort you, my beautiful Aurora, after I shoot through the heart for which you scorned my love.

AURORA: My God! Erast! Must you really fight?

ERAST: Don't worry, dear Aurora! I've been fortified by your faithfulness, and now I have reason and strength—I'm not afraid of this braggart.

AURORA (*ringing her hands*): Oh! Will I ever find peace? Count! Take pity on me!

ERAST: Oh! Don't humiliate yourself by asking something of this monster! I promise you, my dear, you will find peace. (*He takes the pistol from the table.*) Let's go! (*They walk toward the doors. Erast turns and sees that Aurora has fainted. He rushes to her. The Count is about to say something, but at that moment Mrs. Dobrova and Pravdin enter; seeing Pravdin, the Count drops his pistol.*)

MRS. DOBROVA (*seeing Aurora*): My daughter! Dear Aurora!

PRAVDIN (*approaching the Count*): Ah! Your Excellency! Can it be that you've not yet completed all your noble deeds, which my sister has briefly recounted to me? Can it be that, having no honor, you dare to raise a weapon to defend it?

COUNT (*falling to his knees*): Have mercy on me! I'm guilty!

PRAVDIN (*helping him up*): Get up, Your Excellency! Get up! It's unseemly for you to humiliate yourself.

COUNT: No, allow me at least to vindicate myself.

PRAVDIN: I don't need your excuses; I know them. But there's still time to change your ways. You must now learn how to bear shame, and you must feel that it's better to forgive than to beg forgiveness. Make use of this time before everyone knows who you are. (*He hands him a money purse.*) Go into hiding—and remember this moment. If you're not completely lost, then this moment will be a lesson to you for the rest of your life. (*The Count grabs his hand and kisses it.*)

PRAVDIN: What are you doing, Count?

COUNT: I'm kissing the hand of the one who's pulled me from the abyss. (*He exits.*)

PRAVDIN: That's the result of recklessness! An hour ago, he would have probably placed no limits on his pride, and now he crawls at the feet of someone he barely knows.

AURORA (*regaining consciousness*): Erast, Erast!

ERAST: I'll never leave you.

MRS. DOBROVA : What happened to you, my child?

AURORA (*taking her mother's hand*): Ah, Mother! Don't separate me from Erast. No work is too difficult when he's beside me. We vow to take care of you in your old age.

MRS. DOBROVA (*embracing them both*): My dear ones! Happiness is nearest when we least expect it. I was just now sitting in the garden and thinking, with suffering in my soul, about the sacrifice my daughter would make tomorrow. Knowing the love she had for you, Erast, I was astonished at her generosity in forgetting herself in order to do everything for me.

AURORA: That was so, Mother! But I no longer can. Ah! When a person loses the way to happiness, when a dear friend is separated from her by the calamities of fate and she has no hope of living for him, she can still find the strength to sacrifice herself! (*She takes Erast's hand.*) But when she feels the presence of her beloved, when she sees how tenderly he treats her, then, dear Mother, then she can only love, and every obstacle to that love is horrible to her.

ERAST (*kissing her hand*): No, dear Aurora! No one will demand that sacrifice from you.

MRS. DOBROVA: Thank God, we're no longer in such dire straits! Fate hasn't separated you but has brought you together. (*She points to Pravdin.*) Aurora! This is your uncle, whom we've been waiting for so anxiously.

AURORA (*rushing over to embrace him*): Uncle, dear Uncle! Ah! How happy I am! But tell me, Mother, where did you find him?

PRAVDIN: She didn't find me, I found her—in the garden. And together we hurried here. It seems we got here at just the right time. (*He kisses Aurora.*) Now to merit your love, my daughter, allow me to join you in embracing the one your heart has designated as my son. (*They both embrace Erast.*)

ERAST: Oh! Who can describe my joy?

MRS. DOBROVA (*looking around*): Where is the Count?

PRAVDIN: Let's forget about him, my friends! He's gone into hiding, but he'll carry the burden of his villainous deed everywhere he goes, and while we rejoice, perhaps he'll be struggling with his conscience.

ERAST: In truth, I must admit that his is a most pardonable crime. In the heat of anger, I accused him of something that isn't at all blameworthy. Is it possible not to love Aurora, Uncle? Is it possible, having all the advantages in life, not to want to share them with her?

PRAVDIN: Of course, true love can never be blameworthy. It protects a person's heart from weakness and makes it worthy of that emotion! But the source of the Count's love is not as pure as you think. When he found out that I was well off and that Aurora was my heir, he found my power of attorney and used it to deceive my sister.

AURORA: Is it possible? But my heart divined it—I couldn't force myself to love the Count.

ERAST: We have to pity such people. They will never experience true pleasure, but nonetheless such people are necessary. The evil we encounter through them is like a smelting hearth for gold. Heated in its depths, gold is purified and appears in all its luster.

PRAVDIN: And what luster, my friend! Even the clouds of misfortune can't obscure it.

SCENE VII
ERAST, PRAVDIN, AURORA, MRS. DOBROVA, COUNTESS PUSTILGINA, STRADAEV, AND YULIA

COUNTESS: Mrs. Dobrova! I've brought you guests. This poor man is hoping to find his son, and I took it upon myself to show him the way to your house.

ERAST (*approaches his father, while Aurora embraces Yulia*): Father! Sister! Only you were missing for my good fortune to be complete.

STRADAEV: Your good fortune? Oh, thank God! Tell me again, my son! Tell me again of your good fortune! Ah, I had no more hope of rejoicing in this life. Had you left us for good?

ERAST: Yes, Father! I was torn apart and dared to reproach Providence. In my madness, I forgot my helpless father and sought an opportunity to end my life, which had become so burdensome to me. I wanted to, but the Almighty in His mercy stayed my hand. Father! Aurora loved me and loves me still. Her mother and uncle look upon me as their son.

STRADAEV (*raising his hands to the sky*): Righteous heaven! You took heed of a sinner's penitence! This moment is sure proof of it. Where is your Aurora?

AURORA: I've waited so long for you to embrace me, Father!

STRADAEV (*taking her hand and kissing it fervently*): The hand that gave me alms so gladly will surely lead my son along the most delightful path in life. I prayed for your Erast and my prayer was heard. You are united forever.

AURORA: My God! That was you, Father? I gave all my money to you? And look how I was rewarded for it!

ERAST (*showing her the purse*): This is the talisman that returned my Aurora to me. The moment I placed it here (*pointing to his heart*), I decided to fight for you against the entire world.

COUNTESS: Did you say that a little more directly to Count Vetrov? He was preoccupied when he left here, and what's odder still, he didn't pay me a single compliment when he saw me. But I'll take vengeance on him for that. Aurora! I've found the key to his mysterious love for you.

AURORA: Now I have it, too. My uncle has explained the mystery to us.

COUNTESS: Uncle? Oh, I'm truly delighted that he told you first. However, dear Aurora, I pray you don't think my fickle heart was inclined to evil or that I was a party to this deception. I only found out about it today and was looking for an opportunity to tell your mother. Now accept my congratulations. I hope that you'll always be as lovely as you are now. You know that without beauty and money, there's no happiness on earth!

AURORA: No, I don't know that, Countess. My happiness is found in other things.

ERAST: Only mutual love makes our lives perfectly beautiful.

PRAVDIN: True, true, my friend! Mutual love and family harmony are the primary blessings! I hope we won't be wanting for them. (*He takes Stradaev's hand.*) Stradaev! I am rich enough—we can live together. We old people will now take our rest and let our children supply that rest for us.

STRADAEV: I'm not worthy, my good man! (*He wipes away his tears.*) Look! The blind man weeps. This is your reward. Now I no longer fear death. My children have a father who will make amends for the harm I've done them.

COUNTESS (*touched*): For the first time in my life I regret the time I've wasted. I've been living alongside true virtue, but I couldn't comprehend it. Allow me, Madam, to keep my room. Accept me into your family; I feel the only place I'll find pleasure is in your company.

MRS. DOBROVA (*embracing her*): I would be truly delighted! This was all your goodness needed in order to see the vanity of society.

AURORA: When I think about all I've experienced today—all that I've lost and all that I've gained—it seems like a dream to me, a very pleasant dream!

PRAVDIN (*to the audience in the parterre*): Oh, you whose hearts have never experienced joy, you who have lost all hope of good fortune—don't despair! Tomorrow you may awaken in sorrow but sunset will find you in perfect happiness! Believe me, there is no good without reward!

Curtain falls.

THE END

Corinna

As I approached the beautiful city of K., the final rays of the setting sun were playing on its golden cupolas. Admiring the charms of the surrounding countryside, I was carried away by a thousand different things but didn't dare fix my gaze on any one, afraid that in doing so I would miss something else. I ordered the top of my carriage to be lowered, and as I looked around I took pride in Mother Nature and in the fact that I had been chosen to enjoy her. I was unaware that I'd reached the city until the heavy chain of the access gate took me from my pleasant thoughts. I identified myself and then hurried into the city.

Chance led me to an encounter with my dear friend R. I jumped down from the carriage and rushed to embrace him. And as it was still rather early and the weather was beautiful, I ordered my servants to continue to my apartment while I entrusted myself to my friend. "I was going to the garden outside the city," he said to me. "So much the better," I answered, "I would follow you anywhere." "But aren't you tired from your trip?" he asked me. "Oh, no, my friend! Youth and pleasure are companions that are hard to fatigue." Hand in hand, we walked to the garden gates, engrossed in the conversation of true friends. The garden was filled with people of both sexes and the unaffected merriment on the faces of everyone we met predisposed my heart to pleasure. But after walking down several paths, I was stopped by a sight that poisoned my pleasant mood.

An attractive young man, dressed in black, was gazing silently at an empty bench. Enormous tears streamed down his face. In a tone expressing despair, he kept uttering the name "Corinna." But suddenly, as if in oblivion, he began to jump about and laugh very loudly. The wildness of his gaze indicated to me that he was mad.

"What a state!" I said, turning to R.

"And do you know the reason for it?" he responded with a sigh.

"Who is this unfortunate man?"

"Baron N."

"It must be love that's brought him to this pitiful state."

"You've guessed correctly, my friend. And if you want to know the details of his story, no one can satisfy you better than I, as I played a role in his terrible drama." I asked him to tell me the story at once, for the sight of this man forced every heart to extend its sympathy to him. "His story," said R., "is as brief as the period of his suffering. I always compare him to a flower that at the dawn of a beautiful day adorns a clearing. Toward midday it's broken by a violent storm, but its charming bloom, now bent toward the ground, hasn't lost its beauty."

As we spoke, we approached the unfortunate man, who, upon hearing my friend, rushed to embrace him, repeating Corinna's name in a voice full of suffering. When he saw me, he begged me to take pity on him and give him back Corinna. "People have taken her away from me," he said and, seeing that I was crying, took my hand and pressed it to his heart, saying, "My tears are here. But don't cry!" He then exclaimed in a firm tone of voice, "People won't believe these are tears." He embraced R. again and left, saying, "She doesn't cry anymore." This man tormented me, and I begged my friend to tell me about his misfortune. As nothing else could interest me on this walk, my dear friend R. and I began to wander through the streets, and I learned the following from him:

"It seems it hasn't yet been two years since the illness of old Baron N., a local resident and president of the local Assembly of the Nobility, brought his son back home. The latter retired from the army with enormous regret, as his youth and the ongoing campaign made him quite attached to military service. Moreover, what's a twenty-year-old man to do at home, especially one who feels himself capable of great deeds?

"He struggled a long time with melancholy and tried to drive it away with a variety of pursuits. But ultimately his father noticed that with every passing hour he was becoming more withdrawn. Because his illness didn't allow him to introduce his son into the finest homes in the city, he entrusted this task to a friend in the hope that new acquaintances and a desire to be liked would dispel his son's gloom. And in fact, young N. did become more cheerful. I met him at the home of Prince B., my uncle, and, finding in him every merit, became his friend.

"Often, with the candor of a friend, he would complain of his idle life and ask me what he should do. 'Get married,' I would say. 'At my age? Is that warranted? Especially when I haven't chosen anyone?' I tried to convince him that this wouldn't be difficult as he spent his time among the city's most beautiful women. 'Oh, that makes it even more difficult!' he answered, 'because only the heart can choose what is beautiful. And besides, what do you call beautiful? Not that unbearable affectedness that I see every day?' 'But truly, not all of them are like that. What about Miss B., for example?' 'I like her more than all the others because she's your cousin. But admit that she displays a rather unbecoming arrogance.' 'Oh, you're too picky,' I said to him, and with that our conversation ended. N. became visibly less withdrawn, however, whenever he was at my uncle's.

"Miss B., to be fair, was much admired. A brilliant fortune and experience in the beau monde made her an idol of society, and so, having grown accustomed to the awe in which she was generally held, she looked upon sincere praise with disdain and often caused offense with her haughtiness. Although she wasn't a beauty, she possessed many agreeable traits, which she enhanced with the deftness and cunning of a refined coquette. She had been schooled in self-satisfaction and exulted when she saw herself surrounded by a crowd of adoring men who pursued her. Her true character, however, had yet to reveal itself.

"You've seen N. and can judge how he was then, so it's no wonder he attracted all of Laura's attention (that was Miss B.'s name). She immediately tried to chain him to her chariot wheels without any consideration for how those chains would feel. He seemed to put up no resistance, perhaps because he himself didn't know what he was doing.

"When his father was informed of everything by his friend, he suggested that he ask for her hand in marriage. N. shuddered at the very thought of it, but his father's words—'I'll die without seeing you happy'—compelled him to make up his mind that very moment. And while still asleep, I was brought a note from him, which contained the following: 'Rejoice, dear R.! I will soon be your cousin. Laura is my fiancée.' I rushed over to congratulate him but was surprised to see no joy in him. He even sighed as he shook my hand, and it was not until I called him 'cousin' that a pleasant smile appeared on his face.

"The prospect of marriage didn't seem to dispel his melancholy. He appeared more cheerful only when he was next to the high-spirited Laura. It was winter and the wedding was set for May. When spring arrived, preparations for the festivities got underway and Laura, like a small child, leapt about, trying on every article of clothing ordered for the wedding. But N. remained withdrawn and shared in her joy with only a smile.

"At that time Countess L., the sister of Princess B., returned from abroad, where she'd spent the last several years for the sake of her only daughter's education. As her health prevented her from going to the city, she wrote to the Princess and asked her to visit her at her country estate, which was no more than twenty miles away. Preparations for the wedding and the diversions of the city, however, delayed the trip for quite some time.

"At last, one fine morning we set off in Laura's foppish carriage. That day N. was particularly dull, as if he sensed the gravity of that day. Noticing this, Laura told him his gloom upset her. 'If someone saw us, they'd think you were about to be incarcerated rather than married.'

'My gloom is nothing new. It's a part of my nature.'

'But we're visiting a home where you're a stranger and where they'll judge my happiness from your expression.'

'What do strangers matter?! It's enough if you find it true.'

'Oh,' she said, turning up her nose, 'We're not in Arcadia. And what they call domestic bliss is now completely out of fashion!' N. fell silent, but his expression betrayed how much her words had affected him. How could one display such flippancy in a conversation with someone who was sensitive to the smallest kindness? To our chagrin, Laura made jokes the entire way, and N. sat quietly and smiled so as not to reveal how much all this upset him.

"We arrived at Countess L.'s, and as we passed through her charming little house, we found everywhere the most refined taste. We were shown into the parlor where the Countess greeted us with a smile. She then paid each of us a welcome that appealed to the heart's sentiment. Her manner and appearance were so engaging that after knowing her for only a moment, one had infinite trust in her. She combined majesty with naturalness in such a way that when you looked at her you couldn't decide what was most marvelous in her and what was more fitting for her: to obey or to command.

"The room was filled with lemon and peach trees in full bloom. The most beautiful paintings, rare not because of their golden frames but because of the works themselves, were arranged in perfect symmetry. The main wall of the room was decorated with portraits of the Countess and her daughter. In one, the mother was painted with an expression of grief, and her daughter, with angelic innocence, was shown wiping the tears from her mother's eyes. The Countess saw how N. examined the portraits and said in a gentle voice, 'That's my Corinna. She's shown here as a child, but she wipes away my tears to this day.' 'And where is my cousin?' asked Laura. 'She's in the garden,' answered the Countess. 'We've spent our time apart ever since our return. I've had to take care of my disordered household, and Corinna has completely taken charge of the garden.' N. glanced out the window, and I noticed how his expression changed. I walked over to him and caught sight of Corinna walking in the garden. I wish in vain I could describe her to you. The ordinary word 'beautiful' wouldn't give you a full understanding. It's not enough that her height, face, and figure were enchanting—there was an indescribable charm about her!

"When she entered the room, she was even more captivating. The unexpected surprise of finding us there enlivened her face with the sweetest hint of shyness. She cast a glance over all of us and then stopped at Mr. N., whose confusion was evident. The Countess, after introducing her to everyone, asked Laura to be a loving cousin to her: 'You were just children when you were separated. Now, if only you choose to do so, you can find in one another a friend.' Corinna embraced Laura and swore, it seemed with her whole heart, to love her. Laura was otherwise disposed. Her tongue was tied with envy and astonishment. Perhaps for the first time in her life she saw before her a creature who was superior to her in every way, and she vowed to hate her cousin, although she said with feigned kindness, 'That will depend on Corinna!' 'Corinna!' said the Countess, 'you still haven't met Mr. N. He's Laura's fiancé!' 'Cousin!' Corinna exclaimed and extended her hand to him, saying, 'I can't say why, but I feel as though I know you!' N. kissed her hand but was unable to utter a single word.

"Corinna and Laura were inseparable until lunch. The latter, fearing N.'s attention toward Corinna, led her cousin several times from the room. What a useless precaution! When mutual sympathy binds two creatures who have just noticed each other, what is powerful enough to tear that bond asunder? What can stop two hearts that are racing toward one another? Corinna said almost nothing to N. and rarely looked at him. She respected him as her cousin's fiancé and considered her feelings to be a fitting tribute to the familial ties that now united them. Subterfuge and ruse were unknown to her. Her conversation was always simple and persuasive. As soon as she began to say something, her expression would become animated, and her voice, which spoke to your soul, left an indelible impression on it. If I found her to be such a perfect creation, made to bring happiness to a gentle heart, what must N. have felt? His heart, which was drawn to everything refined, was enchanted by her charm.

"After lunch, Laura once again took Corinna away, and we asked the Countess if we might go into the garden. 'I'd be delighted!' she said, 'although you won't find anything entertaining there. The garden was completely neglected, and what's best in it now is the work of my daughter.' And so, N. entered the garden as if it were a sanctuary, where with every step he hoped to find traces of Corinna. Although it was obvious that the garden was very new, taste and selection were nonetheless evident throughout. The linear perspective was intersected by the most meandering paths, which led either to a temple of sincerity or to a monument to the daughters of love.

"Unaware, we walked very far from the house, but our conversation often broke down because my companion preferred to think rather than speak. Then suddenly our eyes came upon a patch of ground where spring seemed to bloom eternal. Everything indicated that this place had received the most attention from the garden's proprietress. A superbly built fence separated it from the rest of the garden and in the center of this level expanse stood a pavilion built in an uncommon architectural style; and it was surrounded by tall oaks, the tops of which were hidden from view.

"We approached the doors of the pavilion and gave each other an inquiring look: Should we go in? But curiosity overpowered us and we extended our arms at the same time to open the doors. This temple was dedicated, of course, to the pursuits of Corinna and her mother. Simple furniture indicated how little luxury was valued here. Bookshelves in each of the corners were filled with books by the finest authors. On the bureau stood a bust of Countess L., and surrounding its small marble base was a wreath made of fresh flowers, which had been placed there by a gentle hand so as not to hide the inscription carved at the bottom of the bust. Delighted, we read these words: 'O dearest mother! Be my inspiration! Every look I cast at your image gives me new strength to imitate you in virtue.'

"You must admit, my friend, this is not one of those pretentious and forced inscriptions through which the intellect strives to display itself. These words appeared to be written in a single stroke by a gentle hand. They revealed the boundless virtue of a heart that has yet to be darkened by a single earthly sorrow and that hopes to protect itself from such sorrows with virtue.

"An unfinished painting on an easel was also a true, ideal reflection of the one who'd painted it. It featured a sacrificial altar, not illuminated, but warmed by a small blue flame. At the foot of this altar was a nest in which a dove was shown covering its chick with its wing. She seemed to be trying to protect it from a storm that was raging in the distance, bending back the treetops in the grove. A woman dressed in white, or rather, Corinna, was on her knees embracing the altar, below which was the inscription 'What sacrifice could represent my gratitude?' 'My God!' exclaimed N., 'her soul is as pure as all her pursuits!' He turned around and caught sight of the sweet image of Corinna. Here she was represented as an adult and again beside her mother, who was gazing at her with a celestial joy, herself surprised at such a collection of pleasing qualities.

"A work basket stood on the table and beside it was an open volume of sermons by Bossuet.[1] Near the sofa were frames with embroidery. Curious at seeing all this, we turned over the frames and found that here, too, art was debating with intellect. Corinna had undoubtedly embroidered the scene for the Countess and in the design had placed the following allegorical picture: a sky-blue temple was covered with the most delicate curtain, which was partially lifted to reveal a charming scene inside. Love, Friendship, and Sincer-

1. Jacques Benigne Bossuet (1627–1704) was a French bishop, writer, and orator.

ity, adorned with beautiful masks, were embracing a cheerful youth, while Truth, lifting the other side of the curtain, revealed the interior of the temple, in which the same passions, now without masks, could be seen in their true form. A tender mother led her child to the temple and put the child into the arms of Truth. And here were embroidered the words 'Under the protection of Truth, what has a heart to fear?' 'Ah, she has yet to learn what there is to fear!' exclaimed N. with a sigh. 'Often Truth itself reveals to us things that, when we're unable to possess them, deprive us of all our happiness!' There was also a piano, and everything was neat and orderly. I confess I can't remember how we managed to leave that beautiful place.

"I would have carried on a conversation about Corinna on our way back, but N.'s curt replies convinced me to be silent. Then suddenly, as we walked down a garden path, N. stopped, pressed my hand firmly, and said, 'Let's listen!' I stopped and heard Laura and Corinna talking nearby.

"Corinna: 'Yes, dear cousin! It seems to me you'll be happy. The bearing of your N. displays the finest attributes.'

"Laura: 'What do you mean, the finest attributes? Not that eternal brooding that's unattractive in a fiancé and intolerable in a husband?'

"Corinna: 'Isn't it up to you to dispel that brooding with friendly sympathy, which can cure not only fits of melancholy but the most varied wounds inflicted by sorrow?'

"Laura: 'And so, instead of a wife, you'd like me to become a nursemaid, amusing my husband with a rattle while I yawn with boredom?'

"Corinna: 'I'm saying what I feel. Personally, I don't understand how someone could wish to entrust her fate to a person toward whom she can display no sympathy. Isn't that the same as intentionally destroying him?'

"Laura (*laughing*): 'That's beautifully put! It's a great misfortune indeed to possess a woman of the greatest elegance and to be the richest man in the entire region! But see here, Corinna, so that I don't entertain any suspicion, are you enchanted by my doleful fiancé?'

"I glanced over at N. and from the glow of his cheeks I could see the intense emotion with which he awaited her response.

"'You have nothing to fear!' said Corinna, 'The appearance of any suffering individual would compel me to say the same. And Mr. N. will be my cousin, and for that reason I wish that you could make him happy.' 'We'll see what fate disposes.' 'Oh, no, no!' Corinna repeated, 'promise me he'll be happy, otherwise I won't let you leave this spot.' N. took my hand and squeezed it tightly. But Laura replied that she was surprised Corinna should give her such advice. Corinna asked her not to be angry and assured her she had no wish to distress her, at which point they got up and left in silence.

"Without speaking, N. threw himself on my shoulder. Now pale, he groaned but didn't say a word. It seemed this conversation had laid the future out before him. But within a quarter of an hour he'd collected himself and was calm. After witnessing such emotions and such an inner struggle, I found it odd to see him in his present state.

"When we entered the parlor, Laura was playing the harp and, raising her voice to the heavens, appeared calm, whereas Corinna looked with sadness at N. 'You must certainly have learned to sing?' asked Laura, moving the harp toward her. 'Very little,' answered Corinna, 'I have almost no voice.' 'Perhaps, something,' urged Laura, already sensing that she would triumph, 'Something. You're among friends.' 'Then you'll have to answer for my mistakes,' said Corinna, who took the harp, tried it out for quite a while, and then, without the slightest affectation, began to sing this song:

Love, they often tell me,
Love is life's great joy.
Don't trust them, others say to me,
For love will happiness destroy!

O heart! How will you now decide,
O, whom will you believe?
If only dreams in love reside,
My gentle heart may be deceived.
How can I hope to find my bliss
In opinions so opposed?
O heart! Avoid the tender traps
To which you'll be exposed.

Love? It seems to me this word
Can only bring despair.
Happy the man who pawns his life,
Entrusting it to freedom's care.

"She sang the final words in a charming, languid voice. 'Everything would indicate you're singing against your own interests,' said Laura, sarcastically. 'Oh, no!' Corinna answered with adorable frankness, 'Actually, I'm afraid of love. I feel somehow that love will make me very unhappy.' 'What a prophecy, my friend!' Poor Corinna! I can never forget her words.

"After we'd left them, from the moment we were seated in the carriage, we began to talk about Corinna. Laura found nothing pleasing in her: her voice was strained, her conversation flat, her face lacked beauty, and her figure grace. In a word, neither the mother nor the daughter was to Laura's liking, and we were glad that she didn't think to ask our opinion. Although she could see in our eyes that we disagreed with her, she didn't stop talking. 'It seems it was unnecessary to have traveled half the world,' she said. 'Her marvelous education is utterly commonplace, but then the student herself is nothing out of the ordinary! Do you know what? This meek creature is in love with a foreigner, and her mother is so displeased by it that Corinna tries to hide it from her.' I glanced at N., who blushed at this lie and in a strained voice barely uttered the words, 'How hot it is!' And then in order to conceal his embarrassment, he tried to lower the curtain but accidentally tore off the blinds. This incident cheered him, and we began to laugh; with that the conversation was interrupted. Never before had a journey seemed so intolerable! As soon as the carriage stopped at the entrance to his house, N. leapt out and, excusing himself because of his father's illness, was immediately gone from sight. I knew that he'd be suffering, but didn't dare follow him."

"And Laura?"

"Oh, my friend! I thought her heart would be grief-stricken over Corinna's advantage and in my heart I excused her. So imagine my surprise! We found a large number of guests in the parlor and among them was the handsome Count Sv., who'd left his regiment abroad and come home to see his family. He was a distant relative of the Prince and so was introduced to Laura as a cousin. This charming cousin possessed all the perfections Laura dreamed of. He was schooled in women and had learned by heart the science of pleasing them; he entangled them in the very same webs they set for him. Laura was the most eligible woman in the city and so, without thinking, he occupied himself with her. But her behavior that evening was to me abominable. Knowing that the Count was, in spite of all his attractions, an unsuitable husband for her—for he was poor and her ambition swallowed up incalculable riches in her mind so that only N.'s fortune could satisfy her—I grasped her intentions and was perfectly livid.

"Someone asked me, 'What is your opinion of Miss L.?' 'She's an angel possessing every perfection!' I answered. 'Oh, what fine-sounding words!' said Laura, joining in the conversation. 'To be pleasing to you and to my fiancé, one must possess only the most modest perfections: two tears in your eyes and the word 'sentimental' on your lips. Those are all the wonderful perfections necessary!' 'I agree,' I answered, biting my lip from vexation, 'What my friend and I find most pleasing in a woman is modesty and a tender heart. But I can assure you, Miss, that even the most empty-headed man will find disagreeable a woman who places no limits on her affectation.' Laura pretended not to understand me. I was upset and left for home at an unusually early hour.

"The next day I had to attend to my obligations in the country. N. wrote me often, but his letters were always short and he never spoke in them of his feelings and never once mentioned the name of Corinna. And so I began to think that he'd listened to reason and that his heart had found peace, when I received the following letter from him:

"'Have pity on your unfortunate friend! I love and am loved, but I'm pledged to belong to another forever! Oh, how horrible these words are, my friend! I'm not afraid for myself—my life will end soon—but for that sweet creature: I've poisoned her entire existence! But allow me to collect my thoughts so that I can tell you everything. I must unburden my heart and then, after I've entrusted to you alone what has become of my life, I shall be silent forever.

'Prince B.'s illness forced us to postpone our wedding for six months. And, as I never found Laura at home, I had absolutely nothing to do in that city; but when it seemed my father's health had returned, I asked his permission to go to the country. This trip was a specious excuse to drop in on the Countess. I hadn't seen Corinna since our first visit and it seemed to me cruel not to gaze upon her once more before giving her up forever. What madness! And why wasn't your friendly hand there to stop me?

'My heart was pounding as I approached that charming dwelling. I found the Countess alone, and she was very glad to see me. She asked the purpose of my visit, and then asked about Laura and my upcoming marriage. But she was silent about the thing my heart was asking. I finally lost patience and don't remember how I brought myself to ask her the question, "Where's my cousin?" "She's in the garden, of course," answered the Countess, "would you like to go find her?" "With all my heart!" I said hurriedly, and flew into the garden. With every step I could hear Corinna's voice and footsteps, but, finding no one there, I went up to the door of the pavilion. It was open, and very quietly I went inside. Corinna was sitting at the desk, drawing. I could have gotten very close but I thought it indiscreet, and so I stopped beside the door and examined her charming countenance. She was wearing a white dress, and her hair was pulled back with gold hairpins to reveal all of her enchanting face. I sighed, which made her turn. Oh, how happy I was at that moment! When Corinna saw me, she cried out and blushed. She wanted to get up but fell back in her chair, unable to overcome her emotions. I rushed toward her impetuously and begged her to forgive me for frightening her. "Oh, no, no!" she answered, trying to compose herself. "You didn't frighten me in the least. I was just surprised at seeing you so unexpectedly!" "And so," I said, summoning the courage to take her hand, "the charming color in your cheeks indicates only surprise?" She looked at me and asked with a smile, "Can't I be happy to see my cousin?" It was impossible for me to answer this question without revealing my secret, and so, in silence, I kissed her hand. "Tell me how it is that I'm seeing you alone," said Corinna. "Whenever I picture you in my imagination, you're always beside Laura." I told her I was going to our country estate and, not daring to deceive her, almost revealed to her the real reason for my trip.

In her innocence she failed to understand the full magnitude of this revelation and, deceiving herself with the thought of my obligation to Laura, she carelessly revealed to me her own feelings.

'What good is a life that consists of a lengthy series of dreary years? Aren't three days enough to give life its essence if those three days are like the ones I spent at that house? I made bold to look at her and to speak to her of my love; I dared gather hope from her enchanting eyes and recognized that heavenly emotion in all her movements. And now that I've renounced everything, can I say that I'm still alive?

'Corinna was the first to notice that it was time for us to return to the Countess. "My God!" she said, "Look how the time has passed, and Mother must be waiting for us." She got up and began to put away her work, which she carefully hid from me just as before. Noticing this, I wanted to take it from her, but she begged me not to touch it, which only heightened my curiosity. "Corinna!" I said, "Although I haven't had enough time to earn your trust, I'm sure you wouldn't want to deny me it." "I trust you in everything, but just this moment I realized that my drawing isn't accurate. I made it too gloomy. Now I see that a little liveliness would improve it. Let me fix it and then I'll show it to you." As she said this, she tried to move, and a portrait of me dropped at my feet. I can't describe to you what I felt at that moment! I wanted to fall at Corinna's feet, but the Countess's voice stopped me in the midst of my delight. "Oh, Corinna!" I exclaimed, pressing her hand against my heart. A frightened Corinna put her other hand over my mouth and asked me for God's sake to be quiet. Ah! She was afraid to hear from me what she'd known for so long. I obeyed her and was quiet, and she managed to put away her work and calm herself before her mother entered.

'It wasn't difficult for the Countess to understand what was going on in our hearts. Foreseeing all the danger posed by our feelings, she didn't let us out of her sight and was always with us. But her presence didn't interfere with our happiness. Our virtuous love provided us with countless moments of pleasure. Ah! I should describe to you every one of those moments because what followed was no longer life! But how can I describe bliss when my heart is being consumed by the cruelest sorrow?

'After spending three unforgettable days there, I prepared to go to my family's estate. Corinna made me promise to stop on my return trip. I painted the most enchanting scenes in my imagination when I suddenly received word from the city that my father had fallen desperately ill. I froze; it was as if in the midst of the most wonderful dreams, I'd been woken by a clap of thunder. The Countess tried in vain to comfort me while Corinna, pale and trembling, begged me to calm myself. But even that dear face couldn't bring me any comfort and caused unbearable pain in my heart. In that state I returned home.

'I found my father scarcely breathing, but he recognized me right away and, seeing my sorrow and tears, asked me to be calm and to carry out his final wish as soon as possible. At first I understood nothing. Then I saw Laura beside his bed in convulsions of grief, and with a shudder I realized what was being asked of me. Hearing of my father's illness, Laura had rushed to our house in the middle of the night and hadn't left my father's side for a moment. You know to what extent she's able to dissemble. So is it surprising that my sick father was charmed by her and insisted that I marry her right then? I suggested to him that I was too torn apart by grief to occupy myself with anything other than him, but he took no heed and tried to convince me that he could die in peace only after I'd joined myself to that virtuous creature. "Oh, Father!" I exclaimed, falling beside his bed, "Father! Listen to your son's secret!" "I don't want to hear anything, and I know that my gentle son wouldn't poison the last moments of my life. I'm dying!" he repeated with a sickly wail. "I'm dying, and my only son won't comfort me!" He fell back on his pillow, and I was beside myself.

'I won't describe all my misfortunes to you in detail. I'll say simply that everything ended for me. I was completely despondent and can't remember what was going on around me. I went to the altar under protest and made a vow that my heart rejected. Ah! How did I live through that terrible time? When I embraced my father's coffin, I was astonished that they'd placed him in it instead of me—although that wouldn't have cooled the flame burning inside me. It would only have hidden me from ruthless people! What horror seized my soul when I came to my senses and the dear image of Corinna appeared before me, reproaching me with her misfortune! Oh! Take pity on me and if possible, come quickly to wrest me from this excruciating situation!'

"Leaving business matters unresolved, I rushed to the city and found my unfortunate friend in exactly the same situation he'd described in his emotional letter. He was terribly altered, but he concealed his grief and even took part in social events, without which Laura could not live. Only when we were alone together did he open his heart to me in friendship. I saw how his suffering increased upon hearing the news that Corinna was ill. 'She's inclined to consumption,' her doctor said, 'and the slightest emotional shock could cause her death!' I didn't tell this to N. and soon learned that she had much improved. As the Countess never left home, my friend hadn't seen Corinna since his wedding.

"At that time the entire city was in an anxious state over the arrival of Prince D., the local Governor-General. Grand balls were planned, and my uncle hosted the first and most magnificent one at Laura's suggestion. And the Count was her helper. N. and I, forgotten by society, had more time to spend together.

"One evening while we were sitting as usual in a corner of the room, we were shocked to hear someone speak of the arrival of Countess L. Fortunately, we were surrounded by people who had no need to pay any attention to N., who was in a terrible state: a deathly pallor covered his face, and his eyes, filled with anticipation, were focused on the doors. He sighed when they opened and the Countess entered with that pleasant demeanor so characteristic of her. Everyone's gaze was focused on her and Corinna—Corinna, whose beauty was indescribable! You know I was always an enemy of those lofty flourishes of the pen, but she reconciled me to them. Corinna was much thinner, but at the same time her emotional suffering and the heavenly meekness of her gaze made her a thousand times more attractive. Her face contained something pitiful that was impossible to look at without feeling emotional sympathy.

"My God! How beautiful true love can make a person! No suffering can disfigure someone who loves and is loved in return. Corinna's first glance was directed at N., and their confusion frightened me. You can imagine what they felt, especially when Laura approached Corinna, impudently recommended her husband to her, and in a

most ironic tone asked her to love him as a relative. The meaning behind these words gave Corinna strength. She collected her wits and
with a majestic air answered that even without that wonderful bond
she would find him worthy of all respect. Inside I was grateful to her
for this answer, which disarmed Laura and cheered my friend. He
responded to Corinna decorously and, having calmed himself down,
returned to me.

"The conversation was of a general nature: almost everyone
was occupied with the approaching social events. With delight, Laura described the amazement their ball would produce on everyone.
Corinna sat near us, and I asked her whether she would be participat-
ing in the city's celebrations. 'Mama would like me to leave the city,'
she answered with a sigh.

'But isn't that against your wishes?'

'I confess that I wish very much to return to my pavilion. At
least there no one will interrupt our sadness, and that's a great comfort!'

'But you're still so little acquainted with our local society, and
there are many delights in your native city.'

'I thought the same when I moved here,' she said gloomily, 'and
I imagined with delight that my life would flow like a quiet stream. But
the moment I stepped foot in it, I was overcome by the stormiest of
seas!'

'So that's what you experienced?'

She threw a glance at me that was filled with surprise. Knowing of my friendship with N., she thought all the secrets of her heart
were known to me, and so my question seemed odd. 'Yes,' she answered, 'I experienced all the sorrows that come when hope of eternal
happiness is betrayed!'

'Corinna,' uttered my wretched friend N., 'imagine what the
person who carelessly deprived you of that hope must feel!'

"All this time Corinna had been afraid to look at N., but now
her eyes unwittingly directed themselves at him. N. turned pale and
made a gesture that indicated he'd forgotten he was surrounded by
people and was ready to throw himself at her feet. His gaze was fixed
on Corinna, and tears rolled down his cheeks. Corinna was in the

same state, and the intense color in her cheeks was the surest proof that his gaze had penetrated her heart.

"I confess to you, I admired the harmony of their hearts! Don't we typically encounter the most evil hatred at every step of our lives— hatred, which people foster among themselves over utter nonsense. Discord has so taken root in this world that love and true friendship now seem an unusual sight.

"Finally, in order to cheer up these suffering individuals, I initiated a simple, extended conversation, which greatly cheered Corinna. She tried to pay attention, but from time to time cast sorrowful glances at N., who rested his elbow on the table, lost in thought. Laura came over to us and jumped into the conversation, telling us by way of news that their ball would end in a masquerade. 'Would you like to dance the quadrille with me?' she asked N. He didn't hear her, so she repeated the question. 'Very well,' he answered, absent-mindedly. 'Oh, I won't accept this unwilling act of condescension, and I have no wish to disturb your charming idyll in any way. Will you play the shepherd and lay a reed pipe and a staff at the feet of your shepherdess?' As she uttered these words, she shot a derisive glance at Corinna. N. was silent, but I couldn't refrain from telling her that Paris was also a shepherd when he presented an apple to the most beautiful woman. 'So then, will Mr. N. judge the beauty of every woman at this ball?' 'No,' I answered, 'my friend wouldn't take on such a difficult task. And besides, he's suffered from the capriciousness of women, so it's enough for him to express his preference for the most beautiful creature within his heart.' 'Be careful that this judgment doesn't shake Troy once again!' she said. Then she laughed, turned on one foot, and was gone in an instant.

"Now Corinna revealed all the magnitude of her spirit. Understanding Laura's contemptuous mockery, she stood up proudly and at once changed her seat. They quickly left and I found a convenient opportunity to dispel my friend's sadness. The next day, as was our custom, we paid a visit to the Countess. Although Corinna didn't appear, the Countess received us very warmly. In her manner there was something so heartfelt that, when you left, you always felt satisfied with her and with yourself.

"Finally the day arrived that promised us so much merriment. Laura in her finery glowed like the northern lights. Everything that could be invented by a mind that swam in a sea of luxury was at this ball. But for me, the nicest thing was that on this day N. was in much better spirits. After his meeting with Corinna, he became more animated, or at the least his imagination, having found some nourishment, made him somewhat less unhappy.

"Corinna was truly the ball's finest decoration. She was dressed simply: a crepe tunic embroidered with pearls appeared to envelop her. On her head were white lilies. N. grasped my hand and in a pained voice said to me, "Oh! What misfortune! To see her but to be unable to throw myself at her feet!" In order to restrain his desire, I gently reminded him of his duty, but he replied, "Do you really think I could forget about her for a single moment? Oh, my friend! With every movement I make, I hear the heavy chains that bind me!"

"When the dancing began, N., who was still in mourning for his father, didn't take part. He complained to me that this deprived him of his last opportunity to get close to Corinna until he noticed that she wasn't dancing either: the local doctor had forbidden her to do so during the first dance. It appeared that love had joined them. Although the Countess never left Corinna's side, I noticed many times that N. was conversing with them both. Although his expression was gloomy, it indicated that his heart was content and, when we met, he even said to me that this evening was unforgettable for him: "Of course I'm still unhappy, but I don't know how to explain the charming feeling that fills my heart!" Laura, it seemed, was too busy with her triumph to notice their quiet happiness, but her petty spirit was even then arming itself with a plan for revenge.

"At one o'clock in the morning, the garden gates were opened. Thousands of little lamps illuminated the garden and lit up the sky with an early dawn. Embroidered monograms glowed before our eyes, and a group of nymphs placed a wreath upon the head of a handsome Apollo. Everyone hurried out to the garden, and sweet freedom burst forth like a bird from a golden cage. Corinna stepped out onto the balcony to look for her mother and, lost in thought, leaned against a column strewn with garlands, utterly unaware that she was now completely alone. Her anguished expression revealed the struggle taking place within her heart. N. and I approached her just as Laura walked past. I thought she was looking for one of the admirers who surrounded her, so I was untroubled. "Are you enjoying the ball?" I asked Corinna. "Absolutely," she responded, casting a look at N., "but I don't know why my heart is so heavy at such a joyful moment. I'm afraid to look at the future, and I can't help but shudder when I think that this will be my last such moment!" "Do you fear the future?" exclaimed N., unable to moderate his feelings. "What terror fills a heart condemned to drag out its days separated from you!" Imagine Corinna's expression! Pale and trembling, she turned up her hands, as if asking for mercy. N. forgot himself and threw himself on his knees before her, embracing her legs and sobbing. We tried in vain to extract him from this situation. His words made no sense and it seemed he was experiencing his first fit of madness.

"Afraid for Corinna, I wanted to close the balcony door, but it had been opened wide by Laura, who, with indescribable malice, exposed them before the best society, and with a loud laugh not only drew attention to them but also sought to denigrate this scene in everyone's eyes. I can't describe to you the state of the Countess when she saw her daughter exhibited before such an audience. Corinna, catching sight of her mother, threw herself in her arms and fell into a dead faint. I wanted to speak, but my voice was drowned out by Laura's mad ravings. Her rudeness so surprised me I couldn't take in anything else around me. I don't know how it all ended, but when I came to my senses the Countess and her daughter were no longer there. N. had also disappeared, while Laura, with the solemnity of a Fury, gave herself up to the festivities she had organized.

"To this day I don't know how I survived that evening. Unable to find my unfortunate friend, I went back out onto the balcony. My heart froze when I recalled what had occurred on that very spot only a few moments before. I embraced the same column that the arms of the unfortunate Corinna had embraced. The garlands were torn down, the lamps extinguished, and the music had died away. "My God!" I exclaimed. "What's the significance of earthly joys? While thousands of despicable souls are enjoying life, two innocent creatures, whose only crime is that they loved tenderly, suffer from the suspicion of others as if they deserved it." From that time on I stopped valuing the opinion of society, which always makes accusations based only on appearances.

N.'s condition dispirited me. I found him in his study. He threw his arms around my neck and wept bitterly. The tears had a salutary effect on him, restoring his reason and unburdening his heart. "Have pity on me," he said. "Go to the Countess and speak to her on my behalf. I can't bear the thought that she thinks I'm a monster intent on destroying her daughter!" I tried to calm him and only after he'd fallen asleep did I decide to leave.

"When I arrived at the Countess's, they told me she wasn't receiving anyone, for Corinna was now desperately ill. I asked to be announced but waited quite a while before this tender mother came out to greet me. When she saw me, she amicably extended her hand. 'Mister R.!' she said, 'Our tears should be mingled as we're now both weeping for people dear to our hearts! You've come from your friend?'

'That is so, Madam,' I answered.

'He shouldn't have done that. My daughter told me everything, and I believe her.' 'Is it true your daughter is ill?' I asked sorrowfully.

'Yes! She couldn't bear this calamity with indifference. Of course, I am myself to blame for the fact that I'm losing my daughter. I schooled her in virtue but failed to moderate her feelings. But how could I have foreseen that the first object of her love would belong to another?' She wanted to say something more, but at that moment she was summoned to her daughter's bedside, and I took my leave and returned to N.

"I spent an entire month in anguish. Corinna was burning out like a candle. I learned from the doctor that her condition was hopeless, although she was still able to stand and went out quite often for carriage rides. In order to hide her illness from N., I had to seek out all means possible to shield him from rumors, but here cruel Laura showed no mercy. In the company of others she told her father she'd heard Miss L.'s condition was entirely hopeless. N. staggered and wanted to leave the room but fell near the door. From this moment his character, which had been melancholy until then, was completely altered. He became gloomy, silent, and terribly distrustful—especially toward me. Whenever I entered his room, he would tremble and look quickly into my eyes as if hoping with a single glance to learn everything that was hidden in my soul.

"One day, in order somehow to divert him, I convinced N. to go out of town to the very park where we just saw him. We strolled there for quite a while and were returning home when N. caught sight of Corinna on that very bench beside which he had just been moaning. It was midday, and the park was empty. Corinna, her eyes closed, was resting her head on her mother's shoulder. Imagine if you can the emotion that filled N.'s heart! I couldn't restrain him. In vain did I explain to him that he would frighten Corinna, but he paid no attention to me. He fell beside the bench and with a moan forced Corinna to open her eyes. She looked at him in silence for some time and then held out her hand to him and said, weeping, 'Unfortunate man!'

'Can you forgive me, Corinna?'

'Shouldn't I be asking you the same?' she responded. 'Ah! We both suffer equally.'

'Oh, Corinna! What a state I now see you in! My recklessness has led you to the grave!'

'It's better to die than to live without the one you love!' she said with a smile. 'Don't pity me! Only in the depths of death can I find peace.'

"She wanted to say more, but her strength failed her and a deep faint covered her face with a deathly pallor. N. thought she was dying and rushed toward her. In his madness he attempted to carry her out of the park, and it took great effort to wrest her from his arms. He fell to the earth, and after confiding Corinna to the care of her mother, I found him in the same position. With all the concern of a friend, I helped him live through that moment.

"The following day, as soon as I awoke, I was summoned by Corinna. She was sitting in an armchair and was delighted to see me enter the room. 'Ah, Mister R.!' she said, 'How obliged I am that you didn't refuse to visit me in these last moments of my life. They don't seem so burdensome when I see before me the most worthy of friends! Yes, you are a friend to me!' she continued, lifting her eyes to the sky. 'Promise me you'll look after him. Only this will reconcile me with the Judge before whom I shall soon stand, and He will certainly demand from me an account of poor N.'s life. Promise me that, my friend!' Her face grew animated, and she lifted her arms. I imagined I saw before me a heavenly creature, and I couldn't help but fall to my knees before her, promising her everything she demanded, which was more than I could fulfill. She asked me to get up and thanked me most sincerely. At this point she turned to her mother, pressed her mother's hand to her heart, and tenderly asked that she not grieve for her. She then moved in a way that indicated she felt a pain in her chest. Her beautiful eyes were covered by the shadow of death. 'Oh, Mother!' she said, falling at her feet, 'this is how I should appear before the Lord! Forgive your daughter so that our Savior can forgive me the sorrow I've caused you! Give me your blessing so that He, seeing your blessing upon me, will remove His righteous anger!' No, I couldn't bear that scene and ran from the room like a madman; but I was stopped by a terrible cry: Corinna was no more.

I rushed to my unfortunate friend so as to shield him from the news of Corinna's death. He was sitting beside his desk, his head in his hands. I hadn't seen him that morning and so involuntarily shuddered when he lifted his head and asked me, 'What happened?' 'Nothing!' I said, trying to be calm. 'How did you spend the night?' 'Horribly!' he answered, 'My heart's troubled. Dear God! Allow me to see her one more time.' I described Corinna's condition to him and said that his presence would hasten her journey to the grave. Only this stopped him. I don't understand what power enabled me to keep him in his room the entire day. He was calm and spoke of Corinna endlessly, remembering every moment he'd spent with her. It seemed he was afraid to focus his imagination on the present even for an instant. And so I suffered for two. The slightest movement in the house worried me, and I feared every word that was spoken in his presence.

"At midnight he calmed down and fell asleep in an armchair, while I, emotionally exhausted, threw myself into bed, fully dressed. But my eyes had barely shut when I was awakened by the sound of closing doors, and to my horror I didn't find N. in his room. I knew where to look for him and without thinking I ran to the Countess's home. I opened the door of the parlor and saw my friend stretched out unconscious beside the lifeless Corinna—Corinna, who even in death was an indescribable creature. In the dark of night, surrounded by burning candles, she resembled a marble statue. Galatea herself, emerging from beneath Pygmalion's chisel, couldn't have been more lovely. But whereas Galatea was being prepared for a life in this world, Corinna was prepared for a life of eternal bliss. The smile that shone on her lips indicated her complete confidence in the peace that awaited her beyond the grave.

"N. was delirious, or rather, in a high fever, which caused us to fear for his life for several days. Even if I hadn't made promises to Corinna and had only happened upon him by chance at this devastating time, I imagine I couldn't have left his side for a moment: he was completely alone. His wife, having forgotten all propriety, gave herself up freely to her dissipation. My unfortunate friend in his delirium was unable to bear the sight of her. He shuddered whenever she approached his bed. Her countenance represented for him all his misfortunes and put him in a terrible state, which recurs even now at every meeting with her, for his madness didn't leave him even after his fever abated on the twentieth day. His favorite outing was to the public garden. It was there he saw Corinna for the last time and so he sits for hours at a time on the same bench where she sat. He's always particularly moved when he sees me: I must surely remind him of that time so dear to him!"

R. fell silent, but my heart was so heavy with pain that only after a very long silence did I ask him, "What has become of the Countess?" "She took Corinna's body to her country estate and although no one thought she'd outlive her daughter, the salutary effects of religion have filled her soul and given her the strength to bear this sorrow. Mourning Corinna, she slowly approaches her own grave.

"Not long ago I was passing near the Countess's estate and wished to see Corinna's grave. It was morning, and so I had no fear I might meet the Countess, which good sense forbade me to do. With what sadness I walked through that garden where my friend had drunk the poison of misfortune. Everything looked as it had before, and it seemed that her perfecting touch had just now gone cold. I imagined Corinna as I saw her the first time. I pictured her loveliness and imagined she'd just begun to live. I imagined this—and then I caught sight of her grave! Not far from the pavilion a simple white cross and a rose bush indicated the place where her ashes lay. Moving closer, I saw an inscription etched on the white stone. I knelt and said a prayer for this beautiful soul, then read the following:

'Innocent hearts! Beware of love! The torments that it brings end only here.'

"It seemed to me that Corinna was uttering those words in her captivating voice from the grave. They cut deep into my heart. An irresistible force led me to the pavilion. Ah! Here, too, I found everything just as it had been: all the paintings we'd admired before were here before my eyes. A mother's tenderness had been unable to shelter the one who painted them from the storms that raged in her life. She vainly embraced the sacrificial altar of happiness while people tore her away from it in order to plunge her in the grave! I examined everything with sympathy. On the piano were the notes of that very song Corinna had sung for us, but she'd crossed out the original words and written two verses underneath:

Ah, no! Love, love alone
Brings happiness in life!
The heart where love is known
Is filled with bliss, not strife.

Can liberty remove
The blessing that I feel?
O, what a sweet word: love!
Now I understand thee.

"I took the song and often, when I'm despondent, I glance at it. It was surely written before N.'s marriage. How short-lived was that happiness so beautifully expressed in this song! What struck me even more was Corinna's portrait. The polar contrast between her charming smile and her grave, which I could see through the open door, caused me to shed tears of true sorrow. Leaving that place, I ran through the garden as fast as I could and rushed to my carriage with a heavy heart. God preserve every one of us from such an awful state! People don't forgive us for the tenderness they mourn in novels."

At this point in the conversation, we reached my apartment. I shook my friend's hand and we parted, but for a very, very long time

I couldn't fall asleep. The pitiful sight of N. kept appearing before my eyes. Perhaps now, as I write this, he's no longer suffering. Perhaps the ghost of the lovely Corinna has summoned him to her heavenly abode.

Emma

"You're truly lovely," Emma said to her sister, Yulia, as she pinned the last feather to her turban. "You'll be the finest decoration at the ball." Yulia warmly embraced her sister and, glancing in the mirror, said that it seemed Emma had used all her skill to show her off in the most brilliant light. "If that proud warrior isn't captivated by you now, then the many interesting things you've said about him must be untrue." "He's too gloomy for me!" Yulia answered, "and truthfully, Emma, whenever I see him I think you alone could reconcile him with us poor women. He holds us in contempt only because he has yet to see your attractive face among us." Emma smiled, kissed Yulia, handed her sister her shawl and gloves, and walked her to her carriage.

Yulia had been widowed at the age of twenty, and although she was good-hearted and sensitive and had sincerely mourned the loss of her elderly husband, the exuberance of her personality soon took advantage of her freedom. Rich and beautiful, she lived as she pleased, and her house was filled with the best society. She and her sister shared the tenderest friendship although Emma had altogether different qualities, and her quietness, which resembled melancholy, was in total contrast to Yulia's cheerfulness. Having been deceived by fortune, Emma learned while in the full bloom of her youth how changeable it was, which appeared to cause her spirit to wilt.

Emma was not a great beauty, but her face expressed such goodness that anyone would wish to be loved by her. She possessed nothing out of the ordinary, but everything she had was of interest. When Emma began to speak, everyone unwittingly fell silent. When her eyes focused on a certain object, it became fascinating for everyone. Her voice and even her gait were sure, unwavering, and firm. In short, someone who spent a day with her would remember her for an entire century. Music and reading were her favorite pastimes, and while Yulia was hopping about at a ball, Emma would be practicing a difficult piece of music or traveling through Greece with Anacharsis.[2] But today, after taking Yulia to her carriage, she found no pleasure in books or the piano. Her sister's words, "When I look at him, it seems to me you alone could captivate him," echoed over and over in her mind, and although they concerned a man she didn't know, Yulia's description—and her own imagination—presented him in the best possible light.

Yulia had not exaggerated. Major L. possessed every virtue. His attractive exterior was enhanced by intelligence, modesty, and most of all by an absentmindedness with which he moved through the ranks of the fair sex. However, there was no sign in him of that unbecoming lack of concern that almost always accompanies contempt for women. It seemed only that he had yet to find the one capable of filling his heart.

That was how, or almost how, Emma herself imagined him. She anxiously awaited Yulia's return, and the noise of her carriage made Emma tremble. She tenderly embraced her sister and with unwitting dread asked, "Did you conquer the unconquerable?" "No, Emma. That's for you alone to do. When you didn't come, he hid and will probably not show himself again in society until you lead him back into it." "So what did you do at that boring ball?" Emma asked. "Boring?!" Yulia exclaimed. "Do you think the retreat of your intransigent knight diminished the charms of our society? A Colonel appeared in his place and, although less attractive, was lively and cheerful, and he spent the entire evening beside your Yulia." "Oh, what inconstancy! Yesterday you talked of no one more that Major L., who, if we're to believe your words, is a phenomenon among men." "And it's true," answered Yulia, "but am I to blame that cautious fate has hidden him from me, perhaps for the sake of your happiness?" "Oh, surely not,"

---

2. Anacharsis was a Scythian prince who in the sixth century BCE traveled extensively in Greece and elsewhere, and earned a reputation for wisdom. He is credited with pithy sayings and didactic poems. In the *Letters of Anacharsis*, a Hellenistic composition, he is made the mouthpiece for diatribes against a corrupt civilization.

exclaimed Emma, sighing. Nevertheless, long after bidding her sister good night, she was still pondering that conversation.

How fortunate is the person who, early in life, meets the one meant for her heart! Youth and love make everything possible for such a person: it seems as if fate is occupied with her alone and strewing flowers in her path. But what grief for a heart that's infinitely sensitive when the breath of sorrow causes it to wither away while still in its youth, and the salutary dew of hope, having nurtured that heart for the tender emotion of love, will be unable to remove the corrosive distrust it now feels toward its prospects for happiness. While still a child, Emma was promised to a certain young man she had grown up with. The constancy of his affection became a habit for her and, although travel separated them, an unbroken exchange of letters and, even more, the tender names they allowed themselves to use made their relationship a pleasant one and nourished their hearts over several years of separation without weakening their attachment. To others who attempted to woo her, she would answer that the one who loved her with such constancy didn't bear the slightest resemblance to those who surrounded her. It was then that she learned of the death of her beloved; her health suffered and society seemed unworthy of her attention.

At that time Yulia's husband died, and at the sight of her emotionally distraught sister, Emma forgot her own grief in order to lessen her sister's sorrow. And little by little this sacrifice brought relief to her heart. Without objection she'd follow Yulia when the latter had errands in the city, but once there, she'd maintain her solitude; she was seen only in the company of her sister's friends. When Yulia's period of mourning was over, Emma's sociable sister began to make frequent outings and received many guests in her home, while Emma kept to her room. Out of love for her sister, however, Emma took a sincere interest in everything that brought Yulia pleasure and, with the attention of a doting mother, sought to ensure that Yulia surpassed everyone in beauty.

This was Emma's general disposition when Yulia returned once from a magnificent ball and extolled Major L. At first, Emma listened calmly; but Yulia's incessant repetition of one and the same thing attracted her attention, and the words that he seemed alone in a crowd made her unwittingly entertain the thought that he was as un-happy as she. For a sensitive heart, this was enough to fuel the imagi-nation, and Emma took as much interest in every ball as Yulia did and always stayed up, awaiting her sister's return. But her absent-minded sister, now occupied with her newfound attachment to the Colonel, completely stopped talking about the Major, and Emma was afraid to question her. It seemed that her dream of happiness had been taken away, a feeling that resembled that of a man who, after finding his way in an impenetrable forest, loses it again.

Yulia and Emma had a friend with a noble heart who had spent his entire youth in the finest company. He knew society as well as he knew his favorite aria from *The Magic Flute*, and when his heart experienced love, it was always for women who were virtuous, intel-ligent, and kind. Such women school a man in the most advantageous aspects of his character, making him attractive at every stage of life. Such a man needn't fear the loss of his youth; he will always be a fa-vorite among women.

Baron G. loved the two sisters and understood them perfectly. With great pleasure he spent almost all his time with them and lis-tened with sympathy when Emma, in her melodious voice, tried to convince him that this world was like a desert to her. But he occupied himself no less with Yulia, who, with adorable playfulness, would hear out his advice and then make a sincere confession of her fickleness, after which she would immediately bring him all her new dresses, and having tried them on one by one, force him to admit that without her vivacity, she would not be as charming as she was. While observing them both, the Baron would often say that he feared Emma's melan-choly much more than the high spirits of her sister, who loved in the usual way: she would receive a declaration of love during the waltz, and then decide her suitor's fate during the quadrille. Emma, on the other hand, didn't treat any of her heart's emotions lightly, and so her love was bound to be excessive.

Not far from the city, the Baron owned a beautiful estate where he spent every spring. During the previous winter he and his young friends had been inseparable, and he had grown so used to their company that he prevailed upon them to go with him. Delighted when they said yes, he thought of everything for the enjoyment of his dear guests. For Emma, there was a music room, a select library, and charming gardens and groves bounded by a majestic river. For Yulia, he planned parties, concerts, and grand balls so that she wouldn't feel their loss when she left the city for his sake. But she wouldn't have missed them: the novelty of the place and the charming surroundings of the estate made her even more exuberant and free-spirited. Even Emma seemed to abandon her melancholy when she left the city, and she involved herself in almost every one of her sister's activities: she took walks, went boating on the river, and danced at the small village festivals, especially when a shortage of partners threatened to ruin the enjoyment of the others. She would stand in for the missing man or woman and never exhibited the slightest constraint. Always gentle and unpretentious, she was loved by everyone who knew her and was given the epithet Humanity's Friend. Emma was truly that and, having a great deal of free time, would wander throughout the estate beginning at dawn, and wherever she met poverty and misfortune, she would leave behind some proof of her goodness.

The Baron's birthday was at the beginning of May, and the most elaborate preparations were underway for it. Invitations had been sent to the city and to the neighboring estates, and Yulia requested that all the young military officers quartered in these places be invited without fail, for without them, she assured everyone, the world would be like a picture without shading. The fact that Yulia was so occupied with the preparations for the ball gave even more free time to Emma, who spent the greater part of the day in the garden and grove.

Once, lost in thought, she wandered very far and found herself on the outskirts of another estate located along the river. A large post road lay alongside the grove, and the loud bells of a passing horseman forced Emma to recollect herself. She was about to return home when she saw terrible flames entirely engulf the hut closest to her. Terrified, she was all the more startled by the wailing of a desperate mother whose only child was caught in the fire. In a frenzy, Emma begged someone to save the unfortunate child, and when she was unable to find any sympathy, she threw herself without thinking into the flames; but a strong hand pushed her back, and a military uniform flashed before her eyes and then disappeared into the smoke of the fire. Wringing her hands, she was beside herself as she waited for the stranger to return and was in a state of indescribable joy when she saw him exit the hut with a crying baby in his arms. The plume in his hat was broken, his hair was singed, and his uniform torn. Everything pointed to a struggle with the terrible element and to his victory over it. "Savior of the innocent!" exclaimed Emma. She wanted to approach him, but involuntarily stopped for the look directed at her by the stranger made her tremble. She had never before met such an attractive man, especially in that moment when his entire appearance was enhanced by his good deed and bespoke a noble character. He stood silently for quite a while and finally handed the rescued child to Emma, saying in a deferential tone: "I couldn't be a simple witness to your benevolence. That child owes its life to you. If I hadn't seen you, I might not have undertaken that act. But your voice, your pleading forced me to fly in the face of a thousand deaths!" Emma couldn't answer him. She kissed the child, gave him to his overjoyed mother, and said, "Every day, no, every hour we'll pray for the man who saved him!" "That's the only reward I hoped to receive!" pronounced the stranger, deeply moved. "When the angels intercede for me before God, He'll grant me the good fortune of seeing you again!" He was about to go when a loud voice called out to him and, afraid that another pair of eyes might destroy the charm of this scene, he said in haste, "We must part!" and disappeared into the crowd.

Emma leaned against a charred tree, lost in thought, and failed to notice anything that was happening around her. The fire had been put out, the people were beginning to disperse, and the sound of their voices was slowly dying out, but it seemed to Emma that the kind stranger was still standing beside her and was still speaking to her. And she would have remained in that dream if the mother of the rescued child hadn't come up to her once again and embraced her around her knees, thanking her for rescuing her child. Emma caressed the infant and, as she left, promised to visit them the next day.

Returning home, she was delighted that no one had noticed her absence or seen her confusion when they asked how she'd spent the day. She told her friends she was tired and went up to her room early, not because she hoped to find any peace there, but because she wanted to dream at her leisure about her adventure. But throughout the night, beginning as soon as she closed her eyes, her room seemed to be engulfed in flames and the stranger was standing there in the middle of the fire, holding the rescued infant.

Everyone was still asleep when Emma reached the edge of the grove. She brought the victims of the fire everything she had and lightened their sorrow with her kindnesses. She sat the baby, which Providence itself had entrusted to her, on her lap and spoke with the peasants who had gathered around her. Cheered by her goodness, they told her about the cause of the fire—how it broke out—and then about the young gentleman who'd thrown himself so desperately into the fire. "A brave gentleman!" said one of the peasants, "God will surely reward such a good deed! My grandson found a notebook with money in it, which the gentleman must have lost. Please take it, Miss. You'll sooner find an occasion to return it to him." He then gave the small notebook bound in Moroccan leather to Emma, which pleased her very much. She hoped to find in it the name of the stranger who interested her so, but when she opened it, she saw only money, some notes on expenses, and a sheet of parchment on which the following words were written: "What gloom! To cross this wide world in a futile search for a heart that will beat in time with mine, to stretch out my hand in vain, hoping to feel true love strike! Oh, dear creature, about whom I've dreamed for so long! Appear before me and light up my soul with a ray of happiness!" She couldn't tear her eyes from the paper. The one who'd written these lines seemed to have been thinking of her. The date indicated that it had been written only a day before she saw him. Having assured the peasant that she would return the notebook, she then gave a reward to the one who'd found it, took her treasure and walked home so quickly it was as if someone were trying to take it away from her. She reread the mysterious sheet of paper often and always found something new in it for her heart.

She anxiously awaited the Baron's birthday celebration, thinking that she could easily find out who owned the notebook from one of the officers present. She wanted to consult Yulia about it but didn't have the courage to tell her of her adventure and so put it off from one day to the next. In any case, if the Baron and her sister had been less occupied with the preparations, they would have easily discovered her secret because Emma's face bore the imprint of her heartfelt emotions. Her former despondency was no longer evident and even her pensive-ness no longer exhibited the sorrow that had burdened her heart. The smile on her lips was proof that no gloomy apparition darkened her mind. She was even absent-minded with her pastimes, often abandoning something she'd undertaken before finishing it so as to walk in the garden and think at peace about one thing only.

Yulia once saw her in that state and, thinking her melancholy had returned, gently asked her to cheer up, at least for the Baron's birthday. "Will I ever feel the happiness," she said, "of seeing you at least once in your life open your eyes with a goal and a purpose?" "It's fate itself," answered Emma, "that keeps me from it, bringing me close to a goal, only suddenly to take away any hope of reaching it." Yulia took those words to refer to Emma's former attachment and with a smile remarked that fate was in that case as capricious as she.

On the morning of the Baron's birthday, there was no one around except for a few of his friends and acquaintances, and so at ten o'clock Yulia and Emma brought him their gifts. Yulia gave him a painting in which Mirth and Joy, in the form of beautiful women, were decorating a bust of the Baron with flowers, with the following verses inscribed below.

> The years bring nothing fearful
> To one who lives with Joy and Mirth.
> Let them abide within you,
> They will crown your days on earth.

Emma's gift, however, was of a completely different kind. Knowing the Baron's heart well, she gave him a list of all the unfortunate people living in the vicinity of his estate. She included only those whom she herself could not help. The Baron was deeply moved and accepted their gifts with tears in his eyes. He embraced the two sisters and said: "So it is, my friends! Joy and Mirth live with me, they appeared to me in the beautiful form of you two, and they adorn what remains of my life. I feel, as if without your friendship, I would be nothing." His young friends knew the value of his love and to show that, they were both very amiable that day, especially Emma, whose cheerfulness was so out of the ordinary that everyone was captivated by it. Heartfelt pleasure enlivened her, and she was so charming that she eclipsed even Yulia with her striking beauty.

As evening approached, everything took on a different appearance. Women changed into ball gowns, carriages clattered up to the entrance, bells jingled, doors opened, and suddenly the entire hall was filled with contented faces. When the music began, Emma, despite herself, felt shy. She'd grown unaccustomed to such crowded gatherings and was afraid to look up lest she catch the glances directed at her. When the first dance was announced, a potential partner approached her and asked, "May I have this dance?" His hesitant tone spoke to something in Emma's heart and compelled her to look up at him. And what do you think she felt when she saw the stranger standing before her? Smiling with pleasure, he repeated his words and added that the hope of seeing her there had made him impatient for the ball. Trembling, Emma could barely get up from her seat, and as they traversed the ballroom she ran into Yulia, who stopped her, looked straight into her eyes, and said, "That's him! Wasn't I right that you alone could bring him into our circle?" She went off, but Emma, confused, paid no mind to her sister's words and followed her partner.

As soon as Emma regained her composure, she reminded him of the lost notebook. "At the time how could I notice such a loss?" he said. "I found out about it from those poor people whose misfortune served the cause of my happiness. Without their misfortune I wouldn't have met you!" "How guilty I feel before those good people!" exclaimed Emma, wanting to cut the conversation short. "I haven't had time since then to visit them!" "You didn't have the same desire that brought me there," responded the stranger. "I was there every day if only to speak about you with people who know you!" Emma felt incapable of saying anything to him. She remained silent for quite a while and then asked him, "Have you known the Baron long?"

"I enjoyed his favor when I spent some time in the city."

"You were in the city?"

"Last winter I spent a short time there."

"And so you know my sister?"

"I had the honor of meeting her several times in society."

"Oh, what a strange coincidence!" Emma exclaimed, wringing her hands. Yulia's words "That's him!" now resounded in her heart and forced her to add, "And so you're Major L.?" The Major was surprised and didn't answer for some time. He finally nodded his head and said, "If that name has merited your attention, then I'm proud that it belongs to me!" At that moment Emma felt all the recklessness of her exclamation and, hoping to correct it, explained to him with adorable candor that she'd heard of him very often from her sister, who said so many good things that she wanted to meet him herself.

If the Major had been more conceited and worldly, he would have understood perfectly from those few words what was happening in the heart of that sweet girl. But he loved her sincerely and didn't dare to think that he was loved by her. He simply experienced the pleasure of seeing her and feeling her presence.

When the dancing was over, Major L. accompanied Emma back to her place, at which point Yulia came up to them and, with her usual cheerfulness, scolded the Major for visiting them for the first time only now when he lived so close to the Baron's estate. "I was away at the beginning of spring," he responded, "but since returning, I've had little time to think of myself. The first thing that happened to me has entirely occupied my heart!" He glanced at Emma, who blushed. Surprised, Yulia looked at them both. She saw that her prediction had come true but didn't understand how or where Emma had met the Major. Finding it impolite to ask her about it at that moment, she couldn't resist saying to Emma that her fortune-teller merited the finest reward, since the pronouncements of the Sybil herself were not as accurate. She left them but kept coming back and often disconcerted them with her pointed remarks.

Throughout the entire ball the Major never left Emma's side and several times returned the conversation to the happy event that brought them together. He insisted that on that very morning a peculiar feeling had filled his heart: "My friend was surprised by my high spirits and said that something good was going to happen to me. What a happy prediction! I caught sight of the fire from a distance and without thinking leapt from the carriage. As I made my way through the crowd of people, I saw you pleading for someone to save the child! I was astonished and deeply moved and at first didn't understand what it was you were asking. But I knew already then that I couldn't deny your request. When you rushed into the flames, I forgot everything and thought only of how I could win your approval!"

"I didn't have time then to say a single word to you, but I can assure you I'll never forget that incident!"

"You promise me more than I dared hope for," responded the Major.

Emma wanted to give him back his lost notebook before he left, but the Major was unwilling to part with her for even a minute and asked her to leave it for another time. "To avoid another scolding from your sister," he added, smiling, "I'll try to come by as often as I can."

When all the guests had gone, Emma, who had no thoughts of sleep, accompanied her sister to her room and asked whether she didn't want to hear her out. "Oh, no! No!" answered Yulia, "Once you start talking about it, you won't stop until morning, and I'm terribly tired. Besides, I want to punish you for keeping secrets!" Emma embraced her, persuading her that she couldn't have brought herself to talk to her about it before, but now that Yulia had guessed everything, she could relate her adventure in a few words. "Alright," Yulia said and, listening with delight, repeated several times: "It was Fate itself that brought you together." Finally, Yulia wished Emma good night and went to bed.

Vain wish! For Emma, the charms of the day drove sleep away almost completely. The last minutes of her sleep were interrupted by a most lovely vision that appeared before her and forced her to get up. She threw on a light dress, opened the doors to the balcony, and stood there for a long time, gazing at radiant nature, which for the first time in her life seemed to her to be blossoming. Remembering that the Baron and Yulia would sleep in late that morning, she decided to visit the victims of the fire and went back to her room to get a shawl and the bag containing the Major's notebook. Though it was still early and she had rather far to go, the familiar route and, even more, her pleasant mood shortened the way. She made it to the edge of the grove without noticing and was surprised to see instead of the burned-out hut a beautiful new home, as if some magical power had placed it on that spot.

Guessing the identity of the magician, she approached the little house with delight just as the peasant woman was coming out, holding her child in her arms. She rushed to meet Emma, kissed her hands, and asked her to come to the housewarming. "I'd be delighted!" said Emma, "But first I'd like to know how you were able to build this cottage in so short a time." "Oh, Miss!" she answered, "God has been kind to me! He sent me two generous people who answered all my needs: first, you, Miss, and then the nice gentleman who saved my Vanya. He visited us right after you and said he'd bought us a house, ready-made, that was being delivered. He asked us to try to put it up before you came. At first we thought we'd have to find workers, but the fine gentleman calmed us. He assured us that he'd instructed the men who were delivering the house to put it up. Every day he came himself to check on the workers; he badly wanted to surprise you. But when they finished and you didn't come, the poor man lost all patience. Forgive us, Miss! Seeing how this wonderful gentleman suffered, my husband and I prayed to God that he'd find you soon and never be parted from you."

You can imagine Emma's composure as she listened to that good woman! She entered that house as if she were entering a temple of love prepared just for her, and she blessed the moment she saw the man who understood her completely. Noticing that there was still much that was lacking in the house, she promised to decorate it. "Oh, I'll have so many things!" said the delighted peasant woman. "The gentleman promised to do the same. I'm expecting him, Miss, and I keep thinking: if only he'd come now. Oh! He'd be so happy to see you!" At these words, Emma involuntarily leapt to her feet and wanted to run away, thinking it improper to wait there for the Major. "Where are you going, Miss?" asked the startled woman. "At least have something to eat. With the money you gave me, I bought a cow and, expecting you and the gentleman, I prepared some wonderful cream. You sit, Miss, and I'll bring some in just a moment." Emma sat down, and while the peasant woman prepared breakfast, she anxiously looked out the window and secretly in her heart hoped for what her good sense would deny her. After eating a little, to the satisfaction of the woman, Emma kissed the child and hurried off.

At first she kept looking back, expecting that she'd be followed, but finally she calmed down and continued more slowly on her way. And as the sun indicated it was still morning, she was in no hurry to return home. Emma picked a few beautiful flowers, then sat down beneath a spreading tree and without noticing began to weave a garland. Her heart was filled with the previous day and with everything she saw that very moment. It's impossible, she thought, that someone who can display his feelings with such tenderness doesn't feel them in his heart! She was surprised that Yulia could complain about his coldness when Emma saw no signs of it at their two meetings. As she thought about all this, she recalled the time when her heart had longed for just such a thing. In the midst of these pleasant daydreams, she was awakened by the clatter of a galloping horse. Lifting her head, she saw the Major, who was lost in thought, only a few feet away. She wanted to get up and hide, but she didn't have the strength and remained rooted to that spot.

As soon as the Major noticed her, he leapt from his horse and approached Emma. The joy that was evident in his eyes prevented him for quite some time from speaking. But then he collected himself and asked her: "To what do I owe the happiness of seeing you?" "To this beautiful morning!" Emma replied, attempting to hide her confusion. "It is indeed a beautiful morning!" said the Major with delight, looking up at the sky. He then lowered his eyes and met Emma's gaze. At that moment, not knowing what she was doing and planning to leave, she placed the garland she'd made on her head, which made her look so lovely the Major couldn't help exclaiming, "I've never seen anything more beautiful than that!" He sat down beside her on the grass and, begging her not to leave, said, "You can command me to go away and I'll obey you, but think of the anguish that would fill my heart if you did." "They'll be expecting me at home," Emma said softly. The Major took out his watch and showed it to her, saying, "It's not seven o'clock yet. Surely, your sister and the Baron are still asleep, so I'm not depriving them of a single minute with you. I confess that when I saw the roof of your house, I dreamed that you, too, were still sleeping." Emma blushed at this remark. She thought it strange to see him up so early after such a tiring evening. Unable to dissemble or pretend, she said she'd slept very poorly, and so got up and decided before the heat of day set in to visit the people she hadn't seen for so long because of the festivities and her own absent-mindedness. "And so you've already been there?" asked the Major. "I'm just returning now, touched by your goodness! You anticipated me in everything. But I can't be upset with you for having surprised me so!" "Surprise isn't the emotion my heart would like to feel from you," said the Major in a barely audible voice. But Emma's confusion told him that she'd heard and understood him. Frightened by the subsequent silence and by the Major's glances, she took the garland from her head and asked the Major, absent-mindedly, "Isn't it pretty?"

"It is!" said the Major, looking at her adorable face, "It's beautiful! For whom did you make it?"

"I was occupied with your noble deed and wasn't thinking of anyone. I didn't make it for anyone."

"Oh, then give it to me as a reward for my deed! The memory of this moment will compel me to search out occasions to do only good in this life!"

With a trembling hand, Emma gave him the garland. Delighted, he took it and, not daring to kiss her hand, put the garland to his lips and then hid it near his heart. Emma didn't know where to look and so was glad when she saw the bag lying at her feet. She picked it up and took the opportunity to change the conversation. "I almost forgot again to return your lost notebook! Please check to see that everything's there." "I won't complain about your stealing," answered the Major, smiling. Opening the notebook, he caught sight of that sheet of paper that was so dear to Emma. He read it over, first to himself and then aloud, and then gave it to Emma and said in a touching voice. "Oh Emma! I've found that person! And although I've yet to feel the warmth of her tiny hand, my heart is full of the happiness only her presence can bring. Won't you take it? I beg of you, take it. When I wrote it, I had a premonition that I would see you soon." He fell silent; the place and his respect for Emma made it impossible for him to go on. Even more, Emma's confusion forced him to stop.

Looking up at the sun, Emma said, "I have to leave you. My friends are probably awake and are expecting me at breakfast. But would you like to accompany me?" She got up. "Circumstances deny me this pleasure," answered the Major, "but tomorrow I'll come without fail." He retrieved his horse, which was quietly eating grass nearby, and, taking it by the reins, walked beside Emma. The entire way they carried on the lightest conversation, which calmed them both. Approaching the garden, Emma said, "And now, farewell!" She wanted to open the gate, but the Major, anticipating her, stopped for a moment and asked, "Would you allow me to hope that the time we've spent together hasn't been unenjoyable to you?" Emma couldn't deceive him at that moment and, in fear of their parting, gave him her hand and said that she considered him the best thing in her life! The delighted Major pressed her hand to his lips and, before Emma could take it away, kissed it several times.

When the garden gate closed and the Major, now galloping away, was hidden from Emma's view, she hastened her steps. Learning that her sister was still asleep, she went to her room and woke her up with kisses, saying, "Is it possible to sleep on such a splendid morning?" Yulia opened her eyes, looked at her sister, and said, "Have you just seen him?" "Who?" asked Emma, blushing. "Major L.—the one you've been taking a walk with." "Oh, dear God! How did you know that?" "From your eyes—they're radiant with happiness," said Yulia, laughing. "If you don't believe me, just look in the mirror." "Oh, I have a feeling you're speaking the truth," said Emma with a sigh. She then sat on the bed beside her sister and recounted every detail of their meeting.

Not once did Emma leave Yulia's side the entire day, and, just like two friends after a long separation who have so much to tell one another, the sisters, who'd been separated from each other by their different interests, were delighted that they could now talk about the same things. Not all the guests at the ball had gone home, and so the friendly conversation of the sisters, to their great displeasure, was often interrupted. And when the Baron asked them to think up something to extend the pleasure of the previous day, Yulia and Emma looked at each other, knowing that for them personally too much was lacking for them to carry out the Baron's request. The good Colonel, who was so interested in Yulia, had also been at the Baron's birthday, and Yulia's attachment to him was more constant than her previous attachments, strengthened perhaps by the attractiveness of Emma's new love. In any case, at that moment the Colonel occupied Yulia's heart.

In this romantic mood, Yulia proposed that they all go boating on the river. "Ah," said the Baron, "let's leave that until tomorrow, and I'll order them to clear the vegetation from the path on my favorite island, which my friends have yet to visit. And if it's nice tomorrow, we'll go there and drink tea and have supper." Only Emma was pleased by this delay, for she remembered that the Major would be with them tomorrow.

But how heavy was her heart when midday arrived on the following day and the Major hadn't come. Yulia intentionally put off lunch but finally, at three o'clock, ordered it to be served. Every time the door opened, Emma trembled and cast an anxious look at each person who entered. Toward the end of lunch, she was struck by the sound of spurs and a saber. "Finally," she thought and glanced at her sister to communicate the feeling to her. She was, however, deceived: it was only the Colonel and his officers. "I've come to say good-bye to you," he said, casting a despondent look at Yulia. "What do you mean, good-bye?!" exclaimed the Baron, "You haven't said hello yet." "What can I do?" he answered. "The thing that burdens our heart is always the first thing said. We received marching orders for tomorrow." Yulia, seeing how pale Emma had become, was more worried for her than she was for herself. In any case, it was impossible for her to feel the pain of parting when the object of her affection was standing there before her eyes. "But can't you stay a few more days?" she asked the Colonel. "No," he said, pulling up a chair and sitting down next to Yulia, "But we've been so advantageously quartered, I hope this will bring us success in our march!" "Please leave aside the compliments," exclaimed the Baron, "and tell us where you're going." "We received the shortest possible orders. They also called up Major L., who will probably be given instructions and sent on ahead." The conversation continued for a long time, but Emma didn't hear it. Her heart felt so constricted, she was afraid she'd fall off her chair. When lunch was over, she went immediately to her room, and Yulia followed her there. The tender friendship of her sister succeeded in lessening Emma's sorrow and even in planting a certain hope in her heart. "Oh, what a blessing a true friend is, who skillfully touches your aching heart and almost always heals it with her sympathy!" thought Emma, seeing how good-hearted Yulia was and, not wishing to separate her from her admirer on their last day together, overcame her sorrow and appeared once again in the parlor.

At six o'clock the entire company, now in high spirits, made their way to the riverbank where large boats had been prepared for the crossing. After boarding the boats, each person found a comfortable spot. They were all having fun except for Emma, who now wore her former melancholy expression. Leaning her elbows against the side of the boat, she gazed into the water and traced on its surface with her parasol the initials that were so dear to her. Occupied by this one individual, her thoughts were interrupted by beautiful music that greeted them on the island. The company's mirth increased even more when they saw the lovely place where Spring, it seemed, had erected her temple. The artfully laid paths led to a large spreading oak tree, under which divans and tables had been placed. Throughout the island turf benches had been made, and, to complete this picture, it should be mentioned that a fire was glowing in the distance, around which cooks were bustling while attentive servants unloaded from the boats everything necessary for dinner. The mixed company dispersed across the island and, as strict etiquette was replaced by simple propriety, each person found an activity that suited his or her taste. A happy Yulia told her sister, who was walking beside her, that the Colonel had come for her final decision.

Wandering away from the others, Emma chose to walk down the most solitary path, which lay close to the riverbank. After walking quite a way, she was completely startled to see on the opposite bank the village her heart knew so well; and the lovely little house, which had been built with such care, stood directly before her eyes, much to her satisfaction. Spotting a bench deep in some bushes, Emma threw herself onto it and relieved her heart with her tears. Oh! After losing all hope of happiness, what could be sadder than to see unaltered those things that bear witness to her former happiness! Emma knew that her solitude would not be interrupted and so she remained in that spot, which, given her mood on that lovely May evening, only fed her sorrow. The sun had already set, but Emma didn't notice and, listening intermittently to the now distant noise, she hoped she'd be forgotten entirely, when suddenly she heard the plash of an oar. She got up and, looking out at the river, saw a boat that was putting into shore several feet away. By the time she noticed it, it was already too late to leave. She then heard the Major's voice ordering that the boat be pulled into that very spot. At that moment Emma couldn't give an accounting of her emotions. Fear mixed with joy forced her to emit a loud cry. Her voice startled the Major down to his very soul, and before his boat reached the shore, he'd leapt onto the bank and found himself beside her. "Emma," he said tenderly, "of course you didn't expect me, but did you think there was anything impossible for someone with the emotions I feel? Could I leave this place without seeing you?"

"They convinced me you couldn't be here," answered Emma.

"Couldn't be here, when I promised you? When I dared to think that you wanted this as much as I, and that you were counting the minutes until this moment? Did I deceive myself in that, dear Emma?"

"No," she said, "I was waiting for you so impatiently, but now I'm at peace."

"Oh, Emma! What did you say? After that, how could I not consider myself a happy man?" He then took her hand, and Emma, deeply moved, didn't think of taking it away. She looked up at the sky and said, "Ah! Why feel this happiness when tomorrow it will be taken away forever?" "Never, never," exclaimed the Major, placing her hand on his heart. "What power can separate us if you don't wish it to happen! Tell me, Emma, do you want me to be completely happy?" "Do I want it? Ah! How can I convince you that I want it with all my heart!" "Oh, Emma!" said the Major, delighted, "And so, will you belong to me forever?" "Yes!" Emma answered, "But can it be that you are to leave me tomorrow?" "No, my dear!" he said, pressing her to his heart with joy. "No! I can remain here and we'll never be parted again." Love and sincerity fueled the conversation for quite some time. Of course, they might have forgotten the entire world if the prudent Emma hadn't recalled that her friends were waiting for her. She wanted to go, but when she realized that she would have to appear with the Major, she was confused.

Guessing the reason for her confusion, the Major told her that his boat was still there and that he could take her over to the shore where her high-spirited friends were dining. But when he noticed that she was about to get up, he held on to her hand. "Oh! Let's prolong this priceless moment, if only for a few minutes more! Dear Emma! Remember that for the rest of the evening I'll see you only in the company of others." "But then we have the rest of our lives!" she answered, smiling. "But what is saddest for me is leaving behind this place. We'll find it again and take note of it," she said, getting up. "No, we need to take note of it this very moment!" exclaimed the Major, pressing her to his chest and planting on her lips the warmest kiss. Then he leapt into the boat and moved quickly away from the shore.

Oh, who can describe what Emma was feeling then! Only a while ago she'd been devoid of all hope, and now, completely happy, she fell to her knees and gave thanks to the One who alone can send us such joy, but not in words—no! She couldn't utter them, but God could surely see into her heart, which was open before Him.

When she returned to the place designated for lunch, she ran into Yulia, whose eyes beamed with the same happiness. "My friend!" she said to her sister, "I looked for you everywhere. You should know of my good fortune before everyone else. The Colonel loves me, and I've promised him my hand in marriage." Emma embraced her tenderly and replied, "This island is surely inhabited only by the blessed! And I will belong to him forever." "But where is he?" asked Yulia, surprised. And then Emma recounted in just a few words everything that had happened to her. They returned to the group and at that very moment the Major appeared. He cast a meaningful look at Emma, then gave the Colonel a piece of paper and explained that their departure had been postponed for two days. "For this good news," said Yulia, now exuberant, "you've earned the greatest reward. Have you not already received it? Your appearance suggests something extraordinary." "You've guessed correctly, Miss!" he replied. "On the way here I met a creature who in a single instant made me the happiest of men!"

How different was Emma's return home from her trip to the island! Sitting beside her beloved, she only took her eyes from him to look up at the sky so as to thank heaven for her good fortune. The moon, which shone directly on the Major, made him so attractive that, while admiring him, Emma asked quietly, "Is it true that he'll be staying several more days with me?" "You should ask instead whether I could live without you for a single moment," replied the Major just as quietly, and noticing how the others were dozing, he put his hand over the side of the boat and with his eyes implored Emma to extend him her hand. The ever-modest Emma, unable to bring herself to do it, indicated with a glance the people sitting around them. "Even now in their dreams, they can't imagine the kind of bliss that fills our hearts," said the Major, "Doesn't this adorable hand belong to me now? I demand my property!" Who, in Emma's place, could resist those words, which were accompanied by a tender look? She gave him her hand and repeated her question: "Can you stay several more days with me?" "I can," he answered. "The general likes me and I explained to him that I hoped to remain in the reserves until dear Emma was mine!" He wanted to bring the hand that he held in his to his lips, but when Emma made a movement to take her hand away, the boat dipped low, and hoping to raise it, the Major lowered his hand that was still holding Emma's into the water. This entirely insignificant incident gave new fuel to their most tender feelings, and love knew how to use it to its advantage: the Major wiped off Emma's hand and then dried it with kisses.

Oh, the most wonderful moment of our life! There's not a pen capable of describing its charms! All the emotions of the heart can be expressed perfectly, except for happy love, which cannot be represented! When they reached the shore, the Major accompanied Emma all the way home, where they had a pleasant moment recalling how they'd parted the day before beside the garden gate. They couldn't have hoped that their very next meeting would decide both their fates. He showed her the garland he'd received from her just yesterday morning and insisted that it had withered from the heat of his heart. They finally parted so that they could see one another the next day with new joy.

Both sisters thought it sinful to keep their happiness from the Baron for so long, and so they went to his room immediately and tearfully told him of their intentions. The Baron was moved and sincerely shared their happiness. He embraced each of them again and again, saying: "O God! How happy You've made me, a decrepit old man, by bringing good fortune to my dear friends in my home. I should think you'd never leave me now, for this place is so dear to you that it must belong to you both. I hope to play here with your children, and surely you'll teach them to love me as much as you do, won't you?" Yulia and Emma were sincerely moved at the sight of his tender concern. They rushed over to him and on their knees vowed to honor him like a father. This sacred appellation was foreign to their hearts for they had lost their parents early in life, but finding in the Baron a true friend, they harbored for him sincere affection of the sort children feel for their parents. "Go to bed, my little ones!" he said, "and tomorrow we'll talk about how and when to celebrate your weddings."

The following day it was proposed that the weddings take place in a month. Although this seemed a very long time to the Colonel and the Major and they found a thousand reasons why this happy day should not be put off, both sisters were implacable. Emma still had many things to do, and Yulia insisted that their weddings be on the same day. The Baron maintained his neutrality, insisting only that the weddings take place at his estate. "Of course, here!" said Yulia. "And I would ask you, Father, not to exclude our beloved island from the festivities." "No," answered the Baron, "We'll have an enormous outdoor party there." "I'm afraid of only one thing, Father" continued Yulia, "that Emma will take all the lovely places on your estate for they are essentially a sanctuary to the birth of her love." "And so, according to that logic," said Emma, "I should prefer the city over every other place." "The city?" asked the Major with surprise as he sat beside her. Emma then recounted to him how she'd loved him before she knew him, and the Major thanked her with the tenderest expressions for that revelation, which, as he said, made him even happier.

On the evening of the next day the Colonel and the Major left to see the General, the former, in order to receive his orders, and the latter, to request a leave. During this separation, their only comfort was the thought that in a day they would see Yulia and Emma again, as the sisters would be moving to the city for several days. However, the very word "separation" had already filled Emma's heart with sorrow, and only the inventive Yulia was able to find a way to distract her from her sadness: she recalled that the Baron still hadn't heard about how Emma had met her beloved, and so, after spending the entire evening recounting the details, Emma fell asleep with the sweetest dreams.

She got up early as she wished to visit the good peasants and to tell them of her fate before her departure. These grateful people were extremely pleased to learn that their final wish had come true. "My God!" said the peasant woman. "Surely there won't be a lovelier couple in the whole world! Ah, Miss, the two of you must come see us more often so we can gaze at you to our heart's content!" Emma promised them this with pleasure and left, saying that she would bring each of them a new dress from the city on the condition they attend her wedding.

Yulia couldn't fall asleep that night, knowing that if she didn't sleep she could see the Colonel a few hours sooner, and by the time Emma returned, the carriage was ready. Although the city, as mentioned before, was not far, for the two impatient sisters the journey seemed too long. Their silence gave the floor to the Baron, who regaled them with his quaint anecdotes, which any other time would have pleased Yulia and Emma, but now they didn't hear even half of them. Before arriving in the city they were met by the Colonel and the Major, who told them that, although the General had done everything according to their wishes, he was unable to extend their leave for more than two weeks. At first the sisters suspected that this was a plot to dispose them to a speedier union, but when they found out they weren't being deceived, they agreed not to oppose the request of the men who were so dear to them.

City life, which Yulia liked so much, was intolerable to Emma, especially now, when the visits she had to make as a bride-to-be took time away from being with the Major, who, no longer distracted by military service, spent every free moment with her. Occupying himself exclusively with her, he discovered with each passing day new merits and virtues in her and thanked fate for having sent him such a friend for life. Emma likewise saw that her heart had made the happiest of choices. In addition to the tender love the Major showed her at every opportunity, she had acquired in him the best possible mentor and friend, and entrusting herself completely to him, she hoped under his guidance to avoid making a single mistake in society.

The time they had to spend in the city passed imperceptibly, and the return trip to the Baron's estate did not resemble in the least the trip there, when Yulia and Emma in impatient silence were rushing to meet their beloveds. The Baron had not failed to take notice of that, and so asked the Colonel and the Major to travel with them in the carriage so that he might at least hear the voices of friends. "You're putting yourself in an unfavorable position," said Yulia. "I'm afraid that in occupying ourselves with these fellow travelers, whom in your goodness you've provided, we may, despite ourselves, forget once again that you're sitting here beside us."

"No need to worry!" answered the Baron. "As compensation, I won't have to see beside me those gloomy faces, which, to be honest, don't suit you at all."

"So ask these gentlemen," said Yulia, laughing, "not to leave us and to love us as much as they love us now. That way you'll never see us with dull faces."

"I doubt that will work, my friend! Women are capricious, and I know many who are made bored and gloomy by their husbands' tender love."

"Oh, dear Papa, what a comparison! Isn't it true, Emma, that even without our companions we'd be amiable, if only to avoid being compared to someone else?" In fact, the high spirits of this charming woman made the trip most agreeable.

Although the Baron took great care to make the weddings as magnificent as possible, the short amount of time allotted to the Colonel and the Major prevented him from achieving his goal, and only a few of his friends were invited at such short notice. For the happy lovers, it was, of course, more pleasant to spend that most important day without a throng of unknown observers. Blessed by everyone, they vowed with true reverence to love one another, and Emma, being religiously inclined, uttered the vow with particularly touching emotion. She felt even in that moment what the loss of this happiness would cost her and asked God to preserve it through her entire life.

As soon as they got up the following day, they received the joyful news that the marching orders had been cancelled and the regiment was returning to its previous quarters. "Fate is playing a perfect joke on us!" said Yulia. "Wanting to please these young men, she invented marching orders so as fulfill all their desires that much sooner." "Are you reproaching her for it?" asked the Colonel, tenderly. "Oh, no!" she answered. "Father is undoubtedly the only one who won't forgive her for preventing him from celebrating our weddings the way he wished." "That's right," said the Baron. "But has any time truly been lost? Please, Madam, leave your kisses and sit down this moment to write out invitations!" "Ah, have mercy, Father," exclaimed Yulia, "we'll write them worse than schoolgirls who've been given a pen for the first time!" "Alright, alright! I'll let you rest today, but starting tomorrow you'll have no peace. I'll prove to you that I'm delighted at your good fortune."

He did, in fact, invite a large number of guests and every day he thought of new pleasures for them. And they made a visit to the happy island. Having learned of the place that was so dear to the hearts of Emma and the Major, the Baron ordered that a beautiful bench be erected and adorned all around with sweet-scented flowers in pots, which made a charming sight. All the trees were strewn with garlands made of the finest flowers, and a small boat rested on the shore. The other bank was illuminated, especially the little house built by the Major, and near it a group of well-dressed peasants danced in a circle. A beautiful evening completed the picture. When the young newlyweds reached the shore, they rushed to find their spot, where, completely enraptured, they embraced and renewed their vows to make one another happy. These promises were faithfully kept.

Yulia's husband, who was promoted to general, had to live in the city, which fully corresponded to her desires and personality. On the other hand, the Major, who liked the quiet life as much as his wife did, retired from military service and, to the Baron's great pleasure, lived on the estate and occupied himself with the sole task of providing peace of mind to the people dear to his heart. They rarely visited the city, but Yulia left behind its amusements from time to time in order to rest amid the circle of her true friends.

Count Gorsky, a Novel

Filled with sincere gratitude for a good deed extended during a time of sorrow, an appreciative Liubov Krichevskaya dedicates Count Gorsky *to Her Highness Princess Emilia Petrovna Trubetskaya.*

BOOK I

LETTER I

From Countess Gorskaya to Sofia Liubskaya
Village of Uspenskoye
January 20, 183—

Again no letters from you! Tell me, dear Sonechka, have you already completely forgotten your childhood friend? Who would have expected this from you, who have shown such extraordinary constancy in your attachment to your friends? Who would have expected that your fickle Liubinka would surpass you in this feeling?

But who is not humbled by sorrow, dear friend! Where is the playfulness, the insouciance of that happy age when we knew sorrow by name alone? And now! It's as if I never knew happiness, as if I was never young; and moreover, what a bitter price I paid for this precocious maturity.

So why do you increase my grief, dear friend? Why do you answer all my appeals with nothing but unbearable silence? Don't you know how much I need the voice of your friendship? Let it enter my heart but once and out of compassion teach it to live without the love of someone dear!

Upon my return from the Caucasus, I wrote to you that my health was much improved. I might even say that I am entirely recovered, if mineral waters had the power to heal the pain of a grieving heart. Nevertheless, I followed all the recommendations of my physician to the letter and was cured of all attacks of my debilitating illness.

I don't remember whether I told you, my dear friend, that among those I met in the Caucasus was a young man who had arrived there from Petersburg. He's serving in the Guards and knows the Count.

Noticing my confusion upon hearing my husband's name, he no longer mentioned him in my presence and so deprived me of the opportunity to find out anything more than that the Count was loved and respected by all.

Alas, that doesn't surprise me, my friend! Who could resist paying him tribute? Who is not attracted by his merits? His personal affairs are not known in society; and who would dare to accuse him on my behalf when I myself do not find him guilty!

I often imagine that my marriage is a dream, and although I'm in a deep sleep, I neither can nor wish to wake up and redeem my present situation at the price of a happiness that is unknown to me. It will, of course, seem strange to you that, despite all the grief this person has subjected me to, I'm afraid not to belong to him even in my thoughts, and I don't complain in the least of the unhappiness he has unwittingly caused.

Isn't he more deserving of compassion than I, for he was forced to enter a union with me, someone he did not know and could not love, when his heart expected to be captivated by love? No, I don't blame him, Sonechka! And I take great pains to conceal all the afflictions brought on by my separation from him.

If you've been receiving my letters, then of course you know that after my father's death and in spite of all my excuses, the Count insisted that I manage the estate. And although I knew that while serving in the capital he was in much greater need of money than I, I never dared propose that he take something to which we held equal claim. So imagine what satisfaction I felt when, much to my surprise, I was able to do him a monetary favor!

You know the kind old man Ivan Ivanovich Pravin? He still manages the Count's entire estate and, despite the disarray in our marriage, often visits and consults in all matters with me as the lady of the house. I've never demanded this, but it pleases me that the old man, who loves the Count like a son, never criticizes him in my presence out of some vain desire to ingratiate himself with me.

Often he even tries to comfort me, assuring me that such an intelligent mind as the Count's will surely come to its senses soon.

Oh, Sonechka! Can I give myself up to that dream when I know how intolerable he finds the ties that bind us!

Yesterday evening I was told that Ivan Ivanovich had arrived. He seemed very sad, and so, afraid that something had happened to the Count, I asked him, "Has he been in an accident?" "No, no indeed, Your Excellency. The Count is in good health, but he's asked me for money I don't have. I recently sent him our entire mid-year profits." "Then take it from me, kind Ivan Ivanovich," I said. "You know there is nothing for me to spend my money on." "That's so, Your Excellency," he answered, combing his head with his hand, "but where will your money go?"

I blushed, my friend, when I guessed his thoughts, but I didn't hesitate for a moment and said that it was all the same to me: the Count could dispose of what I sent him any way he liked. Moreover, he needn't know it was I. "I can't do that, Countess! The Count knows I don't have the sum he requested, and so he'll probably ask where I got it. I can't lie in my old age, nor do I think it necessary. I think it very opportune for you to lend the Count money now, as I gleaned from his letter that he's quarreled with Princess Zelskaya."

Oh, how my heart pounded, dear Sonechka! If at that moment he hadn't needed money but my very life, I would have gladly sacrificed it. But … is the Princess the only reason for our separation?

"It seems to me, Your Excellency," Pravin said to me, "that you would do well if, together with the money, you wrote to the Count yourself. That would be a good thing indeed!" "I don't think so, my good Ivan Ivanovich!" I answered. "I'm not the one fated to bring pleasure and joy to his heart!"

While uttering these words, I couldn't refrain from weeping, and in order to comfort me, the old man repeated several times, "Then I'll write him the honest truth."

Let him write, my friend; let him remind the Count of me. I confess to you that at first I gave myself over to hope, without thinking, and now, although nothing in my situation has changed and my colorless life remains overshadowed by the current circumstances, an inexplicable sense of comfort has entered my heart. Don't prisoners have the same dream—that as soon as someone remembers them, they'll be vindicated?!

Write to me, Sonechka. Answer me, dear friend! At least tell me that you take some interest in your loyal friend,

Countess Liubov Gorskaya

LETTER II

From Pravin to Count Gorsky
Village of Uspenskoye
January 25, 183 ...

Your Excellency Vladimir Nikolaevich!
I had the honor of receiving your letter and was aggrieved that you, dear Count, with your excellent heart, have yet to find the kind of friend who isn't afraid to vex you and would have warned you long ago to keep away from that woman. And now, God willing, money will be enough to correct the evil she's done to you.

Having already sent you all our revenue, I didn't know what else to do. So I was glad when I thought to ask the advice of Countess Liubov Ivanovna. She happened to have some money and was happy to give me as much as necessary, telling me to send it to you as soon as possible so that you'd be calm—kind soul! You see, it's true, Your Excellency, that we seek happiness across the seas, not knowing that it's standing right behind us.

If you need the money for Princess Zelskaya, give her one or two thousand, Your Excellency, but don't let your beautiful soul have her as a friend.

Forgive me, dear Count, for interfering in your business. Please know how much I've loved you from your earliest years, and so I hope that you have no doubt when I tell you I have only one main task in my old age—to think of your happiness and to serve you as the son of my benefactor and protector.

Your Excellency's most humble servant,

Ivan Pravin

LETTER III

From Count Gorsky to Alexander Lvov
Saint Petersburg
February 12, 183 ...

I'd truly intended to visit you, dear Alexander, when a completely un-
foreseen incident kept me in Saint Petersburg. I was given a rather
important commission and was then required to go to Kh. Province.
And so, these two things robbed me of the joy of embracing you. What
can be done, my friend? Although there are so many things deep down
in our hearts that cannot be dredged to the surface without the help
of friendship, we must wait for that happy moment. But before that,
my friend, I'll recount to you in a letter some of the things I've done,
which seem important to me because only now in my twenty-fourth
year have I learned that it's possible, with perfectly sound judgment,
to do stupid things. Indeed, it's not easy to admit this, dear friend! It's
not easy to say that I've been deceived by the one I loved like the first
dream of youth, and once I'd surrendered to the power of this conniving woman, I was unable to see how incapable she was of nurturing a
true attachment.

I can picture how you're frowning at these words, listing for
me all your previous predictions. But it's no use, my friend! Doesn't
a good thing always come at a high price? And experience is worth
several years of your life and a few thousand rubles.

You'll see, Alexander, that I'll make good use of this lesson! I
have proof of it: I've taken leave of Princess Eugenia Petrovna Zelskaya
forever, and this isn't just a moment's whim on the part of lovers, nor
is it the cooling of a fickle heart that has found itself another object.
No, my friend, I now see perfectly that the woman is depraved and will
never be able to devote herself permanently to me.

When we parted, I was sincerely angry with myself that I'd
been her plaything for so long. She, on the other hand, was utterly
indifferent and that very evening was planning to go to a ball. And so
judge for yourself whether this could have been that exalted love that
makes our lives happy.

But that's not all, Alexander! I must tell you all my acts of folly. My gentle Princess, having received several promissory notes from me for a significant sum, suddenly demanded payment. It would have been easy to refute it all, but you know my principles. The Princess nevertheless has an exceptionally kind heart: taking advantage of my blindness toward her, she could have had my entire estate transferred to her name. How can I not thank her for such condescension?

To pay off the promissory notes, I gave away all my cash, sold things I'd purchased to please her but that were still at my place, and borrowed from friends. But it still wasn't enough. At that point I was again forced to bother my good-hearted estate manager, who'd gotten me out of such scrapes more than once before, in particular when some dress affair was approaching and the Princess needed new clothes.

I'd noticed long ago that this poor old man was in love with my wife. He does nothing without her advice, and now, it seems, he rushed to her. Perhaps the sly old man had heard some time ago that she had money, and the Countess, convinced by his eloquence or simply wanting to do me a favor, sent the entire sum and with a kindness I wouldn't have expected, considering her usual coldness. Evidently, this is the effect of the Caucasian waters, my friend!

Ivan Ivanovich is enraptured by her. And you'd laugh at the artfulness with which he praises the Countess, basing his hopes, of course, on my quarrel with the Princess. I don't actually believe that my wife was in some plot with him. Her indifference toward me and, even more, her exemplary upbringing wouldn't allow her to do that. Be that as it may, I'm very grateful to her and I'd rather be indebted to that modest woman than to the coquette I now despise.

I confess to you that I'm in a state of embarrassment over whether or not to write to the Countess. She and I stopped writing to one another a long time ago and since then know almost nothing about each other. When Mrs. Svetlova died, the Countess informed me of it in a most incoherent note, which represented her confusion about what to write. I excused her even then.

You know, Alexander, I don't know that woman's mind, which her grandmother praised, or her heart, which was constricted by illness—or her comeliness, which withered, they say, from bouts of fever. In short, I know her very little, although I lived with her for three long months.

I can't say anything bad about her, my friend, because she was always quiet, meek, and even excessively good. She seemed to want to hide herself in my presence. And so the fact that I had no desire to look at her or to unriddle her behavior is forgivable, especially when, after being compelled to marry her, I failed to see in my wife the slightest hint of love. And in place of that emotion, she exhibited only fear or alarm when she approached me, and even worse than that was the unbearable, icy indifference with which she suffered my rudeness.

But God be with her! Now, by sending the money, she has very artfully reminded me of her and forced me to think that perhaps I was wrong about her. Blinded by Jenny's charms and lured by her cunning, I couldn't—and didn't—want to see anything.[1]

I know what you'll say—what's keeping you from returning to your wife? No, my friend. I don't abide by the saying, "Whatever kills you will cure you." I've lived long enough under the sway of a woman's whims, and who can assure me I won't find even more of that in the Countess? Now at least we don't annoy each other.

This is what results from premature calculations and marriages that are arranged by cold reason alone! If Liubov Ivanovna had been allowed to make her own choice, she would, of course, be happy and might have provided happiness to a husband who was not too discriminating. But is that my fault? Am I happy myself, my friend?

They say that since ancient times Kh. has been famous for the beauty of its women. I'm on my way there and will perhaps find compensation for what I've lost. But this is the problem, Alexander! I don't know if it's my age or the emptiness of my heart, but I've become difficult to please.

A long time ago, the first requirement of my heart was nothing more than rosy cheeks, clear eyes, and a smiling mouth. But now it's all different, my friend! I look around and seek in the most charming face an expressive quality and that exalted dignity that, without severity, puts a stop to our lust and, without frivolity, draws us near.

1. Count Gorsky here uses the English diminutive for Eugenia, Jenny, rather than the Russian version, Zhenia.

Such emotional refinement, isn't that, too, a result of the lessons of Princess Eugenia Petrovna? Oh! I'm very grateful to her. And if I'm ever made happy again by a woman's love, it will surely not be the kind of love she gave me.

Good-bye, my friend. Remembering that you love me despite all my faults encourages me, and I look forward to the future.

LETTER IV

From Mrs. Sokolova to her Sister
Village of Velikoye
February, 183 …

I was delighted by the arrival of your husband, my sweet Aniuta! And as we spent the whole time talking about you and your children, I utterly failed to notice the days fly by. Your husband is already preparing to depart, and I don't dare detain him; I know you must be anxious, having been without him for so long.

I don't know how to tell you, my dear friend, how much your happiness pleases me! Your husband, with tears in his eyes, praised your meekness, and despite his years he loves you tenderly and appreciates your patience with his gloominess, which is a consequence of his disposition, not of any coldness toward you.

However, dear Aniuta, you have cause to reproach him—he's been unfaithful to you more than once. Our beloved Countess Liubov Ivanovna stole him away with her beauty and her attention to him, especially in her home, where she knows how to be affable with everyone. But she occupied herself with Nikolai Vasilievich, in particular, saying that this was a debt she was paying for your love of her.

Your husband will also tell you about my Sashenka. Unwilling to be separated from her any longer, I took her out of the boarding school—but she'll benefit no less here as the Countess has taken her completely under her wing, and Sashenka is attached to her with all her heart.

You can judge, my dear, how much this pleases me! And how could I fail to see the advantage for my daughter's morality when virtue itself is instructing her!

The more I learn about this outstanding woman, the more I'm amazed at how, at such a young age, she has been able to earn general respect and love. Would you believe, Aniuta, that her presence alone makes everyone well-behaved and forces us all to watch ourselves so as not to say something that might displease Countess Gorskaya?

I can't understand, my friend, how it is that such an intelligent man as Count Gorsky is unable to find happiness with her. Let's suppose that her appearance then wasn't in fact beautiful. Nonetheless, she has possessed an angelic goodness from childhood. And now, after her trip to the Caucasus, she's become incomparably more beautiful than before.

Since then, the Countess has lived alone and has become even more modest and careful, as if the eyes of a jealous husband were watching her. Recently, one of our obliging neighbors, amazed by her blossoming beauty, told her that she could now take revenge on the Count. If you could have seen, Aniuta, the majesty with which she replied that she had no right to judge her husband's faults and so knows of no reason for revenge, and that, out of respect for him, she could never permit anyone to speak ill of the man who'd given her his name.

And with this, her gracious adviser fell silent, as did the hope in the hearts of many young men who commonly believe that a beautiful woman who isn't loved by her husband is fair game.

Such an outburst was especially displeasing to Prince Belsky, who's now on leave due to his mother's illness and who, upon first meeting the Countess, appeared to be captivated by her. A very sweet young man, but somewhat frivolous. He is also a neighbor of the Countess and, although not as handsome or intelligent as the Count, who knows? Perhaps she would be much happier with him!

Good-by, my Aniutushka! Kiss your children for me. The little one, they say, looks very much like my Sashenka, so embrace her an extra time for me. Write to me soon and tell me about your husband's trip home and whether he gave you all our kisses.

LETTER V

From Prince Belsky to a friend in Saint Petersburg
Village of Belskoye
February, 183 …

My good Seryozhenka, you heard me grumble when I had to take a year's leave at my mother's behest. You saw, my friend, I almost cried from grief and despair when I bid farewell to all that is or that I know to be charming in Saint Petersburg, thinking that my poor eyes would go completely blind from the absence of anything beautiful.

But I was mistaken! Ah, how mistaken I was, my dear friend! You should fall on your knees and read the rest of my letter in that position because I will now begin to speak only of *her*.

I know you're impatient, Seryozhenka, and most certainly want to know who *she* is. Unless you've already read her name, as you usually read the end of every novel before the beginning, and if the denouement is not to your liking, regardless of the novel's other merits, you'll hurl it under the table.

Confess, my friend, that this same fate threatens my letter. You're afraid you'll find in it some article on processing grain, and it was only her name that saved you from drifting off. And so you probably already know that *she* is Countess Liubov Ivanovna Gorskaya.

Soon, very soon, almost the moment I arrived home, I was already bored and once, sitting at my sick mother's bedside and listening absent-mindedly to everything she was saying, I thought, "What will happen to hapless me in this desert, where there doesn't appear to be a single human soul?" You probably don't need to interpret the kind of soul I had in mind just then. Well, someone to whom I could give my soul, although not forever, just temporarily.

Suddenly a servant entered and announced that Countess Gorskaya had instructed him to ask whether a visit would disturb the Princess. "Ask her to come in," Mother said and, turning again to me, continued, "I suppose you were too lazy to dress today, my friend, but that was a mistake indeed. Please straighten your hair at least. I think you still remember Liubochka Kronskaya? You used to play with her as a child."

Preoccupied with this woman's arrival and thrown into a state of confusion over my appearance, I couldn't at first recall the child with whom I'd played in my earliest childhood.

These old women are truly amazing! Don't they know that when a youth sits upon his balloon, he flies higher and higher and dreams of touching the sky. And when he happens to cast his eye upon the objects he's left behind, they're barely noticeable until eventually he can't see them at all.

I'd forgotten, completely forgotten Liubinka Kronskaya. But who could forget her now in the person of Countess Gorskaya?

I had just finished straightening myself up before the mirror, in response to my mother's request, when three ladies entered: Countess Liubov Ivanovna, Mrs. Sokolova, and her sweet daughter, whom at first I barely noticed as my every glance, my heart, mind, everything fell at the feet of the charming Countess! This lovely creature enchanted me at first glance!

It is mistakenly said, dear Seryozha, that only in the capital can one receive an education and acquire that grace which is the primary adornment of a woman. Don't believe it, my friend! It's a gift of nature, a property of true intelligence.

I agree that for those who don't possess these merits, social skill is necessary and will often—almost always—correct any deficiency. But here you can immediately see the difference between merits naturally acquired and those that are learned.

The Countess has spent her whole life in the country and could have easily become unsociable. And as a beautiful woman, she had no need to learn social skills, for she would have been attractive enough without them. But when she enters the room, my friend, when she begins a conversation with you, you're utterly perplexed as to what is the more preferable quality in her: her enchanting conversation or her captivating beauty.

That's all the description I can give you of Countess Gorskaya. I stood in amazement until she turned toward me and in a most lovely voice said how delighted she was to see her childhood friend once again.... Why not her friend for life? Why hadn't we met two years ago?

And the Count? How could he have left behind such a charming creature? Oh, how angry I am at him! I'm all the more angry because, I don't know why, I thought to tell the Countess that I'd seen the Count before leaving Petersburg. Suddenly, she looked confused, turned pale, and asked in a strained voice, "Was he well?"

She seemed very pleased that I didn't elaborate in my reply and, petting my mother's lap dog, she grew so pensive that she probably didn't hear our conversation.

I don't know what would have become of me if the adorable eyes of Miss Sokolova hadn't bolstered my spirits. I would probably have fallen into depression, so sad was it for me to look at the melancholy Countess. Who was the object of her suffering? Her husband? I could have forgiven this weakness if her husband loved her. But he is a true barbarian. He's destroying her with his infidelity. This is how men are! This is how I am myself!

A few more words about the Sokolova girl. She is a sweet, playful child who quite artlessly forces you to pay attention to her. And when the lovely Countess, after having captivated you with her mind and charmed you with her angelic beauty, flies off to her home—heaven—you will still be able to find comfort on earth. Sweet Sashenka will give you her little white hand and walk with you around a flowering pond and catch a golden-winged butterfly—a dream.

She lives with the Countess and loves her and, as they say, tries to anticipate her every wish, from which she has much to gain. I think you remember Madame Cottin's lovely saying, "I'm not a rose, but I've lived beside one."[2]

The next time I saw the Countess was at Mrs. Sokolova's, whose small estate was in the same village as ours. Once again I saw the same wondrous beauty and the same love for her husband, which I found detestable.

---

2. This is a reference to the French writer Sophie Ristaud Cottin (1770–1807). "Je ne suis pas la rose mais j'ai vécu près d'elle" appears in Letter XVII of Cottin's epistolary novel *Amélie Mansfield* (1802) and is there attributed to the medieval Persian poet Saadi. *Count Gorsky* owes much to the plot of Cottin's novel. It is considered a precursor of Madame de Staël's *Delphine* (1802) and *Corinne* (1807).

One of the ladies, admiring the Countess's blue scarf, remarked that blue was the Count's favorite color. "I always wear blue so that we're united at least in our tastes," she replied with a sigh.

And this sigh penetrated my heart! Ah, if she were some day to sigh like that for me, I would die of joy! Fortunately for me, at that very moment Sashenka was singing very sweetly and calmed me with her voice.

I'm now traveling to the Countess's on my first visit. Bless me, Seryozhenka! Although they say that the end justifies the means, in our craft it isn't bad if the beginning is done well, too. Tell me, please, what you think. I need your answer.

Now admit that my letters are very interesting. It seems you were afraid that their country prose would be heavy and dull, and you probably intended to read them in bed to help you fall asleep. Be careful you don't do that now, my friend! If, as you read my letter, you can imagine the charming Countess, you'll stay awake all night.

It's time now to occupy myself with my toilette and to complete it with all the refinement of fashion and taste. Truly, those whom I now visit are much more deserving of this than an hour spent at the theater, for which we used to toil so painstakingly. Do you remember?

Ah! Yet there's little hope that the Countess will notice the care I take! To compensate, the high-spirited Sashenka will reward me with her attention and perhaps a tender look. Good-bye! I'll write to you again soon.

LETTER VI

From Milovidova to a friend in Moscow
February, 183 ...

Ah, my friend Paulina! How wonderfully you describe the Prince's ball. Happy Paulina! You're surrounded by everything that attracts the eye and gives true happiness to the heart! That maroon and gold dress is charming! How sweet you must have looked in it, my darling friend!

Make me a loan and order me one just like it. I'll send you the money by the first post.

Paul was delighted by your letter. In our backwater it's such a joy to think I could have fun, too. We'll soon leave for Moscow to spend at least *Maslenitsa* like real people.[3]

I would have left these parts for good long ago, my darling friend, but paying off my husband's debts has put me out, although it's very unpleasant and I could have avoided it. After all, the estate is all mine. But my beloved husband's passionate love forces me to be patient in that regard. Otherwise, I'd be doing exactly what I wanted.

It's now decided: We'll visit you next week. Ah, Paulina, I'm ecstatic! For God's sake, prepare for me everything you can find that's fashionable and fine, and try to find us an apartment near you. I want us to be inseparable.

Do you assume that I'm leaving nothing of interest behind? To the contrary, dear heart! Even our desert has almost come to life. Of course, you remember my description of the old and peevish Princess Belskaya, an endless moralizer, whose son is now staying with her. He doesn't resemble her in the least. He's a very nice, graceful young man. We met at the home of our local representative to the Assembly of Nobles, and we seemed to *notice* each another.

I then forced Paul to invite the Prince to our home. He very eagerly promised to come, but only now have I learned why he hasn't yet been to our house. After waiting several days for the Prince, I went to visit his sick mother. And what did I see? I found both of the Sokolovs and a doleful Liubov Ivanovna, Countess Gorskaya, who, while taking the waters in the Caucasus, achieved great success in coquetry. And so, is it any wonder this trio was trying with all their might to keep poor Prince Belsky by their side?

Vexed by this odious pact, I made every effort to draw the Prince to me, and, despite my respect for his mother, the sidelong glances of Mrs. Sokolova, the childish nagging of Sashenka, and even the sighs of the doleful Countess, I was entirely successful: he sat next to me and I triumphed.

3. Maslenitsa is the weeklong festival preceding the beginning of Great Lent before Russian Orthodox Easter.

Hoping to show the Prince how trivial were the charms of Countess Gorskaya, who'd been abandoned by her husband, I constantly extolled my marital bliss and several times repeated that I was passionately loved by my Paul, who cannot live a minute without me. When I noticed that she pretended not to listenmnvcxz to me, I turned to her and asked whether it had been long since she'd received a letter from the Count.

I truly thought she'd burn up from embarrassment. But nothing of the kind happened. She blushed a bit and answered with pride that she had no idea how she was to take my question, "If this is unexpected sympathy on your part, I thank you. If this is a joke, I don't deserve it, and so I forgive you. Ah, but no!" she said, suddenly turning pale. "You must have heard something about the Count? For God's sake, tell me, is he well?"

At this point everyone rushed to calm her, assuring her that the Count was alive and well. And it was terribly vexing to me. I'd wanted to humiliate the Countess in the Prince's eyes, but instead I made her the object of general attention and forced the Prince to tend to her.

And one more thing, the Princess—that old fool—asked me never to permit myself such jokes in her home. "Our circle of neighbors is so small," she said, "that I suppose everyone knows about the Countess's situation. It would be heartless to make fun of it."

What a terrible calamity! Who's to blame for her condition? Must we all suffer because the Countess didn't know how to keep her husband's affection?

I would have made a good many caustic remarks to Princess Belskaya if I hadn't recalled that the Prince would be here for the entire summer. And I did the right thing. Why should I lose the Prince's acquaintance after our return from Moscow? For that I can bear the Princess's rudeness.

We're on our way to the post office, and perhaps before this letter arrives you'll be embraced by

Your happy Bibi

Now that I've acquainted my readers with the main characters of this novel, I will introduce them to the people who created it and to those who gave me the idea to write it.

Perhaps, while reading it, you will lose all patience and begin to blame them, as much as you accuse Count Vladimir Nikolaevich Gorsky, for having unsuccessfully constituted his happiness. Then I will have gained insofar as the guilt won't fall on me alone. I will share it with the respectable Count Nikolai Stepanovich Gorsky and with Liubov Alexandrovna Svetlova.

May they rest in peace! They wanted to make the people dear to them happy, but they didn't know that our happiness is governed by the One who often destroys in an instant all the intricate garlands that twine around the life of newlyweds.

CHAPTER I

Ah, bitter truth needn't always
Torture our gloomy hearts;
And rivers of tears needn't always
Fall over our misfortunes.
For a moment we can forget
Under the spell of beautiful fictions.
Karamzin[4]

It is impossible to find a place more picturesque than the one where the large village of Uspenskoye is located. A wide river flows through it, dividing it into two equal parts, one of which belonged to Count Gorsky and the other to the widow Liubov Alekseevna Svetlova.

Count Nikolai Stepanovich was still very young when the death of his parents forced him to retire from active service and settle in the countryside, where he foresaw, other than troubles and quarrels with his neighbors, no diversions whatsoever.

One thought brought him comfort—that after he arranged his affairs, it would be up to him alone whether to reenter military service, where he was always the favorite of his commanders and loved by

---

4. From the poem "Il'ia Muromets" (1795) by Nikolai Mikhailovich Karamzin (1766–1826).

his comrades. He was soon to learn, however, that country life wasn't always as tedious as he had previously assumed.

His neighbor, Liubov Alekseevna Svetlova, was an intelligent, educated woman, and although she was much older than the Count, her beauty even then could still pose a danger to an unattached heart like Count Gorsky's.

Every day he visited Mrs. Svetlova and, deceived by her age, which she had no desire to hide from him, and knowing of the attachment she held for her deceased husband, he didn't imagine his heart could cultivate a feeling more tender than friendship and respect.

Mrs. Svetlova had a daughter who was at an age that required her to obtain an education. Not having the time to educate her herself, Mrs. Svetlova, albeit with regret, followed the advice of the Count, who persuaded her to take Natasha to Petersburg. Once Mrs. Svetlova had decided on this separation, she no longer put off her departure and, as soon as they arrived in the capital, placed Natasha in the Smolny Convent.

To that charitable institution of our great TSARS, which blossomed from year to year, this most tender of mothers entrusted without worry her heart's last joy, her only child, knowing that there she would meet with the solicitude and kindness of our IMPERIAL MOTHER.

Oh, how many women have I seen who justify these exalted hopes! I've witnessed how they adorn the most select and glittering society. I know them in the sphere of family life as well, where they provide true comfort to their loved ones and receive true love and respect from all who surround them.

While at the monastery visiting her daughter, Mrs. Svetlova made the acquaintance of Prince Glinsky and his family. The Prince's eldest daughter in particular attracted the attention of the remarkable Liubov Alekseevna: her beauty, modesty, and kindness bound Mrs. Svetlova's heart to her. The Princess also fell in love with Liubov Alekseevna, who asked that she keep her informed about Natasha, whom The Princess promised to visit at every possible opportunity.

Completely reassured in regard to her daughter, Mrs. Svetlova returned home with only the slightest sorrow and now, without distraction, occupied herself with her affairs.

In her absence the Count had time to investigate his feelings and, discovering how strong his attachment to Mrs. Svetlova was, decided to make her a proposal of marriage, despite her age.

Mrs. Svetlova heard him out patiently and then asked him to allow her to respond frankly. And when the Count gave his word to listen to her without interrupting, she said, "Having removed those impediments from my side about which you've known for so long, I, as a friend, as your sister, must stop you because you could never be happy with me."

"Is it possible," exclaimed the Count, "that anyone who possessed you wouldn't be happy?" "It's very possible even if your feelings for me weren't simply the result of your being always with me. If I were to deceive myself in this, too, could your young heart be completely happy spending its whole life with someone who had buried her love in the grave? Could your heart find the bliss that was meant for it with someone who has similar feelings but does not share love? Oh, you deserve that heavenly love, my dear Count! Leave me with the joy of thinking that I can envisage the happiness predestined for you."

One mustn't think that the Count immediately took her at her word. He still asked her to think it over and, before doing so, to refrain from deciding his fate. But seeing she was adamant, the Count asked her to advise him on what to do.

"Leave the country for a while. You said recently that you have business in Petersburg. Go there." The Count continued to object for quite a while, but when neither entreaty nor vexation was able to alter her determination, he set the day for his departure.

Mrs. Svetlova gave him letters for her daughter and for Princess Glinskaya, telling him to visit the former, whom he would certainly have visited even without her request, and to make the acquaintance of the latter, as her friend.

The Count promised her everything she requested and, with the unaffected sorrow of a scorned lover, he left for the capital.

At first, he wrote her very often and always of his love and his eternal feelings and, wishing to please her as a mother, filled all his letters with news of her sweet daughter. About Princess Glinskaya, he wrote simply that when he delivered Mrs. Svetlova's letter to her, she wasn't in.

It seemed he had divined Mrs. Svetlova's intention and, hoping to prove that he was more stubborn than she, avoided every opportunity to meet her lovely friend.

They finally met at the theater. From his letter Mrs. Svetlova could see that he was enchanted by her. He then described a Petersburg festivity that he attended with the Glinskys and was very happy to have escorted the Princess, who was able to appreciate everything refined and understood him so well.

Mrs. Svetlova smiled as she read the letter. She predicted that in the future she would receive even more lovely news. And so it was: the Count and the Princess wrote together. They were betrothed and happy.

This is all the kind-hearted Liubov Alekseevna had wanted. And while she didn't possess the vanity of a beautiful woman, she did have the weakness of a tender mother and knew very well how to calculate the success her daughter would have in society now that she was connected to such brilliant homes in the capital as those of Prince Glinsky and Count Gorsky.

Several years went by in that state of affairs until Mrs. Svetlova was informed that her daughter would be preparing for graduation that winter. What mother doesn't await this moment with a trembling heart? Who among them wouldn't rush—in a hired cab, a simple springless carriage or a magnificent equipage—along one and the same road, to one and the same hall in order to embrace her daughter? Their feelings, their delight are the same, for the mercy of the Charitable Mother of orphans adorns their young charges in equal measure. Oh! With what reverence every mother must enter that building! With what gratitude she must send up to the Throne of the All-High prayers for Her, who took under Her protection a barely comprehending child and returned her as a young lady adorned with every gift!

Liubov Alekseevna did not prepare long for the trip. She knew that for Petersburg it was better to take extra money rather than extra luggage. And this presented no difficulty for the wealthy Mrs. Svetlova. And she didn't worry about lodgings as Count and Countess Gorskaya had invited her to go directly to their home.

The Count greeted Mrs. Svetlova as a loving brother who owed his happiness to her, and in the Countess she found the same charming Princess who had captivated her on her first trip to Petersburg. Embracing them both in turn, she was delighted by their happiness. "You still haven't seen everything, my friend!" said the Count, who left the room and then returned a minute later holding their son in his arms. "This is the one who will complete my happiness. Look at what an angel God has sent me!" Having said this, the Count placed on Mrs. Svetlova's lap a plump, red-cheeked, rambunctious boy, who put his little arms around her neck, kissed her, and then asked, "What are you going to give me?"

"What will I give you, my little angel?" exclaimed Mrs. Svetlova in delight. "What can I give you that would make you happy your whole life long?" "Well then, give me a piece of candy," the child said and again embraced her. His answer produced general laughter and they never forgot it.

This child is, as they say, the hero of this novel: Count Vladimir Nikolaevich Gorsky. In his childhood, he was the instant favorite of all his father's intimate acquaintances. His beautiful face and his wit, unusual for a child of his age, attracted everyone and forced them to give him their uninterrupted attention.

When he was treated with tenderness, it was impossible to find a gentler and kinder child. On the other hand, when someone began to oppose him, he stood his ground with great stubbornness. That personality trait changed during adolescence and would have probably disappeared forever had certain circumstances not arisen that were inimical to his desires.

From the moment they met, the child became attached to Mrs. Svetlova. And she knew perfectly well how to make of him all she wanted. Her power over him continued throughout her life.

The Countess, even before Mrs. Svetlova's arrival, had ordered that everything necessary be done for Natalia's graduation. And Liubov Alekseevna was very grateful to her. She could now spend her time without diversion—either at the Smolny Convent or with her dear friends, to whom she became even more attached.

A great deal of Mrs. Svetlova's time was taken up with amusing her little favorite, Volodenka. He would often ask her not to go anywhere and would say that he didn't like Natasha because she took his "old friend" away from him. This is what he usually called Mrs. Svetlova.

The closer the day came for the boarding school exams, the more anxious her mother's heart grew. When her sweet daughter, now crowned with success in comportment and the sciences, fell into her embrace, Mrs. Svetlova experienced a feeling of inexpressible joy!

CHAPTER II

Shakespeare was right:
Love's happiness is fleeting:
Like a sound, it instantly passes,
Like a shadow, always untouchable,
As short as the lightest sleep;
It passes quickly like a lightning flash
That with its brightness
Lights up the earth and sky;
And before we can say: Look there!
And with a trembling heart
Wish to lift our eyes again,
The universe is covered in dark![5]

Oh, how I love the Russian winter! Wherever you look—in the town, in the village, in the city, everywhere—you'll find the same activities, the same ecstatic youth greedily seizing every pleasure.

On a clear holiday morning the village street is crowded with people; conversation, laughter, and songs drown out the hand bell of a passer-by, who looks affably at a brightly colored circle of well-dressed rural beauties, from whose faces the bitter frost has long ago driven away their summer sunburn, as well as all the cares of the work season.

In our small cities, rambunctious youth finds its pleasures increased by the freedom of winter. Now the gatherings, parties, and skating begin. Officers on leave appear, and then a very long and interesting cotillion is held.

---

5. No author is given for these verses. The metrics and style suggest they were most likely written by Krichevskaya herself.

But the festivities at that time are even more varied in our villages, where visiting neighbors, celebrating name days and Christmastide, playing forfeits, and even dancing French quadrilles constitute the noisy joy of the revelers.

And what lively, brilliant pleasures of winter in our northern capital offers our young people.

At the insistence of Count Gorsky, Mrs. Svetlova decided to spend the entire winter in Petersburg. She rightly thought that, before taking her daughter back to the country, she must not only acquaint her with the finest circles of that city's society but also show her the rarities of which the city is full.

Everything that luxury, fashion, and taste could invent was employed in Natasha's wardrobe. The Countess herself always dressed her, and she increased her outings only so as to provide her daughter with greater pleasure—and to introduce her to high society, where, considering all the benefits of her life, she might not come in last.

Natasha came out socially at the same time as her two dear friends, the Kronsky sisters, who, although rich, were left orphans in infancy and so were placed in the Smolny Convent by their brother, who was serving in Petersburg. Ivan Mikhailovich Kronsky justified the complete trust placed in him by his dying parents. He looked after his sisters with the tenderest care and was rewarded with their sincere affection.

While at his sisters', Kronsky had the opportunity to see Miss Svetlova. At first she was merely Natasha, whose pretty face unwittingly drew him to her; and without noticing it himself, he would always select for her the finest piece of the candy he brought for his sisters. As Natasha grew, so too did Kronsky's attention to her. At that time surprises began to accompany the candy, and the meaning of those surprises became more transparent as her beauty increased. And when she wasn't allowed to go with her girlfriends to the convent gates, she always received her portion from them, as well as greetings from Ivan Mikhailovich. This mysterious attachment matured under the protection of innocent friendship.

Several days before her graduation, after a fatiguing review of her lessons, Natasha was relaxing by the gates with the Kronsky sisters. This time Ivan Mikhailovich had the cleverness to arrive directly behind Mrs. Svetlova's carriage. He had not seen Natasha for a long time and found her even more lovely than before. He gazed at her, dreaming of the pleasure he would have when he finally dared to approach her.

When Mrs. Svetlova departed, Natasha remained by the gate with the Kronskys, and her young friends described to her how sweet and kind their brother was. He had prepared an excellent wardrobe for them and had even rented an apartment so that at least for the winter he wouldn't be separated from them. "What?" Natasha exclaimed, "Can it be that you won't always live with him?"

"That's right, my sweet friend," answered the elder Miss Kronskaya, "That's impossible. Our brother is not yet married."

"Get married this winter," said the other sister, "And we'll never be parted from you, and we'll go on outings with your wife."

Kronsky smiled and answered, "It's not so easy to do. Why haven't you, my friend, tried to find me a wife?"

"Ah, yes. But how can we do that? Why doesn't Natasha marry you, dear brother? Would you like that? What a wonderful, happy thought!" she kept repeating, jumping for joy.

As she said this, Natasha's cheeks blushed violently, and when an embarrassed Kronsky held out his hand to her, wishing to say something, she cast a lovely, bashful look at him and stole away.

Is it any surprise now that after Natasha's graduation Kronsky looked for her everywhere she went and that his sisters were inseparable from her and always knew just where the Countess was planning to go with Natasha.

Without fail, at every ball Natasha ran into Kronsky and had him as a partner for all the interesting dances. He knew at which entrance to the theater the Countess's carriage usually stopped. He hired for his sisters a box near the Count's and tried very hard to make his acquaintance.

Could such attention escape a mother's keen eye? Mrs. Svetlova liked everything about Kronsky. His tender solicitude toward his sisters, his respect for his parents' memory, and his modest relations with her daughter bespoke a truly noble soul. She knew that he was a good son and brother, and would surely be a good husband. And valuing domestic happiness about all else, Mrs. Svetlova saw in Kronsky the most advantageous match for her daughter.

She hid nothing from her friends, the Gorskys, and in this instance they soon became a party to her joy and, noticing Natasha's affection for Kronsky, they approved of her choice.

Wishing to please Mrs. Svetlova even more, Count Gorsky quickly made Kronsky's acquaintance at the first ball and, finding him to be a man of great merit, invited him to his home.

Kronsky was quick to fulfill the Count's wish. He visited him the very next day, and soon Ivan Mikhailovich and his sisters had become the Count's frequent houseguests.

Natasha now lost interest in balls and her chief pleasure was the Kronskys' company. Having more freedom in her relations with Ivan Mikhailovich, she told him of her feelings for him, despite herself. But timidity on both sides put a stop to any explanation, and Natasha might have left for the countryside, taking with her only a memory, if chance, which protects lovers, hadn't worked in their favor. Kronsky was supposed to leave Petersburg on work related to his service. Not knowing whether he'd be gone for long, he was in despair. We can resign ourselves to a separation we've already grieved over and gradually come to accept, inventing ways to comfort ourselves. But a sudden, unexpected separation! Ah! How many tears does it cost!

Several days before Kronsky's departure, Count Gorsky held a ball. With what despair Natasha prepared herself, imagining that there and then she would have to bid farewell to Kronsky and, as a consequence, to all her heart's joy!

And so she'd recently suggested that Kronsky, who had taken a leave to accompany his sisters to their estate in the Crimea, travel together with Mrs. Svetlova and spend a week or two at Uspenskoye … Tell me, how could one refuse such a charming picture?

From the beginning of the ball, Kronsky and Natasha were silent and only during the mazurka, which with its many pairs of dancers was as advantageous as a cotillion, could they, away from the others, turn imperceptibly to the subject that occupied them most of all. Kronsky asked Natasha whether she would remember him. "Could you really have any doubt?" said Natasha. "Could I forget that brotherly attention you showed me, equal to that which you show your own sisters?"

"And do you think the same way now?" Kronsky asked. "No, no! I feel that you are dearer to me than life itself!" A frightened Natasha wanted to leap from her chair, but Kronsky, with a pleading gaze, asked her to hear him out. And when Natasha sat down, he said, "Do you remember the plan my sister so expertly devised when you were surprised to hear that they couldn't always live with me?"

"Yes, I ... remember," replied Natasha, with embarrassment.

"So, my lovely Natasha! If you don't refuse to fulfill it and make me the happiest of men, then we won't be separated now for long— we'll be joined together forever. Do you want that, sweet angel?"

A pale Natasha had no idea how to answer! She asked him to speak with her mother and not to forget that he'd given his word to travel together with them from Petersburg to Uspenskoye.

In that seemingly simple reply, there was so much Kronsky found delightful that he didn't insist she decide his fate that moment and assured the young lady he would immediately speak with her mother and know by the answer of the two Svetlova women whether he would be traveling together with them. "Oh! You'll surely be going with us," said Natasha guilelessly. "My mother is so kind, she would never separate us."

What more could Kronsky have wished?

No sooner had the mazurka ended than Natasha rushed to her mother and embraced her. All she could say was, "Dear Mother! I'm perfectly happy!" And when Liubov Alekseevna looked into her daughter's eyes, she knew without asking who was the cause of her happiness.

She knew the feeling that was agitating her child's heart and it found such a lively response in her own bosom that all that had transpired flashed through her mind in an instant. She knew that only moments such as these leave a trace in our lives.

Here one cannot help but recall the pink silk thread with which Nikolai Grech, using his unique artistry and real magic, connected the riggings of an English ship to the heart of his readers, and in an instant everything that was dimly lit in our memory came to the fore.[6]

That very evening Kronsky explained his intentions to Mrs. Svetlova. She gave him her permission and eagerly promised to await his return to Petersburg. Now the lovers would not be separated by such bitter tears. They promised each other to soften this brief separation by writing letters.

Time passed quickly. And before Natasha had enough time to become respectably melancholy, Kronsky returned. He made every effort to obtain a leave, and as it was already spring and the roads were thoroughly passable, they left for the country, having made their final purchases for the wedding.

Only one thing grieved Liubov Alekseevna—that the Gorskys couldn't go with them to be witnesses to Natasha's happiness, which they had done so much to facilitate.

It was sad for Mrs. Svetlova to leave behind her favorite, Volodenka, who was attached to her with all the love of a child. And for a very long time no toys or caresses from his mother could make him forget Mrs. Svetlova.

Is it possible to describe Kronsky and Natasha's journey? Is it possible to depict their blessed state in simple words? No, dear readers! This is not my task. If one of you has ever traveled like these fortunate ones, then you don't need my description. If you've never traveled like this, isn't it better that, instead of many well-chosen words, I wish you just such a happy trip.

Upon arriving in Uspenskoye, Kronsky insisted that his marriage to Natasha take place before his sisters' departure. Mrs. Svetlova had no excuses or objections, and so in a month Kronsky accompanied his sisters, together with his beautiful wife, back to Petersburg.

It seemed that nothing could increase their happiness, but the birth of a charming daughter made them even happier.

What an ecstatic state Liubov Alekseevna was in when Ivan Mikhailovich gave her little Liubinka and asked her to make her as

---

6. Nikolai Ivanovich Grech was a journalist and writer. His most popular novel, *The Dark Woman* (Chernaia zhenshchina, 1834), combined elements of sentimentalism and the adventure novel.

good as his Natasha! "She's yours," Kronsky said, kissing his mother-in-law's hands, "Take her. She'll surely love you as much as I do."

A pale Natasha somehow foresaw that her daughter would be the one comfort of her mother's old age. It was 1812 and Kronsky, although now a tender father and husband, had to forget those happy ties; as a son of the fatherland, he had to forget that he had only just begun to enjoy life.

Racing to the field of honor, he could not, however, part with his wife. And so it was decided that she would follow him as long as the circumstances of that cruel war permitted.

And so it was. Natasha left Kronsky only when the proximity of the enemy and the constant movement of the troops made her feel all the disadvantages of her situation. "I'm leaving, my sweet friend!" she said, embracing her husband. "However, you must know that your life is bound to mine. Whether here or there, we'll see each other soon?"

Kronsky wept and begged her to take care of herself for their child's sake. "She has a mother," said Natasha, "and as long as her mother's alive, she won't be left an orphan. But what will I do in this wide world when I'm deprived of you, my sweet friend!"

Having bid farewell to her husband, Natasha returned to Uspenskoye, almost lifeless. Neither the love of her pious mother nor the innocent caresses of her beautiful child could bring back her peace of mind. Although Natasha prayed constantly, her healing prayers failed to warm her heart, which was now given over to cruel despair.

Her faithful heart was not deceived by that presentiment. On the twenty-sixth of August, Kronsky was killed. The news soon spread, and before long it reached Mrs. Svetlova, who bore it with obedience to the will of the Almighty. She was only afraid that the shock would crush her dear daughter.

To the great happiness of Mrs. Svetlova, the Gorskys came from Petersburg and lived for a time in their village. Their sincere friendship enabled them to find a way of informing Natasha of the loss as gently as possible. But no sympathy could relieve this unfortunate woman's state, and although she survived the worst moment and seemed to be listening to the comforting words of her sorrowful mother, alas!—that silent grief reflected only the loss of feelings and memory.

Have you ever been witness to the grief of a wife sincerely mourning a soul mate, one that could never be replaced by another? Is she mourning his life or her own happiness? Have you ever seen how enormous tears stream down her cheeks, scorching her heart? How she gazes upon all that surrounds her! How coldly she reacts to thoughtful caresses and the love of her family! This is because love has died for her forever, and people's attention oppresses her. Oh! If you've ever seen such sorrow, it won't seem strange to you that Natasha—exactly one month later—left her daughter in the hands of her elderly and inconsolable mother, and with a joyful smile went to the place where her gentle husband awaited her!

CHAPTER III

> I only vaguely knew I was alive;
> And how much agony that knowledge
> Brings the one who learns
> That his beloved is no more!
> How did I manage to survive?
> I do not know whether it was faith
> Or apathy that kept me alive?
> Zhukovsky[7]

What a terrible state Liubov Alekseevna was in! It seemed she'd lost her sanity. In a frenzy, she'd scream, wringing her hands and calling out to her daughter … It was feared such grief would kill Mrs. Svetlova. The Count took her granddaughter in his arms and placed her in her grandmother's lap, saying, "This, my friend, is the one you must live for now!"

---

7. These verses are taken from the 1822 Russian translation of Lord Byron's "The Prisoner of Chillon" (1816) by one of Russia's greatest romantic poets, Vasilii Andreevich Zhukovsky (1783–1852). The lines from Byron's original read: "I had not strength to stir, or strive,/But felt that I was still alive—/A frantic feeling, when we know/That what we love shall ne'er be so./I know not why/I could not die,/I had no earthly hope—but faith,/and that forbade a selfish death."

Ah, that was enough to make Mrs. Svetlova immediately come to her senses, and pressing the innocent child to her breast, she prayed to her Heavenly Father to forgive her mad complaints and to give her the strength to replace the good parents of the poor orphan.

While she shed bitter tears, caressing her laughing grand-daughter, her favorite, Volodia Gorsky, approached and embraced Liubinka, saying: "Don't cry, my little friend"—this is what he called Mrs. Svetlova—"If you're tired of carrying Liubinka, give her to me. She'll be mine. I'll amuse her, and when I grow up, I'll take her to Petersburg and buy her a toy."

In spite of the enormity of her grief, Mrs. Svetlova smiled, and suddenly a comforting thought flashed across her mind. Handing the child to Vladimir, she said: "Take her. I truly believe that you alone will bring her happiness. It absolutely must be so. My friendship with your parents shall be secured by kinship."

The Gorskys, hoping to lessen the sorrow of their friend and believing that fate was speaking through her, willingly supported Mrs. Svetlova's proposition.

This thought was like a joyous ray of light illuminating Mrs. Svetlova's heart. From that moment on, she showed even more affection toward the Count's son, constantly admiring him and telling him he'd grow up to be a perfect man.

Elderly people hold faster to their hopes. They think that their experience makes it impossible for them to be deceived. And for this reason, Mrs. Svetlova, in spite of Volodenka's and Liubinka's ages, saw in them a lovely couple.

When the Gorskys left for Petersburg with their son, Mrs. Svetlova occupied herself exclusively with her orphan. The only variety in her quiet, doleful life was correspondence with friends and the playfulness of her tiny granddaughter who, in the eyes of strangers, was a most beautiful child with a cherubic face.

With the passing years Liubinka became even more attractive. She loved her grandmother with her whole heart, and when she noticed sadness in her eyes, drove it away instantly with her exuberant, lively disposition. For her, there was no punishment that could equal her grandmother saying that she was displeased with her. The pale youngster would shed tears and be inconsolable.

Several years passed in this way and Liubinka was already at that age when it was necessary to think of a good education for her. At first the Gorskys advised Mrs. Svetlova to move to Petersburg and place her where her daughter had been educated. But Mrs. Svetlova had grown so accustomed to country life that in her declining years she couldn't leave it to take her granddaughter to Petersburg. She also couldn't admit to her friends that this child was her only joy, and she couldn't be separated from her for even an hour. And so she asked the Gorskys to find a governess and a tutor whom she could take in and to whom she could entrust Liubinka.

Such a request came at just the right moment. The Countess had recently made the acquaintance of the family of a certain Liubskoy, who had been raised in the house of a grandee and, having learned everything that was taught the grandee's son, knew much more than his classmate. His natural talent completed the rest.

Fate sent Liubskoy a wife who was his equal in merit. Raised with the daughter of Prince S., she lived for many years in the same magnificent house. When the Princess was married and moved with her husband to England, the poor Liubskoys were deprived of their last patronage, and in order to support themselves in a respectable manner, they gave private lessons. So when Count Gorsky proposed that they leave the capital and move into Mrs. Svetlova's house in the country, they happily accepted and found no reason to regret their decision, as they found in their mistress just what they were hoping for.

Mrs. Svetlova had an outstanding and mature mind, which was combined with true virtue. As a Christian, she loved her friends with all their faults. Carried away by exemplary generosity, she showed charity to everyone without question.

Oh, how easy it is for my pen to depict such a devout woman! It is she! It is my incomparable mother. The only difference is that the sorrowful path of my mother's life was much longer: the extreme poverty and the many children that burdened her provided no relief for her early widowhood. Ah! With what patience she submitted to the will of her heavenly Father!

The Liubskoys had a young daughter who, although much older than Miss Kronskaya, became her best friend, and this friendship gradually grew stronger. She was a great help to her instructors, who knew how to make good use of her in their lessons, as well as for the moral development of their pupil.

In order to receive permission to spend several hours with her dear Sofia, Liubinka did everything that was asked of her. In order to study at the same desk as Sofia, she leapt with incredible speed across the distance that separated her from the knowledge her friend possessed. Her gentleness and obedience charmed the Liubskoys and made them love her as much as their own daughter.

At that time Mrs. Svetlova experienced yet another grievous loss. Her true friend Countess Gorskaya died from a severe fever. When the inconsolable Count informed Mrs. Svetlova, he added that his dying wife had made him and Vladimir give their word that unless Vladimir's heartfelt emotions prevented it, then their wish to unite their son with Mrs. Svetlova's daughter should be fulfilled without fail. Vladimir, who was kneeling beside his dying mother, repeated his promise never to take a wife other than Miss Kronskaya.

After that, Vladimir wrote rather often to his old friend Liubov Alekseevna, and although he mentioned Liubinka only as a child, each of his letters supported Mrs. Svetlova's hope. Finally, she received news that he was going abroad for several years.

Liubinka's aunts, too, often sent Mrs. Svetlova information about themselves and at first were very displeased that their niece was being educated at home. But when they visited Mrs. Svetlova and saw her granddaughter, they admitted that she had lost nothing from such an education.

Guided always by true love and not by her kind grandmother's indulgence, she didn't take a step that was not watched with tender care. The Liubskoys, too, pointed out her mistakes not with strict admonition but with meekness and heartfelt affection, and always acknowledging them, she hurried to make amends so as never to make those mistakes again.

Liubinka's beauty also increased with the years. She was perfectly charming, with fair hair and an oval face that possessed an expressiveness and indescribable beauty. Her enormous eyes of a heavenly hue and her small pink mouth were the most beautiful of all. At sixteen she was of rather good height and possessed a figure that can only be drawn and that is rarely seen. Her kind grandmother couldn't stop admiring her granddaughter, who was a beauty.

In one thing only was the respectable old Mrs. Svetlova indiscreet: she planted too early in Liubinka the hope of a union with Vladimir. As soon as she began to understand her own desires, she impatiently wished to know where he was and what he was writing.

She followed his travels abroad in her mind and at the time studied geography with particular diligence. Then when the Count returned and his son was enlisted in the Guards, Liubinka shared her heartfelt joy with her grandmother. When the young Count informed them that he was already an officer and would be visiting them soon, Liubinka was delighted and told everyone she met of this happy news, not with the joy of a child but with the bliss of a passionate heart.

At that time Liubinka experienced her first sorrow. The rich Princess, the Liubskoys' patroness, sent them a large sum of money and asked them to come immediately with their daughter to England for several years.

Liubinka's separation from Sofia and her parents was so touching and she cried so much that Mrs. Svetlova, fearing her health would be adversely affected, exerted all her power and even severity, saying, "You can't forget, my friend, that you're the only solace of my life! And what would happen to me if you stopped rewarding me for my care with your obedience?"

Liubinka fully acknowledged the truth of these reproaches, and so, after sending the Liubskoys off, she and her grandmother were inseparable. Her beautiful heart very quickly learned the benefit and pleasure of intelligent conversation. Recounting her former life to her granddaughter, Mrs. Svetlova imperceptibly planted in her the principles of virtue and genuine piety, which in the remainder of that sweet girl's life would be her greatest comfort.

Once as they were talking at length about Liubinka's parents, she learned of their short-lived happiness and was deeply moved, imagining her grandmother's grief over the loss of her only daughter. Then, feeling all her goodness toward her, an orphaned child, she fell on her knees and kissed her hands, saying, "From now on you won't see a single tear in your child's eyes, dear Grandmother! If sorrow should ever touch me, I'll pray to God for the strength to hide it from you, my incomparable friend! Ah, haven't you tortured your most excellent heart enough looking after me, a poor orphan! It's up to me to protect your peace of mind!"

Oh! At this Mrs. Svetlova shed tears that contained no bitterness whatsoever and, pressing Liubinka to her heart, said, "Don't make promises, my friend! Submit to the will of our Creator so that your hope in His Goodness will always produce patience and not the economy of cold calculation."

Liubinka had long wished to stay with her aunts. They were married and living in the Crimea, where the estate left to her by her father was also located. Now hoping to dispel Liubinka's sorrow over her separation from Sofia, Mrs. Svetlova herself proposed that she go there.

The beautiful time of year favored their journey and new pleasures, never before experienced, diverted Liubinka Kronskaya. What a happy age! How quickly sorrow passes and how shallow are the traces it leaves on a young heart!

Knowing that one of Liubinka's aunts had moved to Kherson Province, Mrs. Svetlova decided to stay with her on the return trip from the Crimea, reasoning that in order to completely satisfy her granddaughter, she must take advantage of the good weather to see the Crimea.

With what childish delight the young Miss Kronskaya visited the picturesque locales of her aunt's estate. Her aunt herself undertook to show her the finest places in the Crimea and was comforted by the fact that Liubinka traveled fearlessly through the mountain precipices and ravines. "Who knows, dear Aunt," she said, "whether fate isn't preparing for me a path in life that's much more difficult than this one. I must become acquainted with all the dangers in advance."

Mrs. Svetlova was in Sevastopol to look at the sea, and the wealthy beauty from the North attracted much attention there. Unconcerned with the commotion, she didn't notice the effects of her beauty and thoroughly enjoyed all the delights of that truly extraordinary life by the sea.

She very much wanted to go on a ship, and so a captain her aunt knew organized a wonderful outing for them at sea. Exuberant and agile, Liubinka wanted to go everywhere and not only to see but to learn the name of every piece of rigging. And although she hadn't yet read *The Frigate "Hope"* and *Lieutenant Belozor*, one could foresee that she would understand all the refinement of the pen that wrote them.[8]

Young Miss Kronskaya left the mountains and cliffs of the Crimea reluctantly. She went to stay with another aunt in Kherson Province, and here she experienced the misfortune that would affect her entire life's happiness. This beautiful flower, which had just begun to bloom, was seized by a malicious autumn wind that no one's health could withstand—and Liubinka came down with a fever.

Do you know what a fever on the banks of a river delta means? It is a poison that extinguishes all sparks of life in a person. He is still alive, but what kind of life is it? He is a vague shadow bent over by disease; his jaundiced skin is not warmed by that scorching inner heat: dull yellow eyes, half-closed from weakness, force you to suffer together with the sick person. Moreover, as the paroxysms increase, his strength decreases, and then the nerves of the unfortunate one are so weakened that he falls into a terrible state. The most skillful doctors are challenged by the fact that the moment the patient begins to improve, the slightest imprudence revives the illness, which almost always returns with even greater ferocity.

A pale Liubinka experienced all of that. In two months' time, in place of her captivating face all abloom, she resembled a bronze statue. Exhausted and disfigured, she left her bed for only a few hours a day so that, sitting on cushions, she could be revived by the air from another room. During this entire ordeal, she never lost her cheerfulness or complained about her state so as not to grieve her dear grandmother; she only asked to be taken back to Uspenskoye.

In this state of suffering Liubinka returned to her childhood home. Her aggrieved grandmother still held out the hope that her na-

8. *The Frigate "Hope"* and *Lieutenant Belazor* were popular naval adventure novels of the day written by the romantic writer and Decembrist revolutionary Alexander Alexanderovich Bestuzhev-Marlinsky (1797–1837).

tive land and, even more, the knowledgeable doctor who had always treated Liubinka would soon cure her disease.

At first, the patient did indeed experience enormous relief. The paroxysms left her and she had hope of being cured soon, but an unexpected incident caused her disease to return with its former strength.

Upon her arrival, Mrs. Svetlova found a letter from Count Gorsky, in which he complained about his ill health. "Only one thing can comfort me," he wrote, "if I could see my son enter your family." And in the next post she received another letter, in which he asked Mrs. Svetlova to order his home to be heated and for all wedding preparations to be completed as soon as possible. His son would be free the following month and they would be in Uspenskoye as soon as the roads were clear. In this letter he referred to Liubinka with all the tenderness of a father.

Although neither of these letters contained a word about Count Vladimir, Mrs. Svetlova was at peace, assuming that in such a matter the father was undoubtedly conforming to his son's will, and so she hurried to inform her granddaughter of the news.

This surprise agitated the sick girl's heart; at that very moment she experienced a severe nervous attack, and the paroxysms of fever returned once again. Even in her exhausted condition, however, she thought constantly of the one to whom she would belong forever and gave herself over to those sweet feelings. The thought that he would find her so disfigured and would fail to recognize in her the little Liubinka with whom he'd once liked to play tormented her! And so we shouldn't be surprised that, although in a state of constant excitement, she carefully followed all the doctor's instructions.

CHAPTER IV

Hearts suffer when they love,
And our merciful God above
Gives us a cross, and in it
Sends us the hope we need.
Kozlov[9]

It is now time for us to look at Vladimir Nikolaevich Gorsky, whom we knew as a healthy, red-cheeked boy, the favorite of his old friend Liubov Alekseevna Svetlova.

Oh! Look at him now at the age of twenty-two. Look at him this very moment: Built like a palm tree and blooming like a rose, he gallops with all his charm and grace along Nevsky Prospect on an indomitable, expensive steed! Look at him at a lively cotillion when he flies over the mirror-like parquet, attracting the gaze of all onlookers and making his dancing partner very proud! Can't you see the charm in all his movements? Can't you hear how much intelligence and wit there is in all his compliments? Ah! Now that you know all this, you must pity Liubov Ivanovna, now lying in a fit of fever.

Count Nikolai Stepanovich couldn't admire his son more. He gave him complete freedom in everything, assuming that Vladimir, bound by his promise to Miss Kronskaya and being sensible, would be immune to the slippery temptations of high society.

Those very reasons seemed to make Vladimir sure of his behavior as well. Noticing with sorrow that the health of the father he loved so tenderly was worsening from one hour to the next, he suggested that they leave for the country as soon as possible. "I'll take a leave," he said, "and then I'll wed. Indeed, dear Papa, I often think I could be a very good husband. Moreover, I'm entirely in your power. Just give the order, and I'm ready to do anything."

But the old Count was wary of giving his son orders. Knowing Vladimir perfectly, he knew how to make him do anything with a single word filled with tenderness, and so he replied that he wouldn't so

---

9. These verses are taken from the enormously popular romantic poem "Chernets. Kievskaia povest'" (The Blackfriar. A Kievan Tale; 1825) by Ivan Ivanovich Kozlov (1779–1840). In this sentimental verse tale, the hero is ultimately redeemed through repentance.

much as ask him let alone order him, "You know too well, my friend, that you're bound by honor and the promise you made to your dying mother. For my part, I won't say anything, my son. But if you've indeed decided to go with me to the country, let's make haste. I feel that I haven't much time left to enjoy the happiness that lies before you."

"Oh! Don't say that, dear papa!" Vladimir cried out. "I won't break my word! It's sacred to me. It seems to me that I already love that little Liubinka, although I don't remember her at all. But my dear friend, Mrs. Svetlova, I can picture her perfectly. In fact, I'd rather wed her. There'd probably be fewer complaints. Young wives are so demanding."

The very day that Count Gorsky, following his conversation with his son, wrote to Mrs. Svetlova of their imminent arrival, Vladimir was invited to the most brilliant ball in the capital.

As he dressed before the mirror, he examined himself with a triumphant air, remembering that his comrades that very day had doomed him to a new conquest. In jest, they took a vote to see who at the ball would capture the charming widow Princess Zelskaya. The majority of votes fell to Count Vladimir, which now obliged him to occupy himself with the Princess.

Princess Eugenia Petrovna Zelskaya, in spite of her age, had preserved her beauty with great care, and compensated with art for that which time had destroyed. She had already noticed Count Gorsky some time ago and was simply awaiting an occasion to catch him in her web. How delighted she was when she saw that the Count didn't leave her side the entire evening. In an instant she saw how easy it would be to defeat his young heart, and with unbelievable cunning put into place a plan of attack.

The poor young man! He could never have thought that such a pretty face could conceal a perfidious heart, and so in the hope of attracting the Princess's attention, and even more of meriting his comrades' approval, he immediately began to scatter compliments and to play with words empty of any emotion. But when this quick-witted coquette cleverly won back flattery from him and poured droplets of sweet poison into his heart, Vladimir didn't have the strength to oppose her, and by the end of the ball he'd fallen completely in love with her.

Between dances, he asked whether she would permit him to visit her at home the next day. Getting his measure with a glance, the Princess said, ingenuously, "But why?" "To have the honor of seeing whether at least something from this incomparable ball remains in your memory." "And if I remember this ball and remember it my entire life, what use is that to you?" asked the Princess, with feigned nonchalance. "My entire happiness depends on it!" replied the Count. "Who's given you permission to enjoy this happiness? Do you know, Count, what a young widow signifies in the minds of fathers? She's a monster who swallows up you young Guardsmen without mercy. And so, tell me, why should I make an enemy of your father? Moreover, they say you're condemned to marry your rich fiancée?"

Vladimir couldn't bring himself to answer in the affirmative; he treated all her remarks as jest and finally asked for permission to visit her the next day, which is just what the Princess wanted.

As carried away by passion as Vladimir was, he nevertheless thought from time to time that he shouldn't sacrifice his peace of mind so easily. He knew very well not only his father's opinion but also society's opinion of Princess Zelskaya, and seeing that she could never be his equal in terms of age or lifestyle, he was thoroughly tormented. Furthermore, he remembered very well that he had only recently repeated his promise to marry Miss Kronskaya. As an honest man, he should have honored his word, but was that possible now that this beautiful woman, whom others could not conquer, was so favorably inclined toward him?!

After that, did it seem strange that Vladimir tarried in asking for his leave and visited his father much less frequently? He had to see the Princess every day, always by chance, and always in a timely fashion. Then with great condescension she invited him to visit her every evening. And in those candid conversations, she took possession not only of young Count Gorsky's heart but of his mind as well.

Is it possible that his father didn't notice what had happened to his son's inexperienced heart? Oh no! He could read his son's heart very well and, from a few words uttered absent-mindedly by Vladimir, learned the object of his son's attention, but he said nothing so that he might devise a plan to bring his son to reason.

One day the young Count found his father completely downcast. He was sitting at his desk and seemed to be at a loss as to what to write on the paper lying before him. Vladimir couldn't help but guess to whom his father wished to write and what was grieving him so. He wanted to leave the room immediately, however, so as to avoid an explanation, but in a gentle voice the old Count asked him to stay a moment.

"I wanted to send for you, my friend! I need your advice. What should I write now to Mrs. Svetlova?" The question made Vladimir blush, and he answered that, although it was certainly not what he wanted, he was prepared to do anything that was required of him. "That's precisely what I need to speak to you about, my friend. You say 'required,' but who would dare to require you to sacrifice your happiness to another's wish? Not your father! Not your friend whose only joy in life is you, my Vladimir!"

The Count wept as he said this and embraced his son, who was touched, and as he seemed willing to listen further, the Count went on: "No, no. I don't require anything more from you than for us to think together of a way to destroy all of Liubov Alekseevna's hope."

"Do you really want to do that, dear Papa?"

"And why not, my friend? At least for a time. Why should we hurry to take from you a dream that you're enjoying so? I'm not asking you whether the source of that enjoyment is pure because I know your heart. It couldn't remain attached for long to someone unworthy, and you'll no doubt return to your promise. But it will be too late for me!"

"But why, Father?" asked Vladimir, shocked by his father's appearance and voice.

"Do I really need to explain that to you, my son?" said the Count. "Haven't you noticed that I grow weaker day by day, and I'm standing on the edge of my grave? And I must see whether my only child will make himself happy forever or, by breaking the promise you gave, destroy the hope of many and your father's peace of mind."

"Enough, my excellent father!" Vladimir cried out, falling at his feet, "How could you think I preferred someone over your peace of mind? Tomorrow, my dear friend, I'll put in my request for leave and, instead of writing that letter, we'll leave for Uspenskoye. Ah, just tell me you're satisfied with your son!"

Could Nikolai Stepanovich be indifferent to such proof of filial love? He pressed Vladimir to his heart and for a long time was unable to say a word through his tears. Finally, lifting him to his feet, he said: "You are my true joy, Vladimir! But once again I repeat to you, my friend, that I don't want any sacrifice, so think this over while you're still free."

"No, no, Papa! I wasn't free even before I promised my dying mother because my father had already made that promise for me. And woe to the son who measures on a scale his own happiness against the honor of his virtuous parents!"

Everything that Vladimir then said came directly from his heart. And who in his place wouldn't feel exalted in sacrificing his love? Who wouldn't think that such an act of selflessness and a forced marriage wouldn't create a stir in society and make him appear even more interesting in the eyes of Princess Zelskaya?

And so it was. Eugenia Petrovna needed his sacrifice. It increased the Count's worth, and as the Princess couldn't and wouldn't have him as a husband, this indestructible barrier to their union would make the Count even more attracted to her. And then she could get everything she wanted out of him.

She greeted the Count's news of his fate with a violent fainting spell. And when she came to her senses, she said she knew all too well what love had been preparing for her; however, she begged him, for her peace of mind, to submit to his fate. "The only thing I fear is that the one for whom you're sacrificing yourself will be unable to appreciate her good fortune and will be unable to love you as much as I do. Ah, then what will you do, my poor Vladimir?" she asked, looking at the Count with all the sentiment she'd learned by rote.

"Then," the Count said, "then I'll seek my happiness with the only one who can provide it. Oh! For God's sake, don't turn me away then! Tell me, I beg of you! Tell me, when I'm separated from you, can I comfort my grieving heart with the hope that you'll always be mine?"

"Don't worry, dear Vladimir! I'm yours forever!"

When he left Petersburg, Count Vladimir Nikolaevich was in a daze. And dare we blame him for the fact that throughout the entire journey his appearance did so little to comfort his traveling companion, who nonetheless held on to the hope that Miss Kronskaya's kindness would cure him of his day dreaming?

But who could cure the suffering Liubov Ivanovna? After receiving the last letter from the old Count, she barely left her bed. There was not even a shadow of that captivating beauty and that unaffected youthful exuberance that everyone liked most of all in her. That sweet smile that always played on her charming lips was no more! Now her pale, exhausted face and lifeless eyes would light up for just a moment when she recalled Vladimir's arrival.

They were to arrive soon and her ceaseless, impatient expectation ignited the first spark of love in the heart of the exhausted sufferer. Every day she would get up, encouraged that her illness would return no more. She would walk through all the rooms—with the help of others—and incessantly look out the windows through which she might catch sight of the Count's arrival. Then, deceived in her hope, she would again fall ill and have to lie down.

One morning before one of her attacks, she was lying on the sofa, exhausted. She laid her head on her grandmother's lap when suddenly from the other room there was a noise that made her start, and at that very minute both Counts walked through the door. Liubinka was trembling, and when she saw Vladimir filled with health and beauty, she involuntarily looked into the mirror hanging opposite them … There was such a difference between them that in an instant everything died inside her, and a timidity that nothing could overcome gripped her heart.

Ah! One could say that this utterly insignificant incident destroyed her life's happiness for, if during her illness she had revealed to the Count all her merits and all the tenderness of her innocent, ardent love for him, she would have probably attracted his attention and, perhaps, with time, even earned his love. What young man doesn't like to inspire passionate feelings and be an object of adoration? But a profound lack of confidence in herself inspired only one thought in Liubinka: She would be an impediment to Count Vladimir's brilliant future and so he must despise her.

During this emotional tumult, her frozen lips had barely placed a cold kiss on Vladimir's cheek, so warm with life, when she fell into the arms of her grandmother. Now you can judge what state the two Counts were in!

CHAPTER V

> They sing … Zarema, though, is far,
> The Harem's queen, love's brightest star!
> Alas, all pale and overwrought,
> She does not hear her praise. Distraught,
> A palm by tempest bent and spread,
> She sadly hangs her lovely head.
> No thing can hearten her or spur;
> Girey has ceased from loving her.
> Pushkin[10]

When they carried the sick young woman away and Mrs. Svetlova had followed her, Vladimir, with a somber expression on his face, asked his father, "Is that my fiancée?" "Yes," answered the Count, "but remember, my son, that you're not yet bound to her by any ties and you can exercise your will."

Such gentle and condescending words always softened Vladimir's disposition. He sat down and said with a heavy sigh, "Now it's already too late, Father! It would be shabby on my part to refuse when I've confirmed my assent with my arrival."

"Mrs. Svetlova loves you, my friend, as much as she loves her granddaughter, and when I tell her everything, she'll surely help us get out of this unfortunate situation."

At the very moment the young Count was about to answer his father, Mrs. Svetlova entered. Her granddaughter's illness did not upset her in the least for she had grown accustomed to it and, moreover, had failed to notice the impression Liubinka had made on her fiancé.

---

10. These verses are known as "The Tatar Song" from the poem "The Fountain of Bakhchisarai" (1822) written by Alexander Sergeevich Pushkin (1799–1837). The translation is by Walter Arndt and can be found in *Alexander Pushkin. Collected Narrative and Lyrical Poetry: Translated in the Prosodic Forms of the Original by Walter Arndt* (Ardis: Ann Arbor, 1984), 255.

No physical exhaustion could erase Mrs. Svetlova's memory of Liubinka's angelic face before her illness. And could Mrs. Svetlova imagine that someone might not see her granddaughter in that way? She gaily approached her favorite and embraced him, saying, "Well, Count, wasn't my prediction right? Have you ever seen anyone finer than our Volodia? He's a real picture! A true Adonis! I can't stop looking at him; I can't stop admiring him. And how that blue collar becomes him! Ah, you are my sweet darling! This is the happiness I've waited for!"

And all these words were accompanied by the tender caresses of a true mother's love. And could kind Vladimir's heart be indifferent and refuse to repay the sincere affection of the one who had pampered him from childhood as if he were her own? Kissing the hands of the kind old woman, he involuntarily thought, "I, I alone am destined to bring happiness to so many virtuous souls!"

He also remembered that Miss Kronskaya had been educated by Mrs. Svetlova and so could only have good morals; therefore, even if she were unable to give him that deceptive happiness of which he was already a devotee, she wouldn't make him entirely miserable.

Such thoughts resigned him to the fate that was designated for him, and that very evening he asked his father to leave everything as it was and try to arrange for the marriage to take place as soon as possible.

The Count was overjoyed and the next day he told Mrs. Svetlova, who was so ecstatic that she was blinded to the overly constrained interaction of the affianced couple. "They still don't know each other," she thought and was calm.

But what was in Liubinka's heart? From the first moment she adored the one with whom she was to be joined forever. But seeing the way he interacted with her, his forced civility, and the sadness written on Vladimir's face, she divined, trembling, that she was not the one destined to make this dear man happy.

The wedding was set to take place in two days—but the night before it was almost ruined when the bride suffered a violent nervous attack.

That day Vladimir was more attentive to her and more cordial. His words revived her pale cheeks, and she felt that the slightest kindness from him would return her to life; and although every glance from him still embarrassed her, she thought she could earn at least his friendship.

They were sitting together when a man arriving from another city handed Count Vladimir a letter. When he saw Princess Zelskaya's handwriting, he blushed and, with trembling hands, there in front of Liubinka, opened the letter's seal. Oh! Now the reason for his coldness was clear to her, and her heart froze.

Under the pretext that she was going to see her grandmother, Miss Kronskaya left the Count and just managed to reach her room when her suffering became terrible! With a cry, she fell before the icon of the Savior and begged Him to give her the strength to bear this torture and to help her understand what to do. She couldn't refuse to marry the Count without revealing his secret, thereby making herself hateful to him. And her grandmother? Ah, she couldn't survive the loss of that which constituted her entire life's hope!

Acute nausea and delirium forced Liubinka to take to her bed, and she only recovered when Mrs. Svetlova's solicitude brought her to her senses. At that moment both Counts entered the room.

After she'd left and Vladimir was alone, he read the Princess's letter, in which she cleverly poured out the poison of her calculated flattery, and fearing that the Count, now intoxicated with her, would abandon his rich fiancée and rush to Petersburg, she entreated him to carry out the will of his father, who in time would come to know the purity of her feelings for his son.

Satisfied with the letter, Vladimir entered Miss Kronskaya's room and, upon seeing her pitiful condition, rushed to help Mrs. Svetlova, who was worried by her illness. Oh! How quickly this concern quieted the storm in the suffering patient's troubled heart! How easily she dispelled all sorrowful thoughts and replaced them again with sweet hope!

The day of the wedding and many of the days that followed passed as usual. Marital bliss did not make the Count or Countess happier. They observed all the proprieties and could not complain about each other, but where was the bliss of newlyweds? Where was that language of happiness understood by them alone? Where were the caresses in the presence of others and the compunction to refrain?

One could see nothing of the bliss with which enraptured hearts take advantage of the right to display their love for each other! None of that was evident and the young bride shed tears in private!

Oh, how passionately she loved her husband! With what intoxication she looked at him, but he couldn't see it! How she trembled at the slightest caress from him, not daring to repay him in kind, and torturing herself in her heart, she repeated constantly, "If I'm obtrusive, won't I just increase his unhappiness and his hatred for me? Let my heart languish—at least it will be at peace!" This is what she often thought, not knowing that such pretense was the principal calamity of married life.

Still, one could hope that their life would gradually change for the better, although with every letter from the Princess, the young Count grew increasingly morose and his wife's illness only intensified his mood. There were moments, however, when they understood each other—until an unexpected blow suddenly destroyed this accord.

The old Count was often at his home in the country. One day a messenger arrived at Mrs. Svetlova's with the news that the Count had fallen seriously ill. In an instant Vladimir was already halfway there, and the carriage sent by the Countess could barely catch up to him. The unfortunate Liubinka would have immediately gone herself if her exhausted powers had permitted her even the slightest movement. How anxious she and Mrs. Svetlova were! Although she was constantly sending for information about the Count, that did nothing to lessen the young Countess's grief. Fate had denied her even this— the opportunity to be with the father she respected so and to care for him together with his son.

At noon, unbeknownst to Liubinka, Mrs. Svetlova received a note from Pravin to the effect that Count Vladimir Nikolaevich was unable to leave his father for even a moment and had asked him to inform her that his father was suffering from pneumonia brought on by a cold and that the doctor despaired of his life; after receiving all the comforts of religion, he was perfectly calm. Ivan Ivanovich added that Vladimir Nikolaevich had asked her to take care of herself and if possible to conceal this sorrow from the Countess.

When Liubinka, exhausted by her illness, fell asleep, Mrs. Svetlova went to say goodbye to her old friend … but found him dead.

Her presence brought no comfort to Count Vladimir. In his despair he saw no one, comprehended nothing, and never once so much as mentioned his wife.

After the old Count's burial, it was impossible to hide his death from the Countess, for when the Count returned home, his expression told her everything. And so Mrs. Svetlova, having taken precautions, informed her of the loss. With what bitter tears the Countess mourned this virtuous man! In addition to his love, he was the last thread binding her husband to this place. And how right was her reckoning! The sorrowful Vladimir spent almost all his time at his father's grave. He often stayed at his estate for days at a time and when he returned offered no justification for his absence, thinking of course that there was no one there to notice and that he was the only one worthy of pity, having no one with whom to share his grief. Almost two months passed in this way.

One day he returned in a state of great confusion and announced that he had received orders to return to his regiment, as his leave had ended. "The Countess's ill health," he said, "doesn't permit me to take her with me. But as soon as I can get away, I'll come for her." Those final words he added when he noticed the deadly pallor on his wife's face.

"When will you leave, my friend?" asked Mrs. Svetlova, whose poor eyesight prevented her from seeing everything that was going on around her. "Tomorrow, dear grandmother. Everything's ready," answered the Count.

The unfortunate Countess leaned her head against the arm of the chair, made an effort to swallow her tears and, gathering the last of her strength, got up, wanting to walk to the door, but she was stopped by the Count's outstretched arm. Ah! This was the first time he tenderly pressed her to his chest and asked her not to cry. "Even if you were healthy, would you leave your grandmother in such a state?" he asked affectionately and added that he would come soon to visit them ... And that kiss, that voice had such power over his wife's heart that her tears disappeared. The Count hadn't imagined he held such power, although at that moment he was amazed at the loveliness of the Countess's gaze, which, it seemed, expressed the full depth of her emotions. His conscience reproached him for exchanging the affection of an innocent heart for the tempestuous passion of an infamous coquette. Believing, however, that he'd always be able to control himself, he promised himself to return soon for his wife.

A bad calculation, Your Excellency! You must have forgotten your youth and that luxurious, charming life that awaited you in Petersburg. You grew up with it, you're accustomed to it, so how could you imagine that this bond, forged over time, could be broken at a moment's wish?

So the Count left and, as we saw from the Countess's letters, didn't return for her or to her for two years. At first he wrote fairly often to Mrs. Svetlova, and his letters, filled with sincerity, brought joy to the old woman. To his wife, however, he addressed only postscripts and, not wishing to deceive her, preferred only cold instructions instead of a husband's tenderness.

It's impossible to describe what the abandoned sufferer experienced and what she felt when she learned that she was to be a mother! Thinking she could never survive this experience, she decided not to inform the Count so that he would have less reason to reproach himself when she died.

She hid her condition even from Mrs. Svetlova, who would probably have rushed to inform the Count and would have scolded him before the Countess even more than previously for not rushing to his wife's side.

One might have thought that this condition would exhaust the Countess's last bit of strength, but, to the contrary, she became stronger, her paroxysms grew less frequent and less severe. Nevertheless, she had grief enough and battled with it constantly.

During the time of her confinement, her grandmother suddenly and unexpectedly fell desperately ill. Countless tears, care beyond her strength, and several sleepless nights spent by her grandmother's bed exhausted the Countess completely and made the doctor, who knew of her pregnancy, fear for her life.

How could this unfortunate woman bear without torment the thought that she would be separated forever from the one who lived in this world for her alone? Mrs. Svetlova saw very well that she had failed to secure happiness for her granddaughter, and blaming only herself, she blessed Count Vladimir, who was still dear to her and for whom she had prepared an unenviable fate, also against his will.

Placing her ice-cold hands on Liubinka's head, she asked with her final words that she carry without complaint the cross the Lord had given her... and in that position she died.

When the Countess recovered after a severe fainting spell, she asked for some paper and ink and that very moment wrote the Count the note he recalled in his letter to Lvov; and when she'd sent it, the doctor noticed that a severe fever had seized her. In her illness, she gave birth to a son who lived only a day.

Amid the torments of her illness, what emotion seized the heart of the poor mother when the weak cry of her son reached her ear—for her child was exhausted from her suffering.

The careless doctor, believing the Countess to be unconscious, ordered the child to be taken away while he was still alive. But when they tried to take him, no human force could extricate him from his mother's arms! And so, fearing that such excitement would be even more harmful to her, they left her with the child.

Oh, how happy she was at that moment! It is impossible to describe the tenderness with which she pressed to her heart the son who perfectly resembled the husband so dear to her! It seemed she'd completely recovered her senses when, looking at his dear little face, she said: "If you're destined to live a day or an hour, then sleep, my sweet angel! Sleep near this heart, to which you alone have been able to return a long-forgotten joy."

She demanded that her son be baptized immediately and named Vladimir. Then, turning toward him, she continually called him by that name, which was so dear to her heart. Such emotion made everyone present fear for her, and rightly so. Having gone several nights without sleep, she barely closed her eyes when she would open them again and look at her son, afraid he'd be taken away. Toward morning her fever increased to such an extent that the doctor was in difficult straits. Finally, her delirium was so severe that they were able to remove the child without protest. She seemed to have entirely forgotten about him.

For several days the Countess's life was in danger. No one expected her to live, and so the joy of everyone who knew her was all the greater when she not only recovered but, except for her weakness and pallor, was as beautiful as before.

The Countess had a favorite place in her garden. It was her favorite because the Count found her there once, pale and exhausted. With tender care, he had led her back to the house, almost carrying her. Having no hope of surviving her child's birth, she'd asked to be buried in that cherished spot together with her son.

And so what joy she felt when, following her recovery, she found the grave of her son there! With heartfelt tears she thanked those who'd been so attentive to her grief and done everything possible to make that place more beautiful.

While mourning the one Vladimir, she thought constantly of the other and of how she seemed to love him even more. Often as she leaned her head against her son's gravestone, she wanted to write to the Count. She wanted to ask him to shed at least one tear on the grave of their child.

Such ideas, which succeeded one after another in her mind, prevented her complete recovery. And so the doctor, fearing that her illness would return, advised her to go to the Caucasus, although the Countess had no wish to leave Uspenskoye, which was now even dearer to her.

At the waters, the Countess's health gradually improved, and when she had completed the entire course of treatment prescribed to her, she returned home, where to her good friends she seemed as if reborn. She had grown taller, filled out, and blossomed to such an extent that she was more beautiful then she'd been before her illness.

Meanwhile, Count Vladimir Nikolaevich was not entirely at peace. His old estate manager, whom he respected, wrote to him very often of his virtuous spouse, and although he concealed from him all that had happened—at her request—he never forgot to remind him of her in every letter.

At first this seemed to the Count to be a reproach, and he felt indignant at the kind old man. He then began to pay no attention to it or, rather, the news that she was comforted by helping the unfortunate reconciled him with himself. From it he concluded that she was able to bear his absence with indifference.

The death of his beloved Mrs. Svetlova shook him. The thought that she had died without assurance of his gratitude was difficult to bear. The Countess's letter expressed nothing but violent grief. He immediately decided to go to his wife and never to leave her again, even if she should drive him away with the coldness he presumed to find in her.

But, unfortunately, together with the Countess's letter, he received the yearly profits from his estate manager. Was it possible Princess Zelskaya would allow him to take them back to Uspenskoye with him? At first an illness feigned by the Princess kept the Count in Petersburg, then her recovery, then her birthday—and the Countess was forgotten, although not entirely; it seemed, however, that she was able to live alone.

Of course, with his intelligence, which increased with the years, Vladimir couldn't remain so blind and slowly but surely came to recognize Princess Zelskaya's perfidy. However, all-powerful habit bound him in chains, which only one incident was able to weaken enough to allow him to break free.

At last that incident occurred, and it was entirely out of the blue. The mercenary Princess, noticing perhaps that the Count's affection for her had begun to wane or simply having her eye on a rich man she had yet to rob, committed that base act that the Count described in his letter to his friend Lvov.

> *Now that I've explained to my patient readers everything they might have found obscure in the letters I presented at the beginning of this book, I believe they will read—more out of condescension toward Count and Countess Gorsky than toward me— the second volume, which, so as not to interrupt the correspondence of our now familiar characters, I also begin with letters.*

END OF BOOK I

BOOK II
LETTER VII

From Count Gorsky to Countess Gorskaya
Saint Petersburg
April 2, 183 …

I received from my estate manager the money you were pleased to lend me. I was very touched by this sign of your condescension, all the more so as I had no right to expect it. I will make use of it in an irreproachable manner and would regard it as a true pleasure to be of some use to you.

I'm guilty before you, Countess, for not having replied to the message in which you informed me of the death of our dear grandmother. What words of comfort could I give you when I myself was inconsolable? Wasn't she for me, as well, a mother who tenderly loved her son? The memory of this virtuous woman will remain sacred to me forever.

From Ivan Ivanovich's letter I learned that you'd returned from the Caucasus and, as he told me, you're perfectly healthy. This is another reason to remember our grandmother: how happy she would be at your recovery! I don't dare attempt to persuade you that I'm delighted with all my heart.

If the bond of friendship that has joined us since childhood seems stronger to you than the bond that was imposed on us under compulsion, then I hope that in remembrance of the former, you'll tell me more about yourself than others do. I can assure you, Countess, that your message brings particular pleasure to the one who has the honor of being

Your obedient servant,
Count Gorsky

P.S. You'll surely forgive me for having decided to send along a package containing a hat, which is so necessary for you on your walks, as well as fine woolens and patterns for clothes. I believe such things cannot be found in your town.

LETTER VIII

From Countess Gorskaya to Sofia Liubskaya
April 18, 183 —,
Village of Uspenskoye

Do you know, my dear Sonechka, whose letter is lying here before my eyes? No! You certainly couldn't know it without seeing me at this moment. From the joy expressed on my face you could probably guess it's from the Count to me. Yes, to me, my friend! I don't want to think that it contains only gratitude for the money I sent him. I know him, and he would never use immodesty where it might seem false; he wouldn't recall our dear grandmother if he didn't want his letter to be pleasing to me, and he wouldn't speak to me of our childhood friendship if he'd banished it forever from his most excellent heart. Allow me to believe, dear Sonechka, that I'm not mistaken.

I don't know how to describe to you the happiness I felt when I received this letter! I was still in bed when they told me that Ivan Ivanovich had come and brought a letter. "Who is it from?" I thought, and with my heart pounding I quickly dressed and left my room. From the smile on the kind old man's face, I guessed the reason for his joy. "Have you guessed who it's from?" he asked, cheerfully, and held the letter up. I grabbed it, ecstatic, and all my sorrows were forgotten.

As I read the letter, Ivan Ivanovich brought a large box into the room and with childlike delight removed the Count's gifts, not knowing that for me the most valuable thing sent by the Count was in his letter. Ah! Why hadn't he added just one more word—the word *love*, which I could find nowhere! All the same, I'm happy, much happier than I was before. Didn't he ask me to write to him? Oh! What an unexpected pleasure it is for me to speak to him of myself.

I think I wrote to you that he's left Princess Zelskaya. Sometime I'll tell you of the base thing she did to the Count. Ah! Perhaps he misses her! And he's alone now and unhappy! My God! Why wasn't it left to me to comfort him! He doesn't know and probably will never know that there's a love in this world that's as pure and constant as that with which our grandmother nourished us.

Evidently, yesterday was meant to be a day of rejoicing, for in the evening I was suddenly brought three letters from you. Where were they lying and who was so cruel to hold them so long? But you are healthy and happy—what more could I want?

I was always angry with your Princess for having taken my friends away from me, and at a time when my grieving heart needed them so. And now that she's providing for your happiness with such care, I'm ready at every moment to reproach myself before her.

How clever you are, Sonechka, to have rejected that rich Englishman and married a Russian. He isn't poor, my friend, if he knew how to find your love. Your honorable parents needn't worry over your financial situation when they have another daughter who doesn't know what to do with her wealth. Not another word about it.

I've copied out for you the Count's letter and am sending it along. Read it, my dear friend! Then you'll know true happiness! You can find his essential traits in every word. Tell me, is there anything over which one can rejoice as wildly as I do now?

Sasha Sokolova is staying with me now. Her sincere affection for me gives me great pleasure; but her carefree youth, her joy, as clear as the sky, mustn't be darkened by my unrealized hopes and my all-too-well-known troubles. Why acquaint her with them when she'll probably never know them herself? With whom can I share all that fills my heart?

Return to Russia as soon as possible, my dear friend! Ah! You alone are able to understand me well and so I like to talk about him only with you. You seem to know him perfectly from my infinite love for him.

Farewell, Sonechka! I'm impatiently awaiting the letter in which you'll tell me you're married and coming back to Russia. I'll sit down and write to the Count, and you can judge how scrupulously I have to weigh every word so as not to say too little or too much—far too much.

LETTER IX

From Countess Gorskaya to Count Gorsky
April 16, 183 …
Village of Uspenskoye

To my misfortune, I have no right to your gratitude, although I can assure you it brought me a joy I hadn't felt in a long while. Knowing your sense of fairness, I never suspected you'd forbid me to consider income that was of utterly no use to me as shared between us, just as we shared the love of our parents. I'm just your manager, Count, and a manager, as you can see, more miserly than our good Ivan Ivanovich.

Your recollection of my dear grandmother brought back to me my entire past, which I'd feared to waken in my heart. But your goodness pointed out to me the one thing that always served as a comfort to me: her tenderness toward me and her love for you.

You wished to know of my health. It's perfect now. Since my return home, I've been careful to attend to it, knowing that without this priceless gift from heaven, one cannot find happiness.

When I was in the Caucasus, I had the opportunity to order a Circassian outfit for you, as well as full attire for your horse. They've all been sent to me now and I'd be very pleased if I could oblige you with them. The hat you sent me is too nice for this wild settlement, but I always wear it so as to have an occasion to thank you more often.

I have two requests of you, Count! And I beg you to be condescending toward them. I dare to think you'll recall how obligated I am to the Liubskoy family. My friend, Sofia, is getting married to a poor man. May I supplement their income? Having no doubt as to your magnanimity, I can easily guess your answer. But it would be nice to receive your approval.

I think my second request will not be so easy to satisfy. If possible, send me a portrait of your worthy father—the one that bears a striking resemblance to you. My imagination will embellish that which is a consequence of the declining years of the one and that which fails to provide for the perfect handsomeness of the other.

I have the honor to be
Your humble servant,
Countess Gorskaya

LETTER X

From Count Gorsky to Alexander Lvov
April 30, 183 …
Saint Petersburg

Something terribly strange is happening to me, Alexander! And there's so much I have to tell you immediately.

Before my departure for Kh., I discovered that my duties required the speediest and most accurate execution, and so I had no time to examine the local beauties. I tried to carry out my orders as diligently as possible, and when I returned, I was truly heartened by the gratitude of my superiors.

I traveled over the holiday and arrived in the capital toward the end of all the festivities. Either from fatigue or simply from laziness, I didn't go anywhere for several days, and so my comrades probably didn't know of my return.

One evening *Fenella* was being performed and I decided to go secretly to the theater; so I took a box and sat alone.[11] With a smile, I realized that it was the same box where Princess Eugenia Petrovna had once showered me with gentle caresses, which at the time I took at face value. I also realized, however, that I had had to pay back this substantial loan the very next day with the money in my money box, which was coveted by the keen eye of my beloved.

Thought after thought was linked together in my mind and the events of my life seemed to change like scenery before my eyes. At the same time, when I was about to rebuke myself for having left the countryside so thoughtlessly, I heard these words from behind me: "Oh! Countess Gorskaya is incomparably finer."

---

11. *Fenella* probably refers to the opera *La muette de Portici* (The Mute Girl of Portici), originally entitled *Masaniella, ou La muette de Portici*. Written by the French composer Daniel Auber and premiered in Paris in 1828, the opera is notable not only for being the earliest French grand opera but also for the fact that the female lead is deaf. In the opera, Fenella publicly denounces the Spanish viceroy to Naples as her seducer and kidnapper, which inspires her brother to lead a revolt against Spanish rule. At the end of the opera, Mount Vesuvius erupts and a forlorn Fenella throws herself into the lava.

I involuntarily started, and from the voice I realized it was Maisky speaking. He'd spent the previous summer in the Caucasus and consequently could have met my wife.

"Evidently, she must be pretty," someone answered him, "if the Count, that lover of beauty, ignores her." "I don't know what caused the Count to do so," Maisky said, "but I can assure you I've never seen a woman who combines every perfection as the Countess does."

"Well then, in the presence of such beauty, I imagine the bitter waters of the Caucasus were like nectar to you." "Yes! If only I'd dared to make love to her." "And who forbade you? Who were you afraid of—surely not her husband? By the way, Maisky, what did she say about her husband?"

Believe me, Alexander, when I tell you that I listened very closely to his answer!

"She never said a word about her husband in my presence, but it seems she is utterly indifferent to the way he's treated her, for she doesn't sigh, cry, or complain to everyone she meets, as usually happens with wives who harbor a complaint against a husband who's abandoned them."

"Why did you let the chance slip through your fingers? Novice! Thank God Prince Belsky's on leave. He's a neighbor of the Gorskys and will probably come to your aid, you artless thing."

I almost left, but I wanted to know the end of the conversation. And they continued, not thinking that a pair of attentive ears was listening to them.

"Actually, she ought to repay the Count in kind," said Maisky's friend. "The poor woman has been miserable for so long! Please, Maisky, tell me, without bias, who's finer: the Countess or Princess Zelskaya?"

"What a comparison! As if it were only the Countess's face that was beautiful? No! Everything in her is charming: her mind, her meekness, her tact, and even that endless melancholy, which hides her lovely eyes the way a cloud hides the sun."

"Melancholy? Why should she be melancholy when she's so lovely? Why shouldn't she come here to Petersburg, if only to see her husband or to tear him away from Princess Zelskaya? It's a good thing indeed that Prince Belsky is there. I guarantee he'll drive away her melancholy."

"Don't bet on it," said Maisky. "Such a frivolous man as Prince Belsky could never win Countess Gorskaya's heart. It's strange indeed that she and her husband were unable to find happiness together. I must admit, I don't know another couple like them."

Here, either the curtain fell or I left. At any rate, I heard nothing more. It's funny, Alexander. Very funny. But I must confess to you I didn't sleep at all that night.

Is it possible that I, I who always wanted to be an honest man, have become so base that I can listen calmly while people make scurrilous conclusions about a woman who's been true to me in all her innocence? And now, won't I be primarily responsible for corrupting her, having given cause to the likes of Prince Belsky?

And isn't the melancholy they spoke of evidence of her love for me? But no! It's a fancy, a whim of my heart. What am I to do with this woman's love? Of course, I could order her to come here, and if she's blossomed as people say she has, then isn't it within my power to admire her without asking her permission? She's my ... Ah! Is this what my heart demands? Is this the love my heart thirsts for?

Farewell, dear Alexander! Evidently Prince Belsky has succeeded, as I still haven't received an answer to my letter ... However, I won't allow myself to play the fool, and so probably won't write another letter. Farewell.

LETTER XI

From Count Gorsky to Alexander Lvov
May 5, 183 ...
Saint Petersburg

I was on duty yesterday and so slept longer than usual; when I woke up, I was informed that a package had arrived in my name. "Who'd remember lonely old me?" I thought, and immediately left for the post office.

I was handed a warped book and then a large box and a letter. I recognized the Countess's hand, and after barely managing to sign my name, I ripped open the seal and read the letter almost the entire way home.

Yes, my friend! I was truly unable to stop reading it. There wasn't even a shadow of those reproaches that I deserve from her. There were no complaints with which I might reproach her. Instead, there was, visible in every word, if not love then sincere and attentive friendship.

The Countess is asking me to send her a portrait of my father, but the one that looks like me. Why does she need that? Why doesn't she tell me directly that she wants to have my portrait? Oh, how she would have pleased me with that! Nonetheless, I'll order the finest artist to paint me in that wonderful Circassian uniform she sent me, and I'll send her that.

Amazing! How could she have gotten my measurements just right? Does she truly remember me so well? The frock was made with expensive blue lapels with bunches of flowers, and the fittings are of excellent work. I think the Countess must have sacrificed the expensive bracelet that adorned her hand, which shook so in mine when we were wed.

Oh! What if she loved me even then, Alexander? Then what a monster I must have seemed in her eyes? And how will I repay the virtuous Mrs. Svetlova for her tender affection toward me?

The Countess also sent me a saddle and bridle for my horse—with restrained but elegant decoration. Such designs and embroidery on the saddle cloth—it's truly a beautiful sight! She's made me into a Persian shah and such a fine fellow that I'd like very much to appear before her in that outfit, seated upon my dashing stallion.

I'll go to her this winter without fail, and meanwhile I'll find out whether or not she wants to see me. Or maybe I'll stay put in my beloved capital. Perhaps you'll think I've grown passionate toward my wife. That would be an improbable love affair!

You mustn't answer this letter in your usual lachrymose style, but with all the attention of a friend. Perhaps I'm being a fool again; if so, don't laugh—warn me instead.

LETTER XII

From Mrs. Milovidova to a female friend
April, 183 ...

I'm still longing for Moscow, dear Paulina! And I can't wait for winter to come so I can fly to your embrace. Although Paul says it will be an enormous expense, what concern is it of his—it's my money. Besides, I don't prevent him from living without interruption in our deserted little town.

Truly, sweetie, I could die of boredom if it weren't for Prince Belsky, whose presence livens up these parts! He's a wonderful, dear young man! He tells me constantly that I'm awful for having grown so beautiful in Moscow!

He seems to have given up on Countess Gorskaya. They almost quarreled over Sashenka Sokolova because she moved back to her mother's—and closer to Prince Belsky.

Ah! How I wish to know all that, my friend! I've already asked the Prince several times why he hasn't been to the Countess's in some time. And I get from him such excuses that it's funny to listen to him ... and I know what it means.

Imagine, Paulina! Count Gorsky, after two years, is finally writing to his spouse. They say he's squandered his entire estate, and so, it seems, he has his eye on his wife's. He recently sent her a hat. A hat, my angel! Such a pretty one, the likes of which I've never seen!

And this is what it means not to know what to wear when. I was recently at the Countess's. They told me she was in the garden, and several minutes later I saw her walking down the path. She was wearing a peignoir bordered with lace, and that charming thing—her straw hat!

How could she wear such a treasure on a walk in the garden? I was truly surprised and couldn't resist telling her that immediately. She laughed and answered, "This is how I'll bring the Count to ruin. Next year he'll have to send me a new one." "And have you really reconciled with him?" I asked. "We never quarreled," she said very curtly.

She's unbearable! Doesn't everyone know how she and the Count live? I don't think he's so stupid as to abandon Petersburg to move back to Uspenskoye.

You asked me, Paulina, whether my constant arguing with Paul has stopped. No, my angel! It cannot be any other way. Is it possible to bear the fact that he's suddenly transformed himself from a passionate lover to a grumbling husband? And over what? The fact that I spend a lot of money on clothes and want to look attractive not just for him? I never foresaw this, you know, and so never promised to sit at home, much less, alone.

Isn't it always the way, Paulina, that these unbearable husbands pester us first with their love and then with boring sermons?

If you'd like to do me a favor, my friend, go around to all the stores and find me the most expensive straw hat and send it by the first mail. I can't stand the fact that I don't have one like Countess Gorskaya's. Farewell, my dear! I am forever your

Bibi

LETTER XIII

From Countess Gorskaya to Miss Liubskaya
May 4, 183 …
Village of Uspenskoye

Now I'm even gloomier, dear Sofia! I've heard nothing of the Count for so long! And what can I expect, my friend? What's there to hope for? Ah! Everything will remain as it was before! A ray of hope shone down for but a moment, and now it's dark again, gloomy again all around me!

And on top to all that, I must tell you, dear friend, of something unpleasant that happened to me recently.

I wrote to you that our neighbor, Prince Belsky, is on leave and living with his mother. He would often visit me and, as he was affectionate toward Miss Sokolova, I thought his visits were for her sake, especially when I noticed that Sashenka was not indifferent to him.

Could I have imagined, my friend, that the Prince, knowing of my attachment to the Count, could dare hope I'd return his love? Ah, at that moment, Sofia, I felt for the first time that I'd truly been abandoned by my husband!

A few days ago, the Prince came over at noon and found that Sashenka and I were about to go for a walk. He gave his horse to a servant and came with us. Right away I noticed that Sashenka was pouting over something he'd done, so I walked ahead.

Wishing to reconcile them as soon as possible, I asked the Prince how he could be so indifferent to coldness from the one he loved. "The one I love?" he said quickly, then stared at me. "Yes, you've guessed it, Countess! I cannot bear coldness from the one I love so passionately!"

Although his words seemed strange to me, I swear to you, Sonenka, I didn't understand them at all and said to the Prince: "So why don't you speak of it to her?" "Would she permit me to do that?" he asked with a voice full of emotion. "The calm expression on that sweet face upon which I now gaze proves to me she doesn't share my emotions in the least!"

Oh! Judge for yourself, my friend, what I felt then! And with all the indignation of insulted virtue, I asked him: "About whom are you speaking, kind sir?"

My tone embarrassed him. Wishing to achieve his purpose once and for all or taking my anger for coquetry, he replied: "About whom if not about you, most charming Countess! Who is more worthy of adoration than you?"

"Prince!" I exclaimed, barely able to control myself, "I will not hear another such word from you! If your offensive thoughts were based on the fact that the Count is not here with me, and that as a defenseless, abandoned wife I'd easily forget my duty, then you're mistaken. I've enough strength to defend myself from your impudence … I repeat, if I have the unpleasantness of hearing such words from you again, then from that moment on we'll be strangers. I took you to be the son of a noble woman, a man seeking the love of my friend in order to provide her with happiness. Could I have thought, Prince, that in order to conceal your objectives, you wished to deceive an innocent heart that is attached to you with all its enthusiasm!"

The Prince was utterly destroyed. He stood there as if made of stone and didn't so much as dare to justify himself before me. And as soon as he saw Miss Sokolova approach us, he asked me to forgive him and to give him time to expunge his impertinent deed from my thoughts.

"For that sweet girl, Prince," I said, "for her alone … so as not to darken that unclouded peace that illuminates her face … I forgive you. But I demand that you act with me as prudently as possible. I love my husband, and no one can destroy or so much as shake that passionate, eternal love!" At that moment Sashenka caught up to us, and we returned home in silence.

The Prince left soon afterward, and we haven't seen each other since. Perhaps you don't approve of such proud severity, my friend, Sonechka! But I shall never repent of it. Why should we leave so much as a spark of hope in a man's heart when we cannot accept his love?

How many women have perished because they were too weak to put a stop to a lover's impertinence! In order to save him and yourself, you must destroy all his hopes immediately.

But don't be worried about the Prince, my friend! His feelings cannot run very deep. He likes to spend his life in jest, and even his love is nothing but the rambunctiousness of a child. If you could see the various and amiable tricks he plays on Sashenka Sokolova, you'd probably think as I do—that they're made for one another. And these feelings that he thinks he has for me were created in error by his heart.

All the same, my friend, I was unable to collect myself for several days after this unpleasant incident. Why don't I have a brother to defend me? Ah! Why has the one who knows how to guide me and who should do so more than anyone else leave me on my own?! It's sad, dear Sonechka, very sad, and so I shall lay down my pen.

LETTER XIV

From Prince Belsky to a friend
May 5, 183 …
Village of Velikoye

Dear Seryozhenka, you're probably impatiently awaiting my letter, thinking that Countess Gorskaya and I are living like two turtle doves. You're mistaken, my friend! At the first mention of my love for her, she forbade me to visit her home and gave me a sermon that left me deaf and dumb for several days.

She said she'd received me, assuming I was in love with her friend, Miss Sokolova. In addition, like the refrain to a song, she kept repeating that she loved her husband passionately.

Is she really a child who failed to notice where my heart was flying? Regardless, I must admit that she's worthy not only of respect but of amazement. Be careful not to say anything to your comrades! Rumors will reach Count Gorsky, and God knows how he'll pout his lips at such a triumph over me.

He truly needs to be taught a good lesson! Isn't it madness to abandon such an angel? And for whom? For an out-and-out coquette!

But don't be sad for me, Seryozhenka! The magic words uttered by the charming voice of the Countess have penetrated my heart and … What a miracle! I realized that dear little Sashenka is in fact a most interesting creature, worth taking into my ailing heart as a physician. Moreover, as others have said and as I myself have noticed for quite some time, she loves me. And so, I shall seek comfort in her!

There's yet another pretty lady here, Mrs. Milovidova. She, too, is an Arcadian shepherdess, passionately in love with her ridiculous husband, who, however, is already so bored by her feigned tenderness that he'd gladly be rid of her for a glass of champagne—as pink and bubbly as his beloved spouse.

Yes! And although sweet Bibi swears her eternal fidelity to the drunken Paul every minute and every hour, she seems less unassailable than Countess Gorskaya. But my word! You want to cleanse your palate with something refined. You don't want to gaze upon those beauties who with every glance are begging, "Praise me!" No! It's time to fall in love, but until then I'll take a few more steps along my old path. I truly know few women like Countess Gorskaya. That's how women should always be. Then who would dare complain that we men are fickle, inconstant, impertinent, arrogant, and that we have grossly corrupted the sacred sentiments of love?

Can you believe it, Seryozhenka! At that very moment when, in a voice that was threatening and uncharacteristic of her, she banished me, she was so magnificently beautiful that I almost fell at her feet. How fortunate is the Count! Indeed, I'm thinking of challenging him to a duel to the death.

Miss Sokolova's mother, who had gone to visit relatives, has now returned, and so her daughter has left her beloved Countess and is now living at her own home, which is so close to ours that I visit them several times a day.

I believe the sensible Countess has concealed my confession from Sashenka because yesterday when we met she smiled at me very affably and said that the Countess had banished her so that she wouldn't forget how to amuse herself at her young age.

In addition, my friend, I had to endure a considerable examination by her mother. I don't know why, but she saw better what was going on in my own heart than I did myself. And when I was forced to confess my adventure with the Countess, she praised her and then, after grilling me at length, told me she'd also noticed Miss Sokolova's attachment to me, which I'd inspired with my behavior, and that an honorable person shouldn't allow himself to play with an innocent heart. But why shouldn't I play a bit? You know, I also took a turn at being the plaything of women.

Did I really come here only to become a hermit? Did I really bring with me a supply of cunning and flattering phrases only to forget them entirely at a single glance from a pair of bright eyes? What boredom indeed—I leave soon for Sashenka's to hear her sing "I love you, I love you!" Farewell!

LETTER XV

From Mrs. Sokolova to her sister
May 183—
Village of Velikoye

After returning from my visit, my dear Aniuta, I failed to thank you for the lovely time I spent in your home. May God bless you, my gentle

Aniutochka, for the exemplary submissiveness with which you bear your husband's whims, so characteristic of his advanced years. For this you've been rewarded with the sincere attachment and love of your wonderful children, for whom as a mother you're both a mentor and a governess. And this is easy for you, my friend, because in your mind you suppose this to be every woman's duty.

I must also learn from you, my friend, how you manage with your limited means to be satisfied with everything and always in good spirits. You always greet those who visit your home with a pleasant hospitality. I'm very glad that my Sashenka resembles you so. I hope that in time her behavior will resemble yours as well.

Now let's talk about my Sashenka, dear sister! When I returned home, the Countess advised me in an amiable conversation to take my daughter from her and, embracing me, said, "You yourself know that it's necessary for Sashenka. Why during the best time of her life should she be locked up in my gloomy solitude? I avoid visits, and I confess they're burdensome to me, while to her," she added, smiling, "they might bring joy and even happiness. Of course, her friendship and her sweet, exuberant personality diverted me greatly, but could I accept happiness for myself if it were to cause someone else so much as a single sigh? In any case, you know I have my own amusements."

So it is, my friend! After she received a letter from the Count, she seemed as if reborn. Once again she began to occupy herself with everything she'd once studied: playing instruments, singing, and drawing.

And so when I left her in her present state, there was no reason to worry that she'd be melancholy all by herself. In this deed one sees the goodness of her heart: She wanted to bring Sashenka closer to Prince Belsky, who now visits us every day, and he grows more attentive to my daughter with each passing hour. Yes, Sashenka loves him very much.

It seems I've told you that our amiable neighbor, Mrs. Milovidova, has become an even more frequent guest since her return from Moscow. It's funny to see how she tries to attract Prince Belsky, and in order to see him more often, she visits us almost every day. I have no fear for Sashenka, as I'm so strongly convinced that people's fate is in God's hands, and His will is stronger and more exact than all our designs.

Yesterday, however, against her will, she forced the Prince to reveal his feelings in front of Sashenka. Mrs. Milovidova uses every device to present the Countess in a bad light, and if she isn't stopped at her first words, she's always ready to badmouth her.

Yesterday she suddenly asked the Prince, "Haven't you noticed that Sashenka has borrowed many of her manners from Countess Gorskaya?" "It seems to me," the Prince replied, "that innocence and goodness always share the same manners. This is why Miss Sokolova resembles the Countess!" Mrs. Milovidova blushed and said with a smile: "Well, Alexandra Vasilevna, aren't you going to thank the Prince for the compliment?"

"I never give compliments to Alexandra Vasilevna," said the Prince, "and I'm sure she knows how sincere my words and my feelings for her are." When he noticed that Sashenka had blushed and was leaning against her embroidery frame, he moved closer to her and talked to her *sotto voce* for quite some time.

You had to see Mrs. Milovidova at that moment to understand her vexation. She moved from chair to chair, leapt up and walked about the room, all the time looking at Sashenka and the Prince. Finally, to my great satisfaction, she left. Although the Prince and my daughter probably didn't notice her, I was completely constrained by her presence.

I also forgot to tell you, my Aniutushka, Princess Belskaya is very affectionate toward my Sashenka, and now that she's once again taken ill, we often visit her. Kiss all your dear children for me, and don't forget your promise to bring them all here on a visit.

LETTER XVI

From Count Gorsky to Countess Gorskaya
May 20, 183 …
Saint Petersburg

I hurried to fulfill your wish by sending you my father's portrait, ordering that he be painted as he looked when he was your father too. And because the changes in him make my resemblance to him less apparent, I took the liberty of also including a portrait of myself, so as not to tax your imagination, in the outfit with which you were so kind to adorn me. I hope that, for the sake of my father, you'll accept the son.

You asked me, Countess, about your desire to improve Miss Liubskoy's lot. What dare I say? Have I truly won the right to be your advisor? My answer is a request that out of kindness you allow me to act on an equal basis with you to provide for your friend. Such condescension will serve as proof that you do not nurse toward me the hatred that I so deserve.

What a pitiful creature is man! Unable to stop himself in ardent passion, he races to destroy his well-being, and when he comes to his senses, it's all too late for him! Who would want to help him, to set him up again? Isn't that true, Countess? Won't you give me an answer to this question?

My good Ivan Ivanovich, whom I've robbed several times, has always been reluctant to share his possessions with me. While you, Countess, describing yourself as miserly, have thoroughly enriched me. Why have you made me into such a splendid Circassian? Moreover, why have you given me to believe that you remembered me while in the Caucasus? That's another question, Countess!

You see, I've already become as wild and impertinent as a Circassian. I'm starting to hope that I'll receive an answer from you. I'll wait for it like an impatient Asian and, as your devoted friend, I'll know how to value every one of your words.

LETTER XVII

From Countess Gorskaya to Sofia Liubskaya
June 21, 183 ...
Village of Uspenskoye

Sonechka, dear Sonechka! What words can describe my happiness to you? You'll have to figure it out all on your own, as my letter will probably make no sense.

Yesterday for some reason I was very sad. Unable to find joy in anything, I went into the garden to my son's grave. My heart always finds peace there. It is as if that angel is interceding for his mother at the throne of the Almighty. Ah! He surely brought me joy again, for no sooner had I wiped away my tears than I saw Ivan Ivanovich standing beside me. "Enough crying, Countess!" he said gaily. "Look at how many presents there are for you!"

With trembling hands I took from him a letter and a small, flat box. Supposing I would find there a portrait of the Count's father who so resembled my husband, I impatiently tore the wrapping from the package and most likely wouldn't have managed if Ivan Ivanovich—foreseeing, of course, what would happen—hadn't brought a pair of scissors with him.

But I was so impatient that I got in his way and scolded him for being slow. At last the box was opened and I saw two portraits. With a pounding heart I pulled out the one and.... And even now I tremble when I recall that inexpressible moment! Imagine, Sonechka! I pulled out a portrait of my Vladimir! Can you imagine the emotion with which I looked at that charming face, transferred onto paper with such exactness and with such perfect skill!

I cried out and, holding onto this priceless object, fell on my knees beside the grave of our child. I don't know, my friend, whether I cried or said something ... They're trying to persuade me I was in a faint, but I don't think so. I was so happy, however, I didn't want to awake from that sleep.

And there was a letter from him. What a letter, Sonechka! Where did he learn the heavenly language in which it was written? Could it be that he drew it from his cold heart in order to delude me with the bliss that now envelopes my entire being? No, my friend! Then every word, every feature of that letter wouldn't have been so intelligible and insightful, as if I were hearing them from his own sweet lips.

I warned you that you'd find no sense in my letter and that you'd have to explain to yourself all that I left unsaid. And so to make that easier for you, I'm sending you a copy of the Count's letter.

When I came to my senses, I saw tears and friendly sympathy on everyone's faces. The Sokolovs were there and Prince Belsky. They happened to come by at just that moment and truly shared my joy ... No! That's not the appropriate expression, my friend! With whom would I wish to share—and who could have understood—what was happening at that moment in my heart?

I was very pleased that everyone admired the Count. He was indeed indescribably handsome in that light blue *beshmet*[12] I'd sent him in which he'd had his portrait painted. Such attention to everything poured an inexhaustible heavenly delight into my soul, and in my mad joy, I even thought he loved me, that he was mine forever!

Wishing to enjoy my good fortune alone, I asked everyone to leave me for a while. And when everyone was gone, I took the liberty of pressing my lips to those of my handsome husband, and when I looked into those beautiful eyes, I thought I saw in them some pity for me.

Why did he ask me, dear Sonechka, to answer his questions? Can I conceal the truth from him? I'll tell him, I'll tell him everything, my friend! I'll express all my ardent love for him, and I'll call him to me.

Unfortunately, I noticed that the package sent by the Count had taken more than a month to get here. He promised to wait for my reply with such impatience that he's probably accusing me of being remiss, or perhaps he doesn't need my answer any more! Ah, why can't I give my letter wings so that the Count could read it sooner!

I must confess to you, Sonechka, that I looked at his father's portrait last of all, but truly with love and gratitude: wasn't it he who destined his son for me?

I had to force myself to leave the garden and go to my guests. With what riches I reentered my home! And all my servants greeted me with congratulations and asked permission to look at the Count.

---

12. Coat, often quilted, worn by various peoples in the Caucasus and Central Asia.

In a word, I've never been so happy as I am now. I'm no longer an orphan in this wide world. Didn't he say that he'd value my letter as a friend? And so, if I should suffer again, I'll call on my friend.

I'm happy to let you know, Sonechka, that the Prince has completely made amends for his conduct through his love for Sashenka. I cannot look upon the good Elena Ivanovna without pleasure: she's so happy about their love.

I am so obliged to Ivan Ivanovich that in truth I can't express it. Not a single father would have displayed toward his daughter sympathy more sincere than that which he displayed toward me. His joy over my good fortune was so sincere that I couldn't help but take notice of it. Weeping, he kissed my hands and thanked God that he'd lived to see that moment.

The old man was ill at the time he received notice of the package. I didn't dare hope that the Count would wish to fulfill my request so quickly, and I couldn't have imagined that my treasure was lying in the post office.

Why are you silent, my dear friend? One mustn't forget a friendship, all the more so in happiness and joy. Learn that from me. To punish you for your silence, I'm addressing my letter to Miss Liubskaya—truly, I don't know whether you're married?

Imagine, I've spent almost the entire day writing to you! My writing desk flaunts something I very rarely take my eyes from. And he thought I'd accept the son for the sake of the father! Isn't it the father I accept for the sake of the son? Read this and rejoice with your friend

Countess Liubov Gorskaya

P.S. Yesterday I didn't have time to seal this letter, and I'm very glad because now I can inform you of a pleasant piece of news. Elena Ivanovna has just left. My dear Sashenka is betrothed to Prince Belsky. This is how it happened:

From my house they went directly to the Princess, who's ill again. Hearing of my happiness, the kind old woman wept and, embracing her son, asked him to give her a daughter-in-law like me so that she might rejoice in his good fortune before she dies.

"If you want that, my dear Mama," said the Prince, "then ask Alexandra Vasilevna to provide me with such good fortune." The Princess embraced Sashenka and asked her not to refuse her son and together to bring her happiness.

Tomorrow the bride-to-be will visit me, and we'll busy ourselves with her trousseau. The wedding is being rushed, as the Princess is very ill and is unlikely to live long. As I put the finishing touches on Sashenka's wedding dress, I begin to imagine it's you, my gentle Sonechka, dressed with the help of a friend, walking toward the altar.

LETTER XVIII

From Count Gorsky to Alexander Lvov
June 10, 183 ...
Saint Petersburg

I must tell you, my friend, about everything that's happened to me today, or else I'm afraid the fullness of my emotions will suffocate me.

Some time ago I sent a package to the Countess, and for quite a while now I've been waiting for the Countess's reply, and that's made me extremely anxious. Even though I believed I loved her without the slightest passion, I must confess that I constantly thought of her and recalled her features.

I even took out a portrait of the Countess, which I'd tucked away, and secretly looked at it and marveled: How could I have failed to notice how agreeable she was, especially her charming little mouth, which once—even in the heat of her illness—attracted my attention and my kiss?

Perhaps her portrait would have captivated my heart back then if, unfortunately, a recent letter from Princess Zelskaya hadn't been lying next to it, a letter filled with ardent love, or rather, if the sick Countess hadn't shuddered and blanched from my kiss as if it were unpleasant to her. Everything, everything was set up in such a way so as to make me guilty before this angel!

When I heard that Pronsky had fallen desperately ill, I went to visit him. All night long he was in a bad state, but toward morning he awoke, and we expected a happy turning point in his illness.

The doctor, whom I found reading a book in his office, told me this. Then he took leave of me courteously but coldly. Of course I wouldn't have noticed it if I hadn't recognized him as the doctor who treated Mrs. Svetlova's household and whom I'd summoned as my father lay dying.

Recalling that he must know my story well, I was embarrassed despite myself—something that always happens when I remember that reproachful time of my life.

So, I thought, this man considers me unworthy of his conversation. But all the same he'll answer me, and I'll find out something about my wife from him.

With that thought in mind, I sat opposite him on the sofa and said that it was very nice to see him. He bowed but didn't say a word. "Did you move your practice long ago?" I asked, determined to endure his rudeness if only to attain my goal. "More than a year ago," he said in the same tone.

"Is practicing in the capital really more restful at your age?" "I'm burdened with a large family, Your Excellency, and I used to lament the fact that, not having a large income, I had to settle in a provincial seat where the methods of educating children were reliable but limited. May the merciful Creator send at least a spark of joy to the sorrowful heart of the woman who corrected all my deficiencies and sent me here so as not to be separated from my children! And even here she looks after me like a member of the family."

I blushed, I blushed all over, and in a barely intelligible voice, I said, "You are, of course, referring to Countess Gorskaya? I'm very glad to hear only good things about her, and I'm not surprised at her charity—I believe it's her only emotion."

"Her only emotion! Your Excellency is very much mistaken. She's capable of many lofty emotions and is capable of ennobling every one of them. I treated her last illness and I can assure you that I know Countess Gorskaya very well."

"So was she ill for long after I left?" I posed this indelicate question, having noticed that he became talkative when vexed. And I succeeded in my intention—he answered me with emotion:

"She wasn't just ill, she suffered without you, Count! She suffered indescribably if you can call the disdain of a deeply loved individual, which she bore without a murmur, suffering. And she suffered when, on the day she buried her grandmother and together with her the last love for her on earth, she gave birth to a son who was no longer breathing."

"A son!" I exclaimed in a frenzied voice. Oblivious to what I was doing, I tried to stand, but my legs shook so that I had to sit back down. I didn't even know I was a father! She didn't even tell me about it! "Oh, where now is the love with which you gladdened my heart?"

"There was love in that, Your Excellency! You can't judge her because ... I don't dare say it ... You've never known the sacred love that gives one the strength to bear everything for one's beloved."

He wanted to continue but saw the deathly pallor on my face and rushed to help me. He was very sorry for having touched such a string in my heart. For a long while I could say nothing; I just pressed his hand. When tears had given some relief to my heart, I asked him in a supplicating voice to tell me every detail about this incomparable woman.

Despite my impatience, he examined me first, then looked at his watch, and sitting down next to me, he exposed my crime before me.

I was loved! And I was still loved when I joined my life with that innocent creature! Her trembling, her pallor—all that was proof of the passionate love she had for me, a love she was afraid to display, thinking that it would make me, now attached to the Princess, only increase my contempt for her.

If she knew how I pitied her during her bouts of illness! How often in my dissipation I imagined her tormented face. And the thought that the ties that bound us were equally burdensome to us both destroyed my happiness! But I'll make amends or die at her feet!

From Pronsky's I went directly to my Colonel and asked him to petition a leave for me of at least one month. He explained to me why this was impossible, and although my heart rejected his explanations, my good sense had to accept them. My kind superior, however, gave me his word that in a month I would be released without fail.

Ah, if you knew how many thoughts I now have and how comforting some of them are! The majority of them, however, are utterly contrary: If her heart understood me, why didn't she answer my letter in which every word was filled with passion? And the proximity of Prince Belsky? Unfortunately, I know from personal experience that it's possible, despite all the rules of honor, to submit to a worthless creature. The Prince, as far as I know, is a rather nice young man. But now everything alarms me, my friend!

They say she has become beautiful. That's all the same to me, Alexander! Let her look as she did when she entrusted her love to me or when she became the mother of my son! The doctor was right in saying that I've yet to know that true, pure love that he called sacred. This lofty emotion is not associated with a single vice. And when we become better, it fills our hearts!

Today I feel unwell and so have called for the good doctor. How invaluable he's come to be! I've reconciled with him, and it looks as though he'll grow to like me and to forgive what I've done to the Countess.

Oh! You're probably rejoicing, Alexander, that I'm now traveling the road your friendship has shown me. From now on you'll see that I'm worthy of it—at least, that's what I wish.

Your friend Gorsky

LETTER XIX

From Count Gorsky to Alexander Lvov
July 20, 183 …
Saint Petersburg

I'm going to her! I'm going, Alexander! But not to crawl at her feet and to beg forgiveness. She isn't worthy of that repentance which only a day ago lived in my heart!

Wasn't my premonition correct that Prince Belsky would succeed with her? Everything is ready for my departure so I can only tell you briefly how I discovered her infidelity.

This morning I went to the post office and received the following answer: "There are no letters in your name." What's surprising in that? She has no time to answer me now that she's healthy, attractive, in good spirits, and … what's more … is laughing at me with Prince Belsky.

Angry with her, myself, and the post, I dropped by to see Pronsky, who's begun to recover after an illness. He asked me to stay for a bit while he, on doctor's orders, went riding. I found a book on his desk and promised to wait for him.

He hadn't gone farther than the porch when I heard Maisky's voice and that of his companion from the theater. Having no desire to waste time in empty conversation, I went into Pronsky's study, which was divided by a screen, and locked the door behind me.

Of course they sat down, also planning to wait for the master of the house. Their lively and merry conversation jumped from one subject to another. I listened to them distractedly when suddenly Maisky asked, "Well, what does Prince Belsky write?"

"What does he write? Should I recount the entire letter with all its ohs and ahs? You can open any novel and read it. There's the well-known ecstasy of a happy lover: she's sweet, divine! I love her and I am loved passionately in return! That's the whole story."

"And does she really love him so?"

"It seems so, if they know how to love in the provinces."

I was trembling all over. Did I really have to listen to such conversations again! I didn't want to listen anymore—I wanted to go home. When I exited the study, I must have been frightening to behold because they looked at me in surprise.

"Gentlemen!" I said, trying to smile, "I humbly request that you not trumpet so the victories of Prince Belsky. He probably won't boast of them the next time!!!"

They both blushed and wanted to say something in response, but I had no desire to hear anything else and so left for the Colonel's.

I didn't want to reveal anything to him and so I invented a hollow tale and begged him for a leave—something for which yesterday I would have gladly given half my life.

Don't ask me, Alexander, why I'm going. I don't think I'd be able to answer you. But you'll soon receive another letter from me. Everything is ready. Farewell! There is no happiness for me on earth!

CHAPTER I

> Molchalin may be bright and bold, it's true,
> But has he got emotions, passions
> To think the world without you
> To be just vanity and ashes?
> And is he sensitive enough
> To have his heart-beat speeded up by love?
> So that whatever he might think and do
> Would be entirely for you?
> That's what I feel, but words just fail me.
> I'm overwhelmed, I'm in despair,
> It's such a feeling that I couldn't wish an enemy.
> Griboyedov[13]

This was the emotional state in which Count Gorsky left for the place where he'd previously thought to find love and happiness. He traveled two days without stopping for a moment. He hurried the coachmen and argued with the stationmasters. This patient and gentle person had become the most cantankerous of men.

My dear readers! Who among you, at least once in your life, hasn't been under the influence of such emotions? Blessed is the man whose impetuous heart is expressed in his every movement, whose gaze tells us all the secrets that are kept at the bottom of his heart! Do not fear this man. He is probably a good friend, a good husband and father, too!

Perhaps the Count would have continued his journey to his destination at the same speed if on the third day his valet, now ill from fatigue, hadn't fallen from the coach box where he was sitting and injured himself. This incident forced the Count to come to his senses.

Always sensitive and kind, he sat the man inside the carriage and refused to travel any farther that night so that the man might rest and catch up on sleep. When the Count himself awoke, his thoughts were refreshed and he was calmer. From time to time even a ray of hope appeared in his clouded heart.

---

13. These verses are taken from act 3, scene 1, of the play *Woe from Wit* (1833), written by Alexander Sergeevich Griboedov (1795–1829). The translation is by A. S. Vagapov (http://zhurnal.lib.ru/a/alec_v/woehtm.shtml).

Perhaps, he thought, Prince Belsky was teasing his comrades. Perhaps, having failed to conquer the Countess, he was slandering her in order to darken her good name. Perhaps … but perhaps it didn't end at that. With all that in mind, the Count undertook nothing decisive and planned to go directly to his estate to learn the details from Ivan Ivanovich.

The village of Velikoye, a large part of which belonged to Prince Belsky, lay along the great road, and at the end of it was a station. And so Count Gorsky was obliged to drive by the Belsky estate.

A heavy rain had been falling all day and, as he was approaching the end of his journey, the road, which wasn't very good to begin with, was now so bad that toward evening one could travel it only with the greatest difficulty.

The Count's impatience grew in proportion to these obstacles. He was once again anxious. The proximity of the place to which his thoughts had been constantly directed for some time now and his present location, where he dare not stop, fearing he might see the horrible specter of his rival, all made him extremely gloomy. Again he began to urge the coachmen to go faster, and several times he wanted to get out of the carriage, thinking that this would hasten his journey.

A thick fog and heavy rain left no hope of reaching the station any time soon. The descent from the hill to Prince Belsky's estate was especially difficult.

The Count recognized the place from a distance, and a thousand thoughts, one more turbulent than the last, crowded his mind, especially when he noticed that the Prince's house was illuminated both inside and out. The lampions and glass shades cast such a dim light due to the rain that it was impossible to make out anything.

There's certainly a big feast going on here, thought the Count, and his heart seethed. He imagined his faithless wife giving herself over to the festivities, and if she could see how he was dragging himself through the mud, she and Prince Belsky would laugh at him!

This ball was being given for her pleasure, the Count imagined, and when he turned his gaze from the house, he saw to his surprise that the church was also illuminated. He was about to ask himself what it could mean when his thoughts underwent a complete change.

As the horses raced down the hill, the carriage pitched from side to side, despite the coachman's skill, then tossed the Count and his servant out near the gates of a respectable cottage. Fortunately, the Count fell into the mud and wasn't injured at all. His manservant, who was underneath him, slightly injured his hand. But the most annoying thing was that the carriage had disappeared from sight.

Not knowing where to seek help or whom to send for his carriage, the Count looked around: was there anyone on the road? But the entire street was completely empty. Only near the church were there some people, as well as several coaches and carriages.

Leaving his valet near the luggage they'd collected after it was thrown from the carriage, the Count entered the house, supposing he'd have better luck looking for someone there. But the house was also empty. He passed through two rather tidy rooms, then, in the next room, which was illuminated by a lamp burning in front of the icons and decorated with greenery and flowers, he saw an old woman dozing by a cradle that held a sleeping baby.

This picture stopped the Count at the threshold for several minutes. The feeling of annoyance and indignation immediately subsided in his kind heart, which was then filled with a quiet tenderness.

Since learning he'd been a father, he couldn't look with indifference at any child. And now the gaze he directed at the cradle brought back all his tenderness for the mother of his son.

Although the old woman was at first frightened by the Count, his gentle voice won her over, and to the question, "Might I find an unoccupied servant who could go after my carriage?" she replied, "It's unlikely, sir, that anyone's still at home besides old, decrepit me. You see, today's a big celebration for us—our own *batiushka*,[14] the Prince, is pleased to be married, and the ceremony in the church, I believe, is taking place right now."

Ah! What a stone was lifted from Count Gorsky's heart! A light shone on his face; he turned his gaze toward the icon, shining in the lamplight, and stood there in total oblivion. Finally, sensing that

14. *Batiushka* is a now obsolete term for "father," and was used to address men in positions of authority, that is, estate owners and even the tsar (*tsar'-batiushka*). It is still used today to address Orthodox priests. In the above passage the term refers to the estate owner, Prince Belsky.

he couldn't stand any longer, he sat down, and after a moment asked the old woman, "Who's your master's bride?"

"Our benefactor didn't look far. He fell in love with a close neighbor, the daughter of the poor widow Sokolova—such an intelligent, pretty girl—even becoming a princess won't spoil her. They hurried the wedding, sir, because the Prince's mother is very sick, and she wanted to see her beloved daughter-in-law before she died."

So many questions crowded on the Count's tongue! Some he didn't dare to ask, while others he didn't voice, as he thought this simple woman would be unable to answer them to his satisfaction. So he only asked: "Did the ceremony begin a long time ago?" "I don't know, sir. Father Ignaty and his wife left a while ago." "So, I'm in the priest's house?" "You are, sir! I believe he'll be back soon."

At that moment the Count's valet entered and said that after resting a bit he'd carried into the house everything that had fallen from the carriage and thought he'd go to the station, where the horses and carriage had probably gone. He'd then try to return immediately to the Count with the carriage.

"Listen!" said the Count, "No one must know that I've passed through here. So, instead of post horses, hire a carriage, whatever the cost, to take us to our village. Be careful not to give anything away, even here in the house!"

His manservant left and the Count was again lost in thought. The emotions troubling his heart were evident on his handsome face: his heart was not entirely at peace. True, his rival was getting married, but didn't he himself wed when he was in love with another woman? Perhaps the Countess herself arranged this marriage, choosing for her beloved a poor girl who meant nothing to him. She's certainly at the church! At the thought of that, he almost went there if only to look at his wife, but then thinking of the alarm he might cause in that holy place, he remained at the house. Suddenly the thought flashed in his mind that Maisky and his friend had never mentioned the object of Prince Belsky's affection by name. Why should it be anyone other than the woman he was marrying now? And why suppose it was the Countess? At the thought, he pressed his two hands against his chest as if he wanted to stop the beating of his heart.

Thus passed a very long hour! Finally, a light appeared along the road from the church. Then voices could be heard near the door in the entrance hall, and into the room walked the priest and his wife, who was cold.

They had only recently moved to the parish and so didn't know their guest at all. And although they were surprised to find him there in their home, they asked him with all the hospitality of kind hosts to sit down again and to allow them to change his rain-soaked clothes.

Shaking off his cassock, the priest said in a pleased voice, "We're happy for the rain. It presages happiness for our newly-wed Prince. I believe it could only be God blessing this wonderful couple. Where there is pure love, there He abides, and with Him there cannot be unhappiness! Sir, no doubt you wish to hurry to the wedding reception?" he asked the Count. "No! I'm going to Count Gorsky's estate on business." "Really? Do you bring some comfort for his virtuous spouse? That would please us! We all love the Countess."

Although the Count was embarrassed by the question, it nevertheless contained the assurance that the Countess hadn't lost people's respect. "Yes! I do indeed have a message for the Countess. However, I probably won't find her at home today. She's no doubt enjoying herself at the wedding?"

"Evidently, you aren't at all acquainted with the Countess. Since being separated from her husband, she doesn't take part in any festivities. Our present Princess, being a very poor girl, owes a great deal to the Countess, and loves her as a friend and a benefactor. All the same, she was unable to persuade her to attend the wedding today."

Now the Count listened in delight—this completely exonerated the Countess in his eyes. He only regretted that at that very moment he couldn't fall at the feet of the woman before whom he was so guilty, having insulted her yet again with his offensive suspicion.

With what impatience he now awaited the arrival of his carriage! And although the priest and his wife entertained him with great zeal, advising him not to subject himself to the night's foul weather and to rest at their home, he declined and leapt with joy when his valet told him the carriage was ready.

When the coachman managed to rein in the racing horses, they immediately stopped with the carriage near the station. And although the carriage was broken in many places, the trunks and suit-cases, which were tightly tied down, remained in place. The Count's manservant hastily repaired all he could, leased new horses, and rushed to his master.

The Count was in a great quandary: where should he go? His heart was drawing him to the Countess. But when he took out his watch and saw how late it was, he had to deny himself that joy, figuring that he wouldn't be able to see her that day.

While bidding farewell to the priest and thanking him for his hospitality, the Count couldn't resist saying to him with feeling, "I'll always remember that under your roof I found peace for my soul."

How different were the Count's thoughts now from those with which he traveled to the village of Velikoye! Nature itself seemed to be taking part in his joy. The rain had passed and a full moon peeking out from behind a cloud illuminated the distant landscape where the Count was now seeking out the Countess's home, and his gaze fixed upon it.

When he arrived at the spot where the road split in two—one road went along a large pond and led to the Countess's home while the other went through a copse and straight to his house—the Count ordered the carriage to be stopped and, after looking at his watch again, thought for a moment. Then in an unintelligible voice, he ordered the coachman to proceed to his house.

Ivan Ivanovich had already been sleeping for a long time. When the Count woke him, the overjoyed old man was unable to collect himself for quite a while. He cried and laughed at the same time, and as he embraced the Count, kept repeating, "Oh my God! Thanks be to You. Now everything will be alright."

The Count easily guessed that his words referred to his reconciliation with the Countess, and he was touched by the love of this old man, who had always wished him true happiness. Wanting to find out about his wife, he asked him, "What do you think, Ivan Ivanovich, will she be pleased?" "How can you doubt that? Only yesterday the Countess was pleased to tell me she'd written and asked you to come, and that since she sent you the letter by relay, she's been counting the minutes."

"What letter? When?" asked the Count.

"I'm an old man," said Pravin, "and because of my ill health, Your Excellency, it took a long time for her to receive your portrait. She thought you'd be worried about her reply, so she sent it as soon as possible. But your arrival will be a surprise for her!"

"I wanted to ask you, my friend," said the Count, "to forbid anyone to talk about me here and in the Countess's house. Ah! So that was the reason for her slow reply. Again I'm guilty before her for not having thought of that."

"Oh! God save us, Your Excellency!" cried out Ivan Ivanovich, involuntarily recalling Princess Zelskaya. But the Count, having guessed his fear, answered him with a smile, "Don't be afraid, my friend! My foolishness is now of a completely different kind." And then he told him what had hastened his arrival here.

"That's better, Count!" said the old man, laughing. "Now you know how terrible it is to share the love of your beloved with another. That's how the Countess has felt for the last two years!"

"Don't remind me of that; do me that kindness! I truly don't know whether she'll forgive me."

"Oh, there's no need to think of that, Your Excellency! If she was so delighted by your portrait, I think she'll be overjoyed—and God knows how—over seeing her favorite in the flesh."

It was very pleasant to hear such comforting words. He then asked Ivan Ivanovich to tell him how his portrait was received. And more than once he interrupted the old man with questions and exclamations that revealed the ecstasy in his heart.

This is how the night passed, and when at the insistent request of the old man the Count agreed to rest, he slept no more than two hours, lying on the sofa.

When he opened his eyes, the Count saw that a bright sun was illuminating the day, which was of such significance in his life. Without alarming anyone, he went out through an open door into the garden to pay his respects to his father's remains. He wished, before seeing his wife, to become reconciled, through his repentance, with the ghost of the man who had entrusted that sweet woman to him.

Returning from there, he ordered the carriage to be readied and immediately set about getting dressed. We must admit he went about his toilette with great care, and the finest tailor in the capital hadn't toiled in vain over his uniform jacket—he certainly would have admired his own handiwork. All the beauty of Count Gorsky shone in Pravin's eyes, and he kept mentioning it, even remarking that the Countess had yet to see the Count in his officer's epaulets—which nicely set off his face.

Although the Count betrayed his impatience over the fact that the carriage hadn't been brought around, he involuntarily winced when they told him it was finally ready. He embraced Ivan Ivanovich and with true reverence asked him to bless him.

Such respect for the old man's affection caused Ivan Ivanovich to weep as he fulfilled the Count's request. And when he led him to the carriage, he stood for quite a while on the same spot, then put his hand to his weak eyes and watched the carriage depart. When he saw that the speeding horses had turned toward the Countess's house, he raised his hands toward heaven and uttered an even more ardent prayer.

Now we must describe the emotion with which the Count approached the house where he would arrive as a criminal. Despite all the Countess's gentleness, he could expect well-deserved reprimands, and, as he imagined all the unpleasantness of their exchange, his facial expression shifted several times.

But when his carriage rolled into the Countess's spacious courtyard, when he stopped near the porch of the house, the Count thought of nothing but the joy he'd now feel in seeing the one he loved. With what lightness he leapt from the carriage, and with what speed he passed through those familiar rooms!

CHAPTER II

And suddenly the Heavens bid
That I should live and feel intensely,
Should cry sweet tears and know
Joy not in my dreams alone.
Kozlov[15]

---

15. These verses are taken from Ivan Kozlov, "Chernets. Kievskaia povest." This is the only literary work that is cited as an epigraph more than once in the novel.

At that moment, Countess Gorskaya was sitting on the sofa in her parlor. Her favorite pastime when alone was to reread the Count's last letter. From the placement of every period, she seemed to discern a new meaning and a new delight for her heart.

Through the open door onto the balcony a cool breeze brought with it the fragrance of the flowers that blanketed her garden.

Not thinking she'd be receiving guests so early, she had not yet dressed. A light, azure-blue housecoat outlined her figure, and her fair, glossy hair was carelessly gathered with a simple comb.

Leaning against the arm of the sofa, she looked pensively at his letter so that the Count, who was now standing by the open door, could easily see her in the mirror.

Oh! What indescribable amazement he felt upon seeing before him, in place of his thin wife exhausted by illness, a captivating woman with fresh, blossoming color on her cheeks, luxuriously full shoulders, not exaggerated by a fashionable beret, and a figure that was tall, erect, and not constricted by stays. He surveyed all this in a single instant, and wishing to fall before her on his knees as soon as possible, he made a movement that produced a slight noise, which made the Countess turn toward the door.

With a joyful cry she rushed toward the Count and, before reaching him, threw herself at his feet. The Countess's ardent, unfeigned joy filled the Count's heart with a delight he'd never known.

Pale and trembling, he pressed the Countess to his heart and carried her to the sofa, where she, not quite in a faint but overcome by her emotions, said nothing for quite a while.

Then, when the Count, drunk with joy, embraced her and in a supplicating voice begged her to forgive him, she placed her head on his chest and, now feeling all the bliss of this divine moment, said, "All is forgotten, my friend! Everything … and if you really love me, then whose happiness can compare with mine?"

As she said this, she was so beautifully charming that the Count, filled with love and joy, wanted to throw himself at the Countess's feet, but she stopped him with a long and tender kiss that completed their reconciliation.

A scene of such happiness is indescribable, so my readers may imagine it as they wish or as they experienced it when they found themselves in a similar situation.

Finally, the Countess recalled that her dear guest, who'd rushed to see her, had probably had nothing hot to drink, and so with a smile she asked him to permit her to pour him some tea herself; but her trembling hands and kisses from the Count, who was sitting beside her, slowed the process considerably.

Wishing to have as few witnesses to their happiness as possible, the Count undertook to help the Countess and in the absence of a servant attempted to serve her himself. Ah! He felt that he was in love for the first time and that he loved her completely.

The bashfulness of his lovely wife and the ever-spreading color in her cheeks increased the flame burning in his heart and obliged him to be modest in his actions. He saw that without respect there was no love, no true happiness, not only between lovers but between spouses as well.

Amid the joy he felt, the Count was somewhat constrained in his conversation with the Countess. Not daring to touch upon the past, he couldn't entirely enjoy the present, fearing that any mention of the past would cause his wife's sweet face to stop looking at him with affection. But the fear soon passed.

The Countess somehow fathomed his thoughts and told him with all the trustfulness of her heart that she'd waited for him, believing that those places rendered sacred by the memory of his father and the affection of their grandmother would return him to her, if only for a while. And once he saw her love and that he alone constituted her entire world, he'd probably stay with her.

"You see, I was right, my friend, because I know you. Give me your word, my dear Vladimir, that we will only recall these past two years in order to persuade ourselves even more fully that we can't live without each other. Let's pretend," she added with a smile, "that we were separated by a cruel foe who took you prisoner. And now you're returned to me even dearer and more handsome."

As she said this, she embraced the Count, and the dear criminal was so passionate and tender, his ardent love was so evident, and his gaze expressed such bliss that with heartfelt emotion the Countess thanked the One who'd given her such happiness.

Their time together passed with incredible speed. And the Countess was very glad she'd thought to ask the Belskys not to make the ceremonial visit of a newly married couple—now she could be alone with the Count for the entire day.

Toward evening their conversation turned to the Countess's former illness. And at this point the Count told her of his visit with the doctor and that he already knew he'd been a father. Pressing her to his chest, he asked her why she hadn't told him. "Because, my friend," answered the Countess, "I knew your heart only too well. Believing I wouldn't survive the birth of our son, could I have called you to me only for you to see us both in the grave?" "Yes, that's true!" the Count replied, wringing his hands. "You're an angel, a perfect angel! You foresaw that if I believed I'd murdered you, I would hate my life. You'll see that I'm capable of earning that exemplary affection you gave to your unworthy husband! Permit me, my friend, to see my son's grave today!"

Having said this, he got up and, extending his hand to the Countess, asked whether she would go with him. "Oh, certainly," she replied, "only then will I be able to thank God for the heavenly joy He's sent me!"

When they arrived at that spot so familiar to us, a bright moon was shining, displaying that place to the Count in such a light that he was touched to the bottom of his heart and exclaimed, "Yes, indeed! There's an angel present here! I feel even more strongly here what my absence denied me! I feel how great the misfortune I caused you was, my adorable wife! Oh! Forgive me!" he said, falling at the Countess's feet. "I beg you, for the sake of this angelic spirit, who is undoubtedly standing over us now, forgive the cruel actions of his father and your husband! Do I need to convince you, incomparable one, that my entire life will serve as proof that I see in everything your virtuous forbearance and that no power will separate us again!"

The Count was in a perfect frenzy. He inclined his head toward his son's grave, and he was as cold as the marble covering it. The frightened Countess used every tender exhortation to make him come to his senses, and when at last she saw that he was calm, she asked him to spare himself for her sake and to come away from that place.

"No, my dear friend! No! Let's stay here! Where else do we belong to each other more than at this place?" And the Countess, feeling the same, was happy to obey him.

The bright, majestic moon, which so often circles the universe, has undoubtedly illuminated many times before scenes such as the one I wish to present to my readers. Nevertheless, I ask them to help me with their imagination.

Amid the fresh, fragrant leaves of the tall poplars, on a lawn covered in sand and turf, arose a pyramid of white marble. On the steps surrounding it stood expensive vases filled with fresh flowers, typically abundant this time of year. The following words were carved in gold into the pyramid, "Here lies all the happiness of my life!," shimmering in the light of the full moon as if displaying their surprising meaning for the last time, for the happy Countess would now replace them with something signifying her new well-being.

On the last step of this monument an elegant grouping was portrayed. A most attractive man in a foppish uniform that outlined his lean frame was lying next to a beautiful woman and embracing her waist with one arm and her knees with the other, searching in her sweet face and on her alabaster neck for a place where he might lay his lips. At the same time, fearing that the air itself might overhear his words and lessen their intensity, he repeated in a half-whisper that she was sweet and beautiful, and that he would love her to the grave!

And she, filled with indescribable bliss, put her arm around his neck, for it seemed to her that the barely perceptible wind might do harm to her darling. And so, to protect him from it, she cast round him the skirt of her diaphanous dress in place of her lily-white arm.

What a pity, what an enormous pity that it was impossible for their beloved old relatives, Count Nikolai Stepanovich Gorsky and Liubov Alekseevna Svetlova, to be present! I believe they wouldn't be indifferent witnesses to this scene and, as is the custom with old people, would begin to repeat triumphantly that they had predicted it. However, probably knowing from experience that outside observers are not much desired in such situations, their shades didn't interrupt the delights of the perfectly happy couple.

Finally, they recalled that it was rather late, and the Count, having received his wife's word that they would spend several hours here every evening, allowed her to take him back to the house, where with attentive solicitude the sweet mistress treated the Count to a generous supper, to which Ivan Ivanovich had been invited.

When the old man witnessed the countless signs of the perfect reconciliation of the couple so dear to him, he was in high spirits and unusually talkative. In vain he sought to involve the Count and Countess in his conversation: they heard nothing, they saw nothing, and lived only for each other.

Moreover, the arrival of Count Gorsky's envoy, or more accurately, confidant, had caused great agitation at Prince Belsky's reception. From the priest, whose house he'd visited, they learned he had a message for the Countess.

Oh, what a noisy conversation there was in Prince Belsky's parlor! Such an event loosened the tongues of many of those who were warmed by the champagne drunk to the health of the newlyweds. One could see the sentiment Countess Gorskaya inspired in her neighbors! And those who didn't rejoice in her happiness were very few.

The young Princess Belskaya, preoccupied with her own happiness, was the last to learn the news of what had happened with the Countess, but because of her sympathy for her, she was the most impatient of all. And eager to know what joyful news this envoy had brought to her friend from the Count, she wanted to fly immediately to Uspenskoye. Only the Prince was able to calm her by promising that they'd go early the next day. Moreover, she remembered the Countess liked to be alone in the first moments of joy or sadness.

This time such respect for her habits was well taken, and the Count and Countess were obliged to it for the fact that no one visited them on the first day of their reunion.

CHAPTER III

With the holy union of two hearts complete,
One soul easily reads the other soul;
It's easy to express with one's lips
What has already been said with one's eyes.
Zhukovsky[16]

The next day the Count and Countess were alone all morning. Their only regret was that their whole life couldn't pass like the time they spent from the first moment of their reunion. Having settled in the parlor, they recounted everything that remained unexpressed from the previous day. They also admired each other in wordless delight.

Just then the carriage of Prince and Princess Belsky stopped near the front entrance. The young Princess ascended the porch and asked the servants who met her whether the Countess had any guests. "There are no guests," a manservant answered cheerfully and opened the doors for the couple.

Wishing to see the Countess as soon as possible, Sashenka hastened her steps, and imagine her surprise when she found the Countess in the embrace of an attractive man.

When the Count married Liubinka, the present Princess Belskaya had been at boarding school, and so she didn't know the Count at all. But could it be anyone else but him? Whose affection could render the Countess's face so radiant? "So this is the confidant sent by the Count!" she exclaimed, attracting the attention of the couple who hadn't noticed her.

16. These verses are taken from the ballad "Elvina and Edwin" (El'vina i Edvin, 1814) by the romantic poet and translator Vasilii Andreevich Zhukovsky (1783–1852). Zhukovsky's work is a free translation of the English ballad "Edwin, and Emma" (1725), by the English poet David Mallet (1705?–1765), who published under the pseudonym David Malloch. The ballad tells the story of two young lovers, Emma (Elvina in Zhukovsky's version), who is beautiful but not well off, and Edwin, whose father, intent on building his wealth, opposes the union. Edwin dies of longing and Emma dies shortly thereafter. The above-quoted verses in Mallet's version read: "A mutual flame was quickly caught:/Was quickly too reveal'd:/For neither bosom lodg'd a wish,/That virtue keeps conceal'd." *A Poem, In Imitation of Donaides, By David Malloch* (Edinburgh: A. Millar, 1725), 61, lines 25–28. The basic plotline resembles that of Krichevskaya's play *Blind Mother* (1818), although Krichevskaya provides a happy ending.

There is no point in describing all the greetings that followed. Having no reason to greet Prince Belsky coldly, the Count was amiable toward him and, with his usual candor, told him right then and there that he was obliged to him for his own speedy journey to the Countess's.

"I ask you, Prince," said the Count, "to be so kind as to convince your friend that I'm not insane." "Truly!" he continued, kissing his wife, "I love my Liubinka without reason and this affliction will remain incurable forever. That fit in which I was rude to your friend has passed completely, and I ask you to forgive me!"

If it had been anyone other than Prince Belsky, that person might not have listened with indifference to the Count's conjecture concerning his love for the Countess. But that slight impression, which the Countess's severity had prevented from becoming a passion, had been effaced from the Prince's heart long, long ago. And now occupied with his own wife, he couldn't even recall whether he had ever loved anyone else but her.

We know the Prince from his two letters. We also know that, for all his fickleness, he was perfectly noble. And so we're not at all surprised that he soon struck up a friendship with Count Gorsky and, justly granting him superiority, eagerly followed his advice.

With every passing day the Count's love for his wife grew. He could no longer be separated from her for a moment. And when the end of his leave approached, he was horrified at the thought that he would have to leave her behind and go alone to the capital.

Although he'd sent in his resignation, it was still quite a while until winter—and how could he live without his dear wife for even an hour, let alone several months? He didn't dare ask her to go with him, knowing how she disliked that place where for such a long time she meant nothing to him.

There was perhaps another reason that made the Countess dislike Petersburg, although she had never displayed the slightest jealousy toward Princess Zelskaya. But now that she'd become familiar with her husband's principles, she was calm.

Seeing the Count's sadness, she fathomed his desire, and despite the fact that she disliked the life of high society, she decided to go with her husband and was just looking for an opportunity to surprise him with this joyful news.

The Prince and Princess Belsky, too, were leaving for Petersburg as the end of the Prince's leave was also very near. And so the Countess, sitting beside the Count and conversing with the Princess about her impending departure, said, "I think, Sashenka, we'll see each other in the capital as often as we do here."

"How so?! Are you really going, too?" asked the Princess in surprise. "How could it be otherwise?" said the Countess. "Especially when I see that my husband wishes it. So why should I, on an empty whim, deny myself the true happiness of being with him?"

She hadn't finished uttering these words when she was pressed in the Count's embrace. "Sweet angel!" he exclaimed, "You were created to bring me joy and anticipate my ardent desires. Ah! Everywhere I go with you I'll inhabit that paradise you've created for me here!"

And so the Countess, despite her attachment to Uspenskoye, left it gladly, imagining that she no longer had the strength to be separated from her husband. We can part with happiness we have yet to experience, but when every hour, every minute of our life is adorned with it, who could remain indifferent to its loss?

After placing his entire world, his joy, and his hopes in the carriage, the Count did not rush from station to station; he did not take care of the post horses as urgently; and he did not anxiously count the miles along the way. His watch, too, remained undisturbed. He'd hardly wound it since arriving in Uspenskoye. He didn't need it at all and often complained that its pace didn't correspond to his desires.

The Count had become once again quiet, cheerful, and infinitely courteous, and those stationmasters who remembered him from his rude behavior toward them earlier were very surprised: was this really Count Gorsky?

Let us now leave our happy couple to travel alone. We've already noted that they are much happier without outside observers, so let us occupy ourselves with those acquaintances from this book with whom our gentle readers will probably bid a final farewell—as I don't dare to think they will ever wish to read my tale again.

Since getting married, Sofia Liubskaya wrote often to Countess Gorskaya, and in one of her letters she informed the Countess that, since her husband, who was attached to the embassy, did not hold a favorable position, she had decided to return to Russia.

Such news intensified Countess Gorskaya's happiness, and now she was even more delighted that she'd decided to go to Petersburg, where she could embrace her friend, who was always dear to her heart, that much sooner.

The honorable Ivan Ivanovich was very pleased when the Count and Countess left their estate entirely under the old man's direction. He was absolutely certain that his effort would be rewarded in abundance by those for whom he toiled, and that his old age would come to a peaceful end in the company of his family.

Princess Belskaya, who was elderly and incurably ill, died soon after her son's wedding, and so the Prince asked Mrs. Sokolova to move into his house and be its mistress.

She was truly happy. Her good-hearted son-in-law loved her as a mother and, while providing her with every pleasure, never let her feel the great difference in their incomes. And when he noticed how she grieved over her separation from her only daughter, he hurried to calm her with the thought that, once he was retired, he'd return to her with Count and Countess Gorsky.

Just after Count Gorsky arrived in the country, Paul and Bibi, that tender couple, quarreled over her extravagance and his gambling losses. No longer holding any affection for each other and having never set any store by the rules of honor, they only needed a pretext to separate forever.

After ordering her servants to give nothing to her husband, Mrs. Milovidova left to visit a friend in Moscow. I don't know how she'll live there, but I believe that a woman who doesn't value the opinion of others and casually exchanges quiet domestic happiness for the empty glitter of high society will be respected by no one.

Paul, who was left behind, had little reason to regret their separation. But as his income was greatly limited, he began to play the role in life that people assume "out of misfortune." And it's a good thing he was advised to reenter the civil service while there was still time, for this saved him from desperate circumstances.

Do we dare to call such a fleeting feeling love, which is a spark of divine fire given to us as a testament of our Heavenly Father's mercy? Let's not slander the sweetest union of man and wife, blessed by God. Their bonds grow even stronger over time and weaken only when death wrenches one from the other's arms.

In the meantime, Count and Countess Gorsky were already in Petersburg. The Count introduced his wife to that excellent society in which he'd always been received. And because the Countess had never been in such society, she was at first timid, as is always the case, for a true mind does not trust itself. But every day she acquired something more from this refined education, and by imitating only that which is considered decent both in the capital and in the country, she was reputed to be a model of perfection.

In the eyes of her husband she was superior to everything he knew and saw. It was enough to see him when his wife was being praised to assess the love he had for her.

In her dress the Countess was also very discriminating. She purchased only things that were tasteful and characterized by a charming simplicity. She was never seen in anything that by imitating fashion alone might have disfigured her delightful face.

As the Count and Countess's means were great and their available income was not diminished in the payment of debts, it was very easy for them to rent the finest rooms in the capital and to have an excellent equipage and a servant. And all this was marked by the couple's uncommon selectivity.

Not finding much pleasure in noisy entertainment and wishing to use her time to see everything that was wonderful and refined in that magnificent city, the Countess, accompanied by her husband, went every day to view something new.

Of course, today that delightful labor of theirs would be eased by having an inspired writer as their guide. But no, no! I don't dare touch with my pen that genius who sketched the panorama of St. Petersburg with his lofty gifts, giving new brilliance and new glory to literature.[17]

The Countess very much wanted to see Princess Zelskaya in order to get some idea of the beauty that had ensnared her husband.

---

17. Krichevskaya may be referring here to Alexander Pushkin's novel in verse, *Eugene Onegin*, much of which takes place in Saint Petersburg. It was first published in full in 1833, four years before Krichevskaya published her novel.

She heard several times from the Count, however, that such a meeting would be unpleasant to him, and so she began to avoid it.

But an utterly unexpected situation brought her together with the Princess. The Countess herself described the meeting in detail to Mrs. Sokolova, and we will soon read that letter, since, having elicited several letters from the characters to begin my novel, I shall end it in the same way.

LETTER XX

From Count Gorsky to Alexander Lvov
September 22, 183 …
St. Petersburg

Have you been complaining, dear Alexander, that I seldom write? Have you really forgotten what our unforgettable poet told us in the sweet voice of a nightingale?

"I loved and so I sang;

I grew happy, so I ceased."[18]

I, too, have stopped singing, my friend! I'm intoxicated with the bliss I now enjoy, and I hurry to redeem the time that I denied myself so recklessly.

But has the language been invented that can describe true happiness? To form an opinion of it, one must certainly see it, and so I ask you to come visit us next month in the country, dear Alexander—we'll certainly be there.

Although I strongly agree that one who loves and is loved is happy everywhere, I would nevertheless advise that person, as a good friend, to take his beloved away to a secluded corner, under the quiet shelter of love and joy, where nothing will interfere with their living for each other; and where the decorum of high society, which is entirely

---

18. These two lines of verse are a paraphrase taken from the short lyric poem "Vorobei i Ziablitsa" (Sparrow and Chaffinch; 1805) by Ivan Ivanovich Dmitriev (1760–1837). In Dmitriev's poem the lines are spoken by the sparrow about the nightingale: "He loved and so he sang; he grew happy so he ceased."

inappropriate to their situation, cannot steal from their life its finest moments, with which I've now become such an incredible miser.

In fact, my friend, what will you do this winter in your solitude? Wouldn't it be better to visit friends? For me that would hold an incalculable number of benefits: I could see you and so wouldn't have to write to you, and I could read in your eyes the realization that there is no finer woman on earth than my wife!

Nor is there a man finer than my husband! I've taken advantage of his absence to join my request to the earnest entreaty of your friend: come see us as soon as possible. If your heart needs the affection of a sister and the friendship of a wife, then I dare to assure you that you'll find both in me.

Respectfully yours,
Countess Gorskaya

Have you grown so wild, Alexander, that the request of such a lovely woman has no effect on you? Don't oppose her, my friend! Indeed, she can make whatever she pleases of us poor men! And I, I am her slave, and am ready for a single smile from her, for a single kiss given to me this very moment, to race to the end of the earth—with her, of course, only with her!

If you're going to be stubborn and refuse to obey us, then expect guests this winter. My wife and I aren't idlers. Then, my friend, there'll be no mercy for you! We'll take you with us, and then we'll have the right to keep you for as long as we want. I imagine you're so frightened by this prospect that you'll come by the first post.

I should alert you, my friend, that you won't need to bring any books. The Countess's library, too comprehensive for a woman, abounds in the best that was ever created by the human mind. And we're now bringing with us from Petersburg a large supply of excellent new works published here this year.

And so, farewell, dear Alexander! Must I paint for your imagination the joy you'll bring to the heart of your ever-faithful friend?

LETTER XXI

From Countess Gorskaya to Mrs. Sokolova
September 28, 183 …
Saint Petersburg

I want to describe to you, my most esteemed friend, something that happened to me recently that is proof that in the midst of the greatest happiness we can experience grief inflicted by individuals to whom we have given no cause to do so.

Do not think, dear Elena Ivanovna, that this has anything to do with the accord between my husband and me: I'm loved by him more than I could have ever imagined. And this incident seems to have increased our attachment to each other, proving to me the sincerity of my Vladimir's repentance!

We'd arranged with the Prince and Princess to go to the theater, and just as we were about to get into our carriage, the Count received an order to appear before the General.

He was very upset to be separated from me for an entire evening, but, having entrusted me to the Prince, he had little reason to worry—although, as he embraced me, he said: "You're so beautiful today that I truly fear rivals. And so, I'll hurry in order to have some time—if only toward the end—to triumph over them!"

I'm writing this to you, my friend, because it's enjoyable to relate how all his jokes are tempered by tenderness for me, and how with a single word he can fill my heart with pleasure for the entire day.

We arrived at the theater rather early and found all the loges already filled, although the curtain was still down. The Prince, who sat between us, was a resident of the capital and so knew every single surname and could name almost every individual about whom we inquired.

That brilliant scene has always delighted me. And the freedom to examine and admire everything beautiful has made the theater for me the first among public places.

As the Prince was amusing us with witty descriptions of several individuals, making Sashenka and me laugh, we heard a woman in the adjacent loge burst into a loud, indecent guffaw. Curious to see who was laughing, I glanced to the side and saw a woman who was no longer young but very beautiful and dressed with great care.

The feathers in her hat shook incessantly, clearly from the movements she was constantly directing toward the young men who surrounded her and filled the loge she occupied.

What a display of impudence in that milieu, where people attempt to hide their weaknesses, rarely revealing them from behind the cloak of decency! What I saw at that moment, I witnessed for the first time. And so I was very surprised and asked the Prince whether he knew the woman.

The Prince glanced into the loge, grew confused, then answered indecisively that he didn't know her at all. His reply made it easy for me to guess who it was, and I said, "Oh, then I'll tell you myself who it is. Isn't it Princess Zelskaya?"

"How could you know that?" the Prince asked me. "By your vague reply. And even more by her behavior. Now I see," I added, "that this woman couldn't have planted deep feelings in the Count's heart. She had to feign too much for their attachment to last even two years."

This is indeed the case, my friend! Now familiar with the noble principles of my husband, who loves his wife's modesty and her innocent, pure affection, I don't understand how it is she didn't reveal herself sooner!

Although I'd wanted to see Princess Zelskaya, I must confess to you, my esteemed friend, that her proximity to me and her impudent, unrestrained laughter deeply disturbed me, and I was unwittingly reminded of the sorrow I'd endured from that shameless coquette.

I anxiously awaited my husband, for I wanted to ask him to take me away from the theater. The Prince wanted probably have done the same for me, but you know how much I dislike ruining other people's pleasure for my own sake. I wanted even less to do that now, as my dear Sashenka was the one enjoying herself.

Imagine my situation and what I must have felt when I heard Princess Zelskaya utter my name! The men who knew me from society must have told her about me. Then, without the least civility, she aimed her opera glasses at me and in the most blasé tone declared, "Yes, she's quite pretty!" And then a loud burst of laughter drowned out her words.

I tried not to let her see that I'd heard her humiliating assessment of me. Ah, how I regretted having gone to the theater without the Count! In his presence, nothing of the kind could have happened. And no doubt, this evil woman, calculating that it would be easier to insult me, searched for just such an opportunity!

When the curtain fell, I relaxed a bit, thinking that we'd return home and I'd find there the love and affection of my dear husband, who would easily erase this unpleasant impression from my heart.

Near our usual exit, however, there was such a crowd that we were forced to stop. At that moment someone called to the Prince, and before I could ask him not to leave us, he was already quite far away.

Perhaps I would have been less anxious if I hadn't heard behind my back the voice of Princess Zelskaya, who seemed to be coming directly toward us. I begged Sashenka to let us move somewhere else, but she rightly pointed out that the Prince would be unable to find us.

We hadn't finished arguing when Princess Zelskaya stopped in front of me and, taking both my hands in hers, said, "There's no need for us to introduce ourselves, Countess! We know each other well enough. Our affection for the same man makes us friends." After saying this, she tried to embrace me.

Although horror and indignation tied my tongue, I still had the strength to avoid her embrace, and with Sashenka's help I thought to free my ice-cold hands, which the Princess still held in hers. And just as she was about to say something else to me, I saw my husband approaching.

"Thank God, there's my husband!" I cried out, overjoyed. "Your husband?" said the Princess, sarcastically. "And has he been all yours for long?" "Since I scorned you!" said the Count, angry and turning pale. He then pushed Princess Zelskaya away from me so discourteously that I was afraid unpleasant stories might come of it. But evidently those surrounding us knew the Princess well enough for no one thought to intervene on her behalf. And the Count was free to put Sashenka and me in our carriage, and he took us home.

Do I need to describe, my friend, the endearments with which my incomparable Vladimir hoped to calm me? Pressing me continually to his heart, he wanted, it seemed, to shelter me there from human evil.

"Let's leave!" he said, "Let's leave as soon as possible for our peaceful refuge, where once again we'll be happy and at peace, and where you won't come into contact with vice, which is unknown to you! Ah! I've never felt as guilty before you as I do now!"

I couldn't understand what had made Princess Zelskaya act in that way with me, so the Count explained. Evidently, she'd wanted people to witness our acquaintance, to which she tried to lend a familiar tone in order to persuade the onlookers that, by bringing the Princess and me together, the Count was indicating how little I meant in his eyes.

Such cunning made me want to leave for Uspenskoye as soon as possible. And as the Count's business is now concluded, it seems, we'll soon be your guests.

No sooner had we left for home than the Prince returned. Not finding us where he'd left us, he learned from his former comrades what had happened to me, and he couldn't forgive himself for having abandoned us. He was, in fact, punished by the fright our dear Sashenka had experienced; it also took her some time to calm down.

The Count was so angry with the Prince that at first he didn't wish to talk with him. But the Prince's goodness and sincere repentance softened him, and in an hour everything was forgotten.

My dear, priceless Mother! The Countess left her letter to you unfinished because she was given a note from Sofia, who has returned with her husband and parents to Petersburg.

You can judge how much joy that news brought our good Countess. Delighted, she read Sofia's note to each of us and wanted to run to her apartment immediately. Only when the Count gave orders forbidding the use of the carriage did she, as if coming to her senses, ask whether he would permit her to go. "No!" he said, smiling. "Because it seems you won't take me with you, and after the incident at the theater, I gave you my word I wouldn't allow you to go anywhere alone. Besides, I, too, would like to see Sofia and her parents. I hope," he added, embracing the Countess, "that you'll reconcile them with me."

"Oh, do you need to ask that, my dear friend!" replied the Countess. "Won't they guess from my face that I'm the happiest of wives? And won't they see from my husband's face that I love him more than life itself?"

And so they left together, but for only a very short time, as the Count refused to allow their friends to live apart from them, hoping, it seems, with this gesture to please his Liubinka, whose slightest wish he anticipated.

We're already on our way to you, dear Mama! I say "we" because we're traveling in a large caravan: the Liubskoys, Sofia with her husband, will also be in Uspenskoye and, I think, will stay for a while. That will certainly please you, dear Mama, as you, too, love the worthy Liubskoys!

Not expecting to find post horses for our carriages, we'll travel with long-distance horses, which will, of course, slow our journey. But I'll divert myself the entire way with the thought that I'll embrace you soon, dear Mama, and will appear before you as cheerful and happy as I was before.

LETTER XXII

From Alexander Lvov to his neighbor
December 11, 183—
Village of Uspenskoye

You know, my esteemed Fyodor Fyodorovich, being accustomed to one place has made this trip very difficult for me. It was only at the persuasion of my dear friend that I undertook to go on this visit, and what's more—for the entire winter!

But now I don't regret it in the least. Not only has my heart found true pleasure, but my mind has also acquired much that is useful and edifying.

My words must surprise you, and you cannot help but ask, "What can a gloomy misanthrope learn by gazing at two young people in love with each other?" They're truly my teachers, my esteemed friend!

You know Count Gorsky. He's improved much over the years and is now, as they say, a real man. But despite his natural intelligence, good sense, and even insight, despite his infallible principles, instilled in him in childhood, he, like many young men, slipped along the path of life, and abandoning true happiness, chased after its shadow.

As he began to lose faith in everything good in the world, his intelligence, dulled by the studied phrases so essential to society life, didn't know where to find nourishment. His heart, drowned in false emotions, might have come to despise the very words *love* and *friendship*. He could have easily lost himself forever, but he was saved by an exemplary wife!

Oh! If only I could describe her more precisely! How I would like to prove to women that they hold domestic bliss in their hands! And if they don't know how or—God forbid!—don't wish to create and nourish it, then, in most cases they are themselves to blame.

You have to agree, my esteemed friend, that when men lose their inner peace, they don't fall into despair but instead find thousands of ways to replace that loss. You also have to agree that women always suffer more from marital discord. And how do they repair the situation? Do they turn to humility and meekness, or to faith, which is an endless source of consolation for every calamity in life?

No! They multiply their complaints and cries, often insincere, and their reproaches, often exaggerated and unproven. They extinguish the final spark of harmony between them and their husbands, in the end irrevocably destroying their happiness.

And what happens when they have children? I always tremble when I hear of such ruinous cases! What criminals they make of these innocent creatures! If by chance their children's morality cannot be tarnished, are they any less guilty for having forced them to violate the most sacred law which commands them to love their parents?

I've digressed too far, my esteemed friend! I only wanted to invite all unhappy wives to look at Countess Gorskaya or someone like her, for to my great comfort I know other wives like her.

Abandoned by her passionately beloved husband, she not only refrained from torturing him with reproaches but even considered herself guilty before him for failing to protest their union.

Perhaps you believe she's cold and unfeeling and that she was able to bear that misfortune with indifference. To the contrary. I repeat again that, sincerely loving her husband, it took great effort for her to hide her tears, which she shed in secret, even from her friends. Fearing lest someone think or speak ill of her husband, she showed him true, unfeigned respect, and forced others to love him too.

While separated from the Count, despite all the advantages of her income, she lived very quietly, and despite her stunning beauty she was so modest that she could have probably stopped with a single glance the impudence of those who considered themselves justified in tormenting her.

Instead, like the happiest of wives, she preserved the sacred bonds that tied her to her unfaithful husband.

And what a triumph for her virtue when that husband, with total repentance and with ardent love, threw himself at her feet! And she, she alone comprised his happiness.

And now when the grateful Count gives her preference in everything and in his passion submits to her without question, she protects the happiness she now enjoys, not for a single moment of triumph but for her entire life.

Sweet without affecting arrogance, obedient without being lowly, she allows her husband to be the head of the house. She tries to be the first to please him in everything and with subtle art shows that this is not slavish obsequiousness but her heartfelt pleasure, as well as a necessary link in the chain that holds fast their marital happiness.

In a word, esteemed neighbor, I needn't rejoice in this union of virtues, nor enlarge upon them in my descriptions, because you yourself have in your daughters lovely girls who are ready to make someone happy. Read my letter to them, and whatever I failed to express, your father's heart can add.

I could not have received a warmer welcome here, and I enjoy utter freedom in my diversions. My dear hosts are attractive, healthy, cheerful, and welcoming toward all who surround them, and they treat me as a true friend. Their house isn't filled indiscriminately with all kinds of guests. Of course, they receive everyone amiably, but their select group would satisfy the strictest observer and most sensible person. I am indeed delighted by my friends' way of life, and if I should find a woman like Liubov Ivanovna, I would marry her, despite my brutishness, utterly confident that she would make me happy. I remain respectfully yours,

Alexander Lvov

THE END

Ртищеву. На совет: прочитав Волтерово описание природы, описать сад его

Чтобы изобразить сердечные нам чувства,
Не нужно здесь вводить чужих умов искусства.
Что внутри души нашел, то в рифму положи,
Лишь только нежностью свои стихи вяжи.
Не ладится ничто!—я в том невиновата;
Грамматика сердец словами не богата;
К тому ж, малиновка не ходит занимать
Напевы соловья, чтоб слухи восхищать;
А так же как и он в кусточке попевает
И ту же самую природу прославляет.
К чему же мне теперь, чужой слог прибирать,
Чтоб истину души красивей описать?
И сад мне твой сравнить с Эдемом Олимпийским,
Стараясь подражать напевам всем витийским.
Где вкус и разум твой с природою сливался.
Не только я, кто век стихами занимался,
Прекрасней сад твой не можешь описать,
Как только от души *твоим* его назвать.

К раме без картины

Картина не ума и тонкого искусства,
Картина самого, приятного в нас чувства;
Смотревши на нее—что хочешь воображай;
И милое глазам и сердцу—представляй.

To Rtishchev. On the Advice That, after Reading a Description of
Nature by Voltaire, I Describe His Garden

To represent the feelings of the heart,
You needn't introduce the skill of other minds;
What you find inside your soul—put that into your rhymes;
Weave verses out of tenderness alone.
If "it's just not working out!," the fault is not my own:
The grammar of the heart is poor in words.
A robin won't take the sweeter song
That to the nightingale belongs,
But will, just like the other, in a little bush sing out
And praise the same works that nature's strewn about.
So why should I adopt another's style
To describe more beautifully the truth of someone else's soul,
Or to compare your garden to an Olympic Eden,
Imitating melodies so Byzantine?
Where your mind and taste have joined with nature,
I, who for a decade now have written verse,
Cannot more beautifully describe your garden
Than you, when you name it from *your* heart.

To a Frame without a Picture

Not of intellect and keen ability,
A painting's made of our most pleasing sentiment.
Look there, imagine what you want to see
And picture what makes heart and eye content.

Белый листочек бумаги

Один писатель рассуждал:
«Младенца сердце,—он писал,—
Есть беленький листок бумаги».
И так—кто хочет для отваги
Со мной и с ним поспорить в том?—
Я не берусь играть умом,
Но так про это рассуждаю,
И вот чем доказать желаю:
Что тот писатель не солгал,
Он точно истину сказал.
Ах, правда!—что чище сердца
Во всем невинного младенца?
Пока судьба не расписнет
И букв пером не проведет;
Пером, починенным страстями,
Большими четкими словами
На белом том листе: Люблю!
«Покой на век истреблю!»
Судьбе лишь трудно расписаться,
А то не трудно униматься;—
Она в том точная есть я.
Стихи есть страсть моя!—
Но в том не сходны мы с судьбою,
Что час толкуясь с головою,
На силу рифму приберу;
Так можно отдохнуть перу.
Судьбы ж перо не отдыхает,
Она всегда насобирает,
Чтоб весь листочек исписать;
И так уметь рассчитать,
Тебе порядочно расставить
И жалость—нежность,—не оставить
И горесть—ревность поместить;
И все, что чувством может быть.
Под старость так лист измарает,

A White Sheet of Paper

A writer once put forth:
"The heart of an infant child
Is a white sheet of paper."
Who has the courage to argue
The point with the two of us?
I won't play witty games,
But do contend
And wish to prove:
This writer didn't lie.
He said nothing but the truth.
Ah, yes! What is purer than
An infant's guiltless heart?
Until fate then writes upon it,
Passing over it with its pen,
Which, ruled by passions,
Will write in letters large and clear
 "I love!" on that white sheet,
And "Peace is gone forever!"
It's difficult for fate
To start to write, but not to stop;
And it's the same for me,
For writing poetry is my passion!
But unlike fate,
After pondering how
To tidy up a rhyme,
I can give my pen a rest.
But the pen of fate is never still.
Always gathering
To fill the page,
It knows just how to tally up
And neatly to arrange
Your sympathies and tenderness,
Your jealousies and sorrows, too,
And every feeling there could be.
But in old age, the page grows dim

Что вряд ли кто и прочитает.
И время быстро убегая
По части с книг судеб стирая
Для жизни данный нам предел,
Стереть: *умри!* хоть не хотел.
И время букв тех не стирает,
Судьба какие начертает
Чернилом черным на сердцах;
Тому так быть. Я в сих словах
Свое писанье заключаю,
Понравится ль кому?—*не знаю*.

На ополчение 1812 года

Что быстро в воздухе несется?
Что громко в сердце отдается?
Кому внимают все, оставя мир, забавы?
Молве, парящей к нам;—неся в руке щит славы,
Любовь к отечеству, прямое благородство;
В другой неся плач жен, оставленных сиротство.
И я сидя в углу, со слезами ей внимаю,
Всем лучшим: дружбою, ей жертвовать желаю.
Не могши в руки взять, вместо иголки шпаги,
Чтоб сердце облегчит, беру я лист бумаги.
Ужасной правды друг!—тебе ли победить,
Что Вера и Любовь старались ополчить?
Кого ведет на брань Надежда с упованьем,
А вслед летят сердца с чистейшим сим желаньем:
Чтоб не оставил их в селении Творец,
Бог мира, Бог земли, —премудрый наш Отец.
Сражайтесь! Он всегда невинных охраняет;
Не вас, так ваших чад наградой увенчает.
Молитвы каждый час, мы будем возносить:
Победы без меча—и мира вам просить.

And hardly anyone will read it then.
And time, which races by so fast,
Erasing from the books of fate
The limit set for every life,
Says, "Die," no matter what you wish.
But time cannot erase
The letters etched by fate
In blackest ink in people's hearts.
So be it. And with these words
I end this piece—although,
Will someone like it? *I don't know.*

On the Militia of 1812

What speeds so quickly through the air?
Resounding loudly in our hearts?
Whom do we heed when peace and pleasures now are gone?
Rumor, swooping down upon us, carrying in one hand the shield of
glory,
Love of the fatherland, and pure nobility;
While in the other, the lament of wives, now left with orphans.
Sitting in a corner, I listen to her and weep.
I wish to sacrifice to her the finest thing I have: my friendship.
Unable to wield a sword in place of needle,
I take a sheet of paper to relieve my heart.
Horrible friend of truth! Can you vanquish that
Which Faith and Love have rallied arms against?
Or those led into war with confidence by Hope,
In whose wake fly hearts with one pure wish:
That they be not abandoned by the Creator of the Universe,
God of the world, God of this land, Our Most Wise Father.
Now fight! For He protects the innocent
And will reward your children, if not you.
And every hour we offer up our prayers:
To ask for victory without the sword—and peace for you.

Днепр, 25 мая, вечер

С унынием в душе на стол облокотясь,
Смотря на шумный Днепр, я думаю о вас,—
О вас, любезные!—с кем сердце б быть хотело,
С кем горесть, радости делить оно умело.
По вас, под шум Днепра по вас теперь грущу,
Прошедших радостей в душе моей ищу;
Прошедших радостей?—Нет!—месяц освещает
Теперь шумящий Днепр, и в бездне вод играет
Его приятный луч!—На что ж мне говорить
И счастие свое прошедшим находить?
Кто вами, милые! все сердце наполняет,
Тот многих радостей в сем мире ожидает.
Не только подле вас—и здесь, среди степей,
Где камень и в земле—и в сердце у людей,—
И здесь, —когда об вас, родные! вспоминаю,
И скуку, и тоску, и грусть позабываю.
Ах! вы есть у меня,—есть с добрыми и Бог!—
А кто любивши вас, душой не добр быть мог?
И так,—хоть скучно мне—хоть грустно и без вас,
Но все—все то легко,—мне грустно лишь по вас!

Гр—рию О—чу Кв—к, ответ на его стихи 17 Сентября

Благодарю тебя, мой милый добрый друг!—
Счастливой женщины, пред-будущий супруг!—
Благодарю тебя за все, что мне желаешь;—
Но жаль, что лично ты меня не поздравляешь
В тебе я думала увидеть всех родных,
Твой взор бы уменьшил тоску мою по них!—
А будто как на то, какой же был пирог!
Хотя Григорий же нам есть его помог,
Хотя был тут и Иван, Василий и Эразм,
И многие еще, манят мой нынче глаз,
Для сердца ж никого!—Одна моя Лизета

The Dniepr. May 25, Evening

With sadness in my heart, my elbows propped upon the table,
Gazing at the noisy Dniepr, my thoughts all turn to you,
To you, my dearest ones! With whom my heart would like to be,
With whom it shared its joys and sorrows.
For you, beneath the Dniepr's roar, I grieve for you,
And look for past joys in my heart.
Past joys? No! The moon now illuminates
The noisy Dniepr, and its delightful rays
Play in the water's depths! So why declare
My happiness is past?
One whose heart is filled with you, dear ones,
Has many joys before her in this world.
Not only by your side, but here, amid the steppe,
Where the stony earth is heavy, as are people's hearts,
Even here, my dears, when I remember you,
I forget all longing, sadness, and ennui.
Ah! You are with me, just as God is with the good!
For can a heart that loved you so be wicked?
And though I'm bored and sad without you,
It's all so simple—I'm only missing you!

To Gr—ry F—ch Kv—ka in Answer to His Verses of September 17

Thank you, my dear, good-hearted friend!
You are the future spouse of a lucky woman!
Thank you for all you wished for me;
But what a pity you couldn't tell me that in person.
I hoped to see in you all those dear to me;
Your gaze would have made me miss them less!
As if for that, oh, what a pie we made!
Although Grigory helped us eat it,
And Ivan, Vasily, and Erasm, too, were here,
And many more to draw my gaze,
There was no one for my heart! Lizaveta

Была Эгидой мне противу лести света.
Друг милый!—Ты за что меня так расхвалил?
За что в число меня добрейших поместил?
Ах! много уже лет я в жизни проводила,
Но доброе творить себя не научила!
Добро ли то еще, что я добро люблю?
Меж тем я без него часы свои гублю.
Добро ли, что тебя наилучшим почитаю,
Однако же в добре тебе не подражаю.—
Тебя—тебя хвалить … но где сыщу я слов?
Молчу—и чту тебя. Твоя сестра *Любовь*.

Еще песня

Скрепись, скрепись ретивое сердце!
Вмести в себя злую грусть мою.
Слезы не лейтесь—и вздох не лети.
Слезы не умалят тяжелую грусть,
Вздох не убавит кручины моей;
Люди лишь узнают, что милого жаль.
Люди не судят по сердцу других,
Люди лишь судят по мыслям своим.
То им не больно, что рвется другой,
То им не горе, что их не крушить.
Умолкни же сердце!—кому пожалеть?
Бедный на свете, не должен любить!!

Истина

Кто в мире не любил,
Тот верно и не жил.—
А кто любил, да не терпел,—
Тот истинной любви и в сердце не имел.

Was my only aegis against wordly flattery.
Dear friend! Why did you praise me so?
And place me among the very good?
Ah! So many years of life I've lived,
But haven't learned to create goodness!
Is it goodness just to love the good?
In any case, I waste my time without it;
Is it goodness to revere you as the best?
Although your kindness I could never imitate.
To praise you ... where can I find the words thereof?
In silence will I honor you. Your cousin Liubov.

Another Song

Brace yourself, my zealous heart!
Make room for savage gloom.
Let tears no longer flow, and all my sighs be still.
No tears can lift the burden of my gloom,
Nor sighs reduce the sorrow that I feel.
They just reveal I grieve for one I loved.
People cannot judge with another's heart,
But do so with their views alone.
They cannot feel another's pain
Or grief that isn't tearing them in two.
Be silent, heart! For who will pity you?
The poor of this world ought not to love!

Truth

One who's never loved
Has never truly lived.
While one who's loved and felt no pain,
True love that heart did not contain.

На вопрос: От чего я много сплю?

Кто счастье лишь во сне встречает,
Кто в нем покоен может быть,
Тот день скорее убивает,
Чтоб больше хоть во сне пожить.

С берегов Терновки

На миг узнала я блаженство!
На миг проглянул счастья свет;
На миг земное совершенство
Было пред мной ... и боле нет!

На миг все райское слетело;
На миг и жизнь была милей,
И небо лучше голубело,
И солнце было посветлей.

На миг и гость полунебесной
Приют мой скромный посетил,
И мне с улыбкою прелестной
Надежду счастия сулил.

Он был! и нет следов, что было!
И все, что льстило, все взято! ...
Одно: *прости!* всю жизнь затмило ...
И я по-прежнему—ничто!

1824, Октября 18
Село Уплатное.

In Answer to the Question: Why Do I Sleep So Much?

One who finds happiness in sleep
And is at peace but there,
Will sooner kill the day away
To live the more in slumber's care.

From the Banks of the Ternovka

For a moment I knew bliss!
For a moment a happy world appeared;
For a moment earthly perfection
Lay before me ... but now no more!

For a moment paradise flew down;
And for a moment life grew sweet,
The sky more blue,
And the sun shone brighter then.

For a moment to my humble haven,
There came a half-heavenly guest,
And with a smile so charming,
Held out the hope of happiness.

He came! But now no trace of it remains!
And all that gratified is taken!
One thing, "Farewell!," has darkened all my days ...
And now, as before, I am nothing!

October 18, 1824
Uplatnoe Village

Bibliography

Primary Sources

Krichevskaia, Liubov' Iakovlevna. *Dve povesti: Korinna i Emma* [Two Novellas: Corinna and Emma]. Moscow: V Universitetskoi tipografii, 1827.

_____. *Graf Gorsky* [Count Gorsky]. Kharkov: V Universitetskoi tipografii, 1837.

_____. *Istoricheskie anekdoty i izbrannye izrecheniia izvestnykh liudei* [Historical Anecdotes and Selected Sayings by Famous People]. Kharkov: V Universitetskoi tipografii, 1826.

_____. *Moi svobodnye minuty, ili Sobranie sochinenii v stikhakh i proze* [My Moments of Leisure, or Collected Works in Verse and Prose]. 2 vols. Kharkov: V Universitetskoi tipografii, 1817–1818.

_____. *Net dobra bez nagrady* [No Good without Reward]. Kharkov: V Universitetskoi tipografii, 1826.

_____. "R ... vu [To R ... v]." *Ukrainskii Vestnik* 4 (1816): 90–92.

_____. "S beregov Ternovki [From the Banks of the Ternovka]." *Ukrainskii Zhurnal* 19–20 (1824): 47.

Secondary Sources

Andrew, Joe. *Narrative and Desire in Russian Literature, 1822–49: The Feminine and the Masculine*. New York: St. Martin's Press, 1993.

_____, trans. *Russian Women's Shorter Fiction. An Anthology, 1835–1860*. Oxford: Clarendon Press, 1996.

Anonymous. "Modest i Sofiia" [Modest and Sofia]. *Russkaia sentimental'naia povest'*, ed. P. A. Orlova, 183–298. Moscow: Izdatel'stvo Moskovskogo Universiteta, 1979.

Barker, Adele Marie, and Jehanne M. Gheith. Introduction to *A History of Women's Writings in Russia*, ed. Adele Marie Barker and Jehanne M. Gheith, 1–15. Cambridge: Cambridge University Press, 2002.

Berger, John. *Ways of Seeing*. New York: Penguin Books, 1977.

Bour, Isabelle. "The Reception of Jane Austen's Novels in France and Switzerland: The Early Years, 1813–1828." In *The Reception of Jane Austen in Europe*, ed. Anthony Mandel and Brian Southam, 12–33. London: Continuum, 2007.

Fainshtein, Mikhail Sh. *Pisatel'nitsy Pushkinskoi pory: Istoriko-literaturnye ocherki* [Woman Writers of Pushkin's Time: Historical-Literary Notes]. Leningrad: Nauka, 1989.

Gilbert, Sandra M., and Susan Gubar. *The Madwoman in the Attic: The Woman Writer and the Nineteenth-Century Literary Imagination*. 2nd ed. New Haven, CT: Yale University Press, 2000.

Greenleaf, Monika. *Pushkin and Romantic Fashion: Fragment, Elegy, Orient, Irony*. Stanford, CA: Stanford University Press, 1994.

Harussi, Yael. "Women's Social Roles as Depicted by Women Writers in Early Nineteenth-Century Russian Fiction." *Issues in Russian Literature before 1917: Selected Papers of the Third World Congress for Soviet and East European Studies*, 35–47. Columbus, OH: Slavica, 1989.

Heldt, Barbara. *Terrible Perfection: Woman and Russian Literature*. Bloomington: Indiana University Press, 1987.

Hodgson, Katherine. *Written with the Bayonet: Soviet Russian Poetry of World War Two*. Liverpool: Liverpool University Press, 1996.

Kelly, Catriona. *A History of Russian Women's Writing, 1820–1992*. Oxford: Clarendon Press, 1994.

——. "Sappho, Corinna, and Niobe: Genres and Personae in Russian Women's Writing, 1760–1820." In *A History of Women's Writings in Russia*, ed. Adele Marie Barker and Jehanne M. Gheith, 37–61. Cambridge: Cambridge University Press, 2002.

King, Noel J. "Jane Austen in France." *Nineteenth-Century Fiction* 8, no. 1 (June 1953): 1–26.

Kvitka[-Osnov'ianenko], Grigorii. "O novom sochinenii Liubovi Krichevskoi [On a Recent Work by Liubov' Krichevskaia]." *Damskii Zhurnal* 18 (1827): 314–15.

Levitt, Marcus C. Introduction to *Early Modern Russian Writers, Late Seventeenth and Eighteenth Centuries*, ed. M. Levitt, ix–xviii. Dictionary of Literary Biographies, 150. Detroit, New York, and London: Bruccoli Clark Layman, and Gale Research, Inc., 1995.

Lotman, Iurii. "Russkaia literatura na frantsuzkom iazyke." In *Iu. M. Lotman. Izbrannye stat'i: V trekh tomakh*, 3: 350–368. Tallinn: Aleksandra, 1994.

Makarov, M. N. "Materialy dlia istorii ruskikh zhenshchin-avtorov [Materials for a History of Russian Women-Authors]." *Damskii Zhurnal* 51–52 (December 1833): 145–150.

Makedonov, L. "Khar'kov." *Entsyklopediia* [Encyclopedia]. Ed. I. E. Andrevskii. Vol. 74, 109–17. St. Petersburg: F. A. Brokgauz—I. A. Efron, 1903.

Maynieux, André. *Pouchkine: Homme de lettres et de la littérature professionelle en Russie* [Pushkin: A Man of Letters and of Professional Literature in Russia]. Paris: Librarie des Cinq Continents, 1966.

Miller, Nancy K. *The Heroine's Text: Readings in the French and English Novel, 1722–1782*. New York: Columbia University Press, 1980.

Neshumova, T. F. "Krichevskaia, Liubov' Iakovlevna." *Russkie pisateli, 1800–1917. Biograficheskii slovar'* [Russian Writers, 1800–1917. Biographical Dictionary]. Vol. 3, 158–59. Ed. P. A. Nikolaev. Moscow: Bol'shaia Rossiiskaia Entsyklopediia, 1994.

Orlov, P. A. Introduction to *Russkaia sentimental'naia povest'* [The Russian Sentimental Novella]. Ed. P. A. Orlov, 5–26. Moscow: Izdatel'stvo Moskovskogo Universiteta, 1979.

Shakhovskii, S. Introduction to *G. F. Kvitka-Osnov'ianenko. Povesti* [G. F. Kvitka-Osnov'ianenko. Novellas], 3–11. Kiev: Radians'kii Pis'mennik, 1954.

Tompkins, Jane. *Sensational Designs: The Cultural Work of American Fiction, 1790–1860*. New York: Oxford University Press, 1985.

Tosi, Alessandra. *Waiting for Pushkin: Russian Fiction in the Reign of Alexander I (1801–1825)*. Studies in Slavic Literature and Poetics, 44. Amsterdam and New York: Rodopi, 2006.

Zborovets', I. V., and O. P. Nasonova. "G. F. Kvitka-Osnov'ianenka i L. Ia. Krichevs'ka." *Radians'ke Literaturoznavstvo* 11 (November 1978): 40–45.

Index

Alexander I (of Russia), 23n, 4, 7
Anacharsis, 10, 142
Andrew, Joe, 10, 10n, 16n, 19n, 25n, 33, 33n, 36n
Anna Ioanovna (Empress of Russia), 6
Anonymous, "Modest and Sofia," 24
Auber, Daniel (composer), 219, 219n
Austen, Jane, 28, 29, 29n; *Emma*, 29, 30n; *Pride and Prejudice*, 29, 29n; *Sense and Sensibility*, 29, 30, 30n

Baer, Brian James, 22n
Barker, Adele Marie, 3n, 6n
baroque literature, 1
Berger, John, 32, 32n
Bestuzhev-Marlinsky, Alexander, 10, 198n; *The Frigate "Hope,"* 198, 198n; *Lieutenant Belazor*, 198, 198n
bible societies, 5, 7
Bossuet, Jacques Benigne, 123, 123n
Byron, George Gordon (Lord), *Prisoner of Chillon*, 192n

Cathedral of the Dormition (Kharkov, Ukraine), 6
Catherine I (the Great) (of Russia), 2, 4
Caucasus, 6, 165, 173, 178, 213, 215, 218, 220, 231, 233n
censorship, 7
Chekhov, Anton, 36
Christianity, 9, 26, 27, 41, 194. *See also* bible societies, pietism, and Russian Orthodox Church
Classicism (literary), 1

Crimea, 188, 197, 198
Cottin, Sophie Ristaud, *Claire d'Albe*, 28n; *Amélie Mansfield*, 176, 176n

Damskii zhurnal (Women's Journal), 12, 14, 14n, 28n
Dark Woman. See Grech, Nikolai
Dashkova, Ekaterina (Princess), 2, 4
Davydov, Stepan (composer), 92n
Decembrist Revolt, 4, 198n
Dmitriev, Ivan Ivanovich, "Vorobei i Ziablitsa," 258n
Dniepr River, 39, 43–4, 275
Dnieprovskaia rusalka (opera), 91, 91–2n
Donauweibchen, Das (opera). *See* Kauer, Ferdinand (composer)
drame larmoyante (*see* lacrymose drama)
Dostoyevsky, Fyodor, *Poor Folk*, 20n

Early modern (period), 1, 1n, 2
Elizabeth II (of Russia), 6
Enlightenment, 23, 24

Fenella (opera). *See* Mansuella, *La muette de Portici*
Fielding, Henry, *Shamela*, 35

Galatea, 32, 138–9
Gan, Elena, 19n, 36, "Society's Judgment," 24
Gheith, Jehanne M., 3n, 6n
Gilbert, Sandra, 11, 11n
Golden Age (of Russian Literature), 4
Golovkina, Natalia, 5

gothic fiction, 29n
Grech, Nikolai, 189; *The Dark Woman*, 190n
Greenleaf, Monika, 5n
Griboyedov, Alexander, *Woe from Wit*, 240, 240n
Gubar, Susan, 11, 11n

Harussi, Yael, 11n
Heldt, Barbara, 16, 16n

Idealism, German, 36
Izmailov, A.E., "Poor Masha," 20n

James, Henry, 36

Karamzin, Nikolai, 5; "Il'ia Muromets," 180, 180n; "Poor Liza," 17, 20n
Karlinsky, Simon, 92
Kauer, Ferdinand (composer), *Das Donauweibchen*, 91n
Kelly, Catriona, 4, 4n, 5, 6n, 8n, 11n, 13, 14, 14n, 15n, 16n, 27n, 32, 32n
Kharkov, 2, 6–8, 9n, 12, 13, 14, 17n, 26n, 34, 37
King, Noel, 29, 29n
Kozlov, Ivan, 10; *Chernets. Kievskaia povest'*, 200, 200n, 248, 248n
Krichevskaya, Liubov, career (literary), 4, 8–9, 10, 11–13; education, 9–10; family 8, 11. *See also* Kvitka-Osnovianenko, Grigory (Hrihorii)
Krüdener, Yulia, 5
Kvitka-Osnovianenko, Grigory (Hrihorii), 7, 8, 8n, 9, 9n, 10n, 12, 14, 14n

Laclos, Pierre Choderlos, *Les Liaisons dangéreuses*, 25

lacrymose drama, 33
Levitt, Marcus, 1, 1n, 2
Little Russia, 2, 12. *See also* Ukraine
Lotman, Iu.M., 5n

Magic Flute (opera), 144
Makarov, M.N., 12, 28, 28n
Mallet, David, "Edwin, and Emma," 253n
Malloch, David (pseudonym). *See* Mallet David
Mansuella, La muette de Portici (opera). *See* Auber, Daniel (composer)
Maynieux, André, 11, 11n
Miller, Nancy K., 19n
Milonov, N.P. "The Story of Poor Maria," 20n
"Modest and Sophia." *See* Anonymous
Montolieu, Isabelle de (translator), 29, 29n, 30, 30n
Moscow, 2, 4, 6, 7, 12, 17n, 24, 27, 37, 177–79
Moskvina sisters, 14

Nabokov, Vladimir, 39
Nasonova, O.P., 10n, 12
Napoleonic Wars, 5, 7, 12, 191
neo-sentimentalism, 16n

Odoevsky, Vladimir, "Princess Mimi" 21, 24; "Princess Zizi," 21
Orthodox Church of Russia, 6, 178n, 242n. *See also* bible Societies, Christianity, and pietism

Paul I (of Russia), 4
Perks, Eloïse (translator), 29n

pietism, 5. *See also* bible societies, Christianity, and Orthodox Church of Russia
Pletnev, Pyotr, 11, 12
pre-romanticism, 3n, 36
Prisoner of Chillon. See Byron, George Bryan (Lord). *See also* Zhukovsky, Vasily (translator)
Pushkin, Alexander, 1, 2, 3n, 4, 5, 5n, 6, 10, 11, 13n, 22n, 33, 206; and *Eugene Onegin* 258n; and "The Fountain of Bakhchisarai," 206, 206n, 258n
Pygmalion, 32, 139

Rastrelli, Bartolomeo (architect), 6
Richardson, Samuel, *Clarissa*, 35; *Pamela*, 35
Romanova, Maria Nikolaevna (Grand Duchess), 11
romantic irony. *See* romanticism
romanticism, 3n, 5, 5n, 7, 10, 22, 35–7; and irony, 5, 5n
Rostopchina, Evdokia, 36; "Money and Rank," 36n
Rousseau, Jean-Jacques, *Lettre à M. d'Alembert sur les spectacles*, 25; *La Nouvelle Heloïse*, 30n
rusalka (water sprite), 91n. *See also* *Dnieprovskaia rusalka*

Saint Petersburg, 2, 6, 6n, 7, 12, 18, 19, 25, 37, 166, 169, 174, 176, 181–84, 186, 188–191, 193, 194. 204, 208, 211, 214, 215, 219, 220, 221, 224, 230, 235, 238, 255–58, 258n, 260, 263
sentimentalism, 1–3, 3n, 5, 14–15, 15n, 16, 16n, 17, 17n, 19–20,

20n, 21–24n, 25, 27, 27n, 29, 29n, 30, 32–37
Sevastopol, 197
Shakespeare, William, 185
Smolny Convent, 181, 184, 186
Staël, Madame de, *Corinne*, 28, 30, 31n, 39, 176n; *Delphine*, 176n

Tolstoy, Leo, 22; *War and Peace*, 3
Tompkins, Jane15, 15n, 16n
Tosi, Alexandra, 223, 229, 256
Trubetskaya, Emelia Petrovna (Princess), 10, 165
Turgenev, Ivan, 22

Ukraine, 1, 2, 6, 7, 7n, 10, 13; and nationalism, 7. *See also* Little Russia
Ukrainian nationalism. *See* Ukraine.
Ukrainskii zhurnal (Ukrainian Journal), 7
Ukrainskii vestnik (Ukrainian Herald), 1n, 7, 8, 13, 13n, 23n
University of Lviv (Ukraine), 7

Vagapov, A.S. (translator), 240n
Volkonskaya, Zinaida, 5
Voltaire, 23, 269
"Vorobei i Ziablitsa." *See* Dmitriev, Ivan Ivanovich

War and Peace. See Tolstoy, Leo
Woe from Wit. See Griboyedov, Alexander
woman question. *See* Women.
Women; agency of, 2, 4, 25–8, 31, 37; education of, 9, 9n, 10, 22–3, 35, 41, 120, 126, 175, 181, 194–5, 257; *See also* Smolny Convent; and modesty

topos, 13–15; and the woman
question, 19; and writing, 3, 3n,
4, 4n, 5, 6n, 10n, 11n, 12, 16n,
36n

Zborovets', I.V., 10n, 12
Zhukova, Maria, 19n, 36
Zhukovsky, Vasily (translator), 10;
    "Elvina and Edwin," 252, 253n;
    Prisoner of Chillon (translation),
    192, 192n